Successful Fundraising

Second Edition

Successful
Fundraising

Second Edition

A COMPLETE HANDBOOK FOR VOLUNTEERS AND PROFESSIONALS

JOAN FLANAGAN

CB
CONTEMPORARY BOOKS

Library of Congress Cataloging-in-Publication Data

Flanagan, Joan.
    Successful fundraising : a complete handbook for volunteers and
professionals / Joan Flanagan.—2nd ed.
        p.   cm.
    Includes bibliographical references and index.
    ISBN 0-8092-3846-2
    1. Fund raising—United States.   I. Title.
HG177.5.U6F58   1999
658.15'224—dc21   99-24136
                                                                          CIP

Cover design by Scott Rattray
Interior design by Amy Yu Ng

Published by Contemporary Books
A division of NTC/Contemporary Publishing Group, Inc.
4255 West Touhy Avenue, Lincolnwood (Chicago), Illinois 60712-1975 U.S.A.
Copyright © 2000 by Joan Flanagan
Printed in the United States of America
International Standard Book Number: 0-8092-3846-2

00 01 02 03 04 QV 20 19 18 17 16 15 14 13 12 11 10 9 8 7 6 5 4 3 2

Also by Joan Flanagan
The Grass Roots Fundraising Book

17.15

Contents

Introduction

Change is one form of hope. To risk change is to believe in tomorrow.

—Linda Ellerbee
Move on: Adventures in the Real World

I HAVE BEEN RAISING MONEY AS A volunteer since the Eisenhower administration and working as a professional fundraiser since the Nixon administration. Trust me: this is the best time yet to be asking for money for a good cause.

Every day brings some new marvel of technology that makes it faster, easier, and more fun to find information on donors and prospects. Fascinating websites enable citizens from around the world to access the know-how of the best fundraisers. High-tech changes can liberate fundraisers by enabling them to spend more time at the best part of their job: building relationships with the people who share the values and vision of our organizations.

This book is intended for the professional fundraiser. You may be working exclusively as a fundraiser, or be the executive director responsible for raising the budget (or seeing that it gets raised). Unlike for-profit corporations where the boss rises through the ranks in a relatively intentional career trajectory, most often the boss of a nonprofit organization starts in a program as a nurse, a counselor, an organizer, or an administrator, and eventually has a bold idea that outstrips the agency's budget. Therefore learning to fundraise precedes being able to achieve your goals. You may start out slow and the next thing you know you're a full-time fundraiser or the CEO of your own agency, responsible for a large staff and an even larger budget, and eager to learn more about fundraising. This book is for you.

This book is also for the serious volunteer. You may have come from the "Who me?" school of leadership development, where after you present a great idea to the president of an organization, he or she takes you by surprise and says, "Great idea—why don't you take the lead on that?" Power in any organization goes to the people who raise the money, so any savvy volunteer knows that raising money is the surest route to leadership. Whether you are called to be president of a growing organization, cochair of the building campaign, the person responsible for raising money for the twenty-fifth class reunion gift, or the organizer of the first planned-giving committee, this book will give you what you need.

If you or your organization is new to fundraising, you would do well to start with my other book, *The Grass Roots Fundraising Book*. It can help the greenest rookie get started with special events, membership drives, and annual campaigns. However, if you and your organization already have some experience raising money and now want to raise bigger gifts and bequests from more people, this book is for you.

The fundraising examples in this book come from successful fundraisers working for a wide range of nonprofit organizations. You can adapt their ideas to fit your organization, then share your success story with your brother and sister fundraisers so the profession will continue to flourish.

Acknowledgments

IN ADDITION TO WHAT I AM ABLE TO OFFER as an experienced volunteer, fundraising consultant, and executive director, this edition of *Successful Fundraising* is immensely improved because of the good advice and great examples I have absorbed from the leaders who attend my workshops. Professor Jean Hunt once told me that the most important quality you need to be a good teacher is humility. I always capture a few new ideas and discover inspiring stories from every class.

I interviewed successful fundraisers and grant makers from the U.S., Canada, England, Holland, France, Bermuda, New Zealand, and South Africa at the 50th Annual Conference of the Council on Foundations, the International Conference of the National Society of Fund Raising Executives (NSFRE), and the Nonprofits and Technology Conference. Some of the experts who enlightened me were Kurt Aschermann, Marcia Bittner, Kim Bobo, Darryl Burrows, Sylvia Clark, Valecia Crisafulli, Carl Davidson, Shelley Fabares, Davis Fisher, Tracy Gary, Jennifer Gormley, Barbara Helmick, Vivienne Jones, Ann Kaplan, Kim Klein, Lucy Knight, Valerie Lies, David Love, Judy Margolin, Milton Murray, Paul Nebenzahl, Dan Novak, Gina Spagnola, Pam Swenk, Mal Warwick, Ken Weber, Judy Wilson, and Ken Wolfe. My research was helped immeasurably by Gayle Barr, Barbara Kemmis, and Sierra Collins at the incomparable Donors Forum of Chicago.

For the preparation of this new edition, I am especially indebted to the outstanding people I have had the privilege to work with at Contemporary Books. Trade Division editor Danielle Egan-Miller challenged me to transform the text into a book that was newer, bigger, and better than the first edition; assistant project editor Kristy Grant managed every step from manuscript to book; copyeditor Maki Wiering asked intelligent questions that helped me clarify the text; and senior graphic designer Amy Yu Ng made every page look great. Thanks for all you do.

Fundraising in the Information Age

The Road Ahead for Fundraisers

1

Imagination will be a key element for all new applications.
—Bill Gates
The Road Ahead

THIRTY YEARS AGO THE MOTHERS CLUB at Lakeside School in Seattle, Washington, held a rummage sale. There was nothing unusual about that—volunteers have excelled at fundraising events in the New World since the Pilgrims raffled off the first turkey. What was unusual was that these moms used the proceeds to buy a computer terminal and rent time on a big computer somewhere else. Two of Lakeside's students, Bill Gates and Paul Allen, used their lunch hour to teach the cumbersome computer how to play tic-tac-toe. You know the rest. A few years later, Bill dropped out of college, Paul quit his day job, they created the Microsoft Corporation, and designed the software that launched a zillion computers to sit on every desk in the world.

From the rummage sale to the information revolution, today there are more good ways than ever before to raise more money for charities. Successful fundraisers can build on what we already know such as direct mail and membership dues, and learn how to master the new techniques such as websites and Internet auctions. Of course, the tried-and-true system still works the best: give your own donation, ask people you know face-to-face for money, and then send a prompt and personal thank-you note. This is the most basic, and the most successful, strategy for fundraising for any cause.

This is a wonderful time to be a fundraiser. The Internet and E-mail technologies have become simple enough, dependable enough, and affordable enough for most businesses and households to be on-line. Five years ago the average Joe did not know the Internet from *Dragnet*. Today he has a website at www.joeschmoe.com. Smaller charities are mastering the art of endowments, rural counties are running efficient community foundations, and the largest institutions keep leapfrogging over each other's multibillion-dollar capital campaigns. Best of all, more good people are choosing fundraising as a career.

The rest of this book will give you the best tested ideas on how to raise dependable money from a variety of sources. But before we look at the nuts and bolts of raising money, let's look at the larger fundraising environment that affects our work.

Fundamental Principles of Fundraising

Whether you are raising money from your next-door neighbor, the program officer at a family foundation, or the CEO of a computer company, there are three fundamental principles that guide fundraising today. Successful fundraising must be:

- Built on the widest possible base of donors and members

- Focused on creating long-term relationships with your best donors

- Driven by donor choice

We will start by looking at each of these three basic truths of fundraising today to understand how to design the best overall strategy. Next we will explore where the money comes from, who it goes to, and what we can learn from the best fundraising sector. Then you will learn how to design a long-range fundraising plan, from selling the first bumper sticker to getting your biggest bequest.

Last will be a synopsis of how the book covers the information you need to be a successful fundraiser.

Build a Broad Base of Small Donors

The first step of fundraising is to find a broad base of small donors. They may give once a year to a well-organized annual campaign, or become members who pay their dues once a year. The easiest way to upgrade small donors is ask them to pledge every month, every paycheck, or every week. Twelve, twenty-four, or fifty-two small payments will add up to a much bigger gift with very little difficulty for the donor and only one request for the fundraiser.

More important, a broad base of small donors can give your organization permanence and political power. No one can turn off your funding if it comes from thousands of people who want your mission to succeed.

Develop Long-Term Relationships with the Best Donors

The best donors are the ones most committed to your organization over the long term. Many people, whether rich or poor, will make a small "test" gift to see what you do with it and, frankly, how you treat your donors. If you track results, share stories about the people who benefit, and create several easy options to give bigger gifts, many of your small donors will become major donors. As they gain more confidence in what the organization can do, they can and will work with your fundraisers to share their assets through a bequest or a life income plan.

Offer Donors Choices

Fundraising via E-mail and on websites is popular because that is how a lot of donors *want* to be asked. The revolution from a United Way monopoly on workplace solicitations to thousands of charities gaining access to American employees has proved that people *give* more money when they *get* more choices. The largest charities may have dozens of giving clubs at different dollar levels or for different causes. Even the smallest charity can ask its prospects in three different ways six times a year.

Donors Demand Ethical Fundraising

The most important message that fundraisers have received from their donors is a desire for more emphasis on ethics in fundraising. The depth and breadth of the reaction to the United Way scandal in the 1990s hurt not only the local United Ways and alternative workplace solicitation plans, but also fundraisers across the board. Donors were reacting not just to one rogue boss's misuse of funds, but also to the long history of overzealous supervisors intimidating their subordinates rather than involving them as prospects and peers.

Now every branch of every organization must prove that every fundraising transaction is handled with respect; not simply because it is right, but because otherwise the donors will not give. As charities' annual reports to the Internal Revenue Service (IRS) become available on the Internet, we will see even greater demand for accountability from the nonprofit sector.

In sales they say, "You don't want to make a sale; you want to make a customer." In the same way, successful fundraisers want to find a lot of small donors and develop as many of them as possible into big donors. To make that happen will require not only the most sophisticated fundraising techniques, but also the most basic human values of respect and cooperation.

Where the Money Is Now

An organization's independence comes from its diversity in fundraising. If your money comes from several different income streams, you know you will always have the revenue you need for your core budget, especially for salaries. No organization needs to use every strategy, but successful fundraisers can combine several techniques that work well. Choose a mix of ideas to make the most money in ways that are consonant with your values.

Private Money

State, local, and federal government grants and contracts pay for about 26 percent of the bills of nonprofit organizations. Of course, this is much higher for some kinds of charities such as hospitals and colleges and much lower for others such as community organizations. The advantages and disadvantages of public funds are discussed in Chapter 14.

The rest of the charitable dollars—74 percent—comes from individuals, foundations, and corporations. An association of the largest professional fundraising firms, called the American Association of Fundraising Counsel (AAFRC) Trust for Philanthropy, has kept track of the trends in private philanthropy in America since 1955. Their excellent publication *Giving USA 1999* reports that Americans gave away $175 billion to nonprofit organizations in 1998. This is more than the total national budgets of most of the countries in the world. Even this enormous figure is very conservative because it does not include informal giving such as alms to street people, most in-kind contributions, or gifts to organizations too new, too small, or too radical to incorporate.

Individual Givers

Individuals gave 85 percent of the charity dollars in America in 1998. Living individuals gave 77 percent of donations, while bequests—gifts specified in the wills of deceased donors—represented another almost 8 percent of gifts (see Figure 1.1). Gifts from individuals have been going up in dollar terms for three decades and are always the force that drives the increase in American philanthropy. Bequests, on the other hand, wax and wane depending on who dies when. The 1997 figure included a $4 billion bequest from the estate of David Packard, one of the founders of the Hewlett-Packard computer company.

Obviously, smart fundraisers start where 85 percent of the money is. Asking for gifts from living individuals builds a broad base of small donors and builds your organization's political power at the same time. Donors who have proved their loyalty become the best prospects for major gifts and bequests, so the more small and medium-sized gifts you get, the more good prospects you have for bigger gifts and bequests.

Bequests are the fastest-growing source of funds and show the most promise. Giving by bequest has gone up almost 1,000 percent since 1967, and experts predict that money from bequests will triple in the next ten years.

Foundations and Corporations

The remaining 15 percent of American donations in 1998 came from foundations and corporations. About a dime out of every dollar came from foundations; about a nickel out of every dollar came from corporations. Foundation giving was high because of a red-hot stock market. Typically, foundations' share of total giving is between 5 and 8 percent.

Foundations can give more when their investments do better, but less when the market is doing poorly. Most foundation grants support human services, education, and health care. Only 5 percent of grants go to organizations serving women and girls. Less than 5 percent go to African Americans, Hispanics, Native Americans, and Asians and Pacific Islanders. Two percent of foundation grants go to religious congregations.

Because so few grants go to religious organizations, the importance of grants to secular organizations is actually much higher. Foundations and corporations account for almost a third of the funds that did not go to religion: foundations contributed almost 20 percent of funds to secular nonprofits, and corporations gave about 12 percent.

Most corporate contributions support the groups that help companies recruit executives (the arts and higher education), hire a competent workforce (elementary and secondary schools and literacy programs), improve their public image (recycling), or deliver services (United Ways). (Note that Figure 1.1 represents only money given through corporate giving programs or corporate foundations. Corporate sponsorships represent more money, but they are reported as marketing or advertising expenses, not charitable gifts.)

Foundation grants can make great venture capital to start new programs, and corporations can be terrific partners for good programs in their communities. But in every year and in every community the big money comes from gifts and bequests of individuals.

FIGURE 1.1 **Giving 1998: Sources of Contributions**

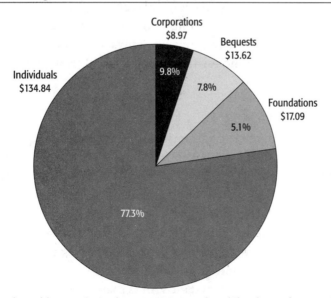

Grateful acknowldgment is made to AAFRC Trust for Philanthropy for permission to reprint chart.

Where the Money Goes

Through the magic of accounting, *Giving USA* shows that more money goes out to charities than comes in from donors. There are two reasons for this. First, the total amount reported includes other sources of money that were not reflected in the four donor categories, such as grants from the 1,400 United Way campaigns, the 100 women's funds, or the growing number of investment company charitable gift funds. Second, some money is counted twice because it is recycled. For example, much of the money donated to religious organizations is redonated for peace and justice causes.

The *Giving USA* figures also reflect the trend in the 1990s of starting many new foundations. Hundreds of smaller towns and rural counties started their own community foundations. Billionaires such as Microsoft CEO Bill Gates, Quantum Fund CEO George Soros, and media mogul Ted Turner started their own well-publicized mega-multimillion dollar foundations. Turner even gave his wife Jane Fonda $10 million so she could have her own foundation. So, to reflect this trend, *Giving USA* created a new category for giving to foundations.

Most Donations Go to Religion: Lessons We Can Learn

Note that most money by far—about 43 percent of the total every year—is given to religion and religious causes. There are eight reasons for this—seven reasons that your group can apply and one that your organization cannot use.

What Will Not Work for Secular Organizations: The Best Premiums

One reason religious congregations make the most money is that they offer the very best premiums. You give them money, and they give you inner peace now and eternal life later. This is mighty hard to match with a baseball cap or even the best cookbook in Carson City.

What Any Organization Can Copy from the Best Fundraisers

On the other hand, think about the following ways that religious congregations ask for money, and use your imagination to apply these to your own cause.

FIGURE 1.2 **Giving 1998: Contributions Received by Type of Organization**

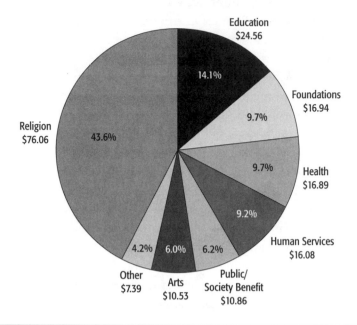

Note: Percentages represent "allocated" giving and add to more than 100%.
"Other" includes Environment/Wildlife, $5.25 (3.0%), and International Affairs, $2.14
(1.2%).
Grateful acknowledgment is made to AAFRC Trust for Philanthropy for permission to
reprint chart

Ask Often

Congregations ask for money at least fifty-two times a year, every week
on the Sabbath. If you count extra requests for the youth group, the
building fund, the Spring Fling, the Fall Fair, and the missionaries, congregations probably ask sixty to seventy times a year.

How many times do you ask your donors? Twice a year? Four times?
Ask more often and you will get more money and more committed
donors.

Especially if you want to raise money from low-income people, it is
vital that you give them the opportunity to donate small amounts of
money many times a year. Rich people buy what they want with one
payment. Poor people buy what they want by making a down payment,
stretching out the financing as long as possible, then paying a small

amount every week or month. If they can buy a car this way, why not let them buy your group's great work in the same way? Ask often.

Aim High

Many congregations ask members to tithe—to give 10 percent of their family's income. Some churches now suggest a "modern tithe," with 5 percent going to the church and 5 percent to other worthwhile causes. Some also gently remind their wealthiest members that for some people 10 percent is selfish, and they should be giving much more than 10 percent. For heaven's sake, even foundations give out 5 percent. How high do you aim? How much do you stretch in your own giving and how effectively do you challenge others to give a significant amount to the organizations that really matter to their lives?

Ask Everyone

Congregations ask everybody: the oldest member of the congregation and the stranger who just walked in, the millionaire who paid for the new organ, and the bag lady. Do you ask everyone? Or do you make choices for other people, eliminating your wealthiest prospects because "we can't bother them" and your low-income prospects because "we know they can't give." Practice what you preach; offer a menu of choices and let the donor decide.

Especially if you're working in a low-income community, the religious model has a lot to offer you. Very often the church or mosque is the only institution in a very low-income or minority community that is respected by the local people—because it is the only one they pay for. If you want to build a permanent successful organization made up of poor people, be sure they are asked to pay for the work it does.

Ask in Several Different Ways

Congregations give their members many different ways to give. People might make a weekly pledge; donate extra amounts or buy tickets for high holidays; contribute for special flowers or music; give memorials in memory of departed members; buy merchandise such as cookbooks from the women's organization, recordings from the choir, or T-shirts from the youth group; purchase tickets to special events; make a major gift for the building; and remember the church, temple, mosque, or synagogue in their wills. How many different ways do you ask your donors to give?

Ask for Time and Talent as Well as Money

Congregations provide many ways to volunteer. Clergy know volunteering is good for building fellowship. Fundraisers know it is good for building the bottom line, because volunteers give more than twice as much money as nonvolunteers. Volunteers can teach, sing, read, care for babies, clean up, make refreshments, drive the seniors and disabled members, usher, count the money, prepare the programs, greet newcomers, sell merchandise, offer tours, and serve in the worship. How many *different* ways do you ask people to volunteer?

Involve Many Volunteers in the Annual Campaign and Capital Campaigns

Most Protestant congregations involve 5 to 20 percent of the active members each year in their stewardship campaigns to ask for annual pledges from the other members. Capital campaigns to build or restore the buildings will involve another 5 to 10 percent of the church leaders. Except for very large capital campaigns, almost none use professional fundraising staff. (Even St. Paul's Cathedral's successful $6.5 million campaign to rebuild their buildings after the bombing of the Murrah Federal Building in Oklahoma City used only very limited professional consultation but enormous effort by the local leaders.) Of course skills are transferrable, so the knowledge your volunteers already have from working with professionals on sophisticated campaigns for their schools, hospitals, or diseases can be used for your organization as well as any religious congregation.

Think Long-Term

Most religious congregations ask people to join for a lifetime, ask their family and friends to join, and seriously consider leaving a legacy to the congregation as part of their commitment to stewardship. If you can foster the long-term development of your donors from newcomers, to donors, then to major donors and planned givers, you will get much more dependable funds and much more significant involvement of your people.

Who Are the Best Prospects?

Individuals give over 77 percent of the money in America, as we know from the Giving USA research. To make it easier to ask, you need to know which individuals give and how you can find the people who will give to your particular organization.

- Forty-eight percent of the money comes from households with incomes under $50,000. Do not think you need millionaires and movie stars to do good fundraising. Even if you are working in a low- or middle-income community, you can raise the money you want.

- Over 77 percent of Americans reported they gave money to charities in 1995. This means that if you ask ten people, at least seven can say yes.

- Thirty-eight percent of Americans say they wish they had given more money. This means out of every ten people who gave to you last year, four want you to ask them more often or to ask for a larger amount of money.

- Fourteen percent of Americans revealed they would have given money, but nobody asked them. Think of it! This means that if you ask ten people, one of them is a charity virgin. That person is not giving to any other cause. If he or she likes your cause, you can get all of that person's charity dollars.

How much does the average person give? Although many synagogues and churches urge people to give 10 percent of their income, in reality the average American gives between 1 and 2 percent of his or her income. Figuring most conservatively, if you can estimate someone's income, project that 1 to 2 percent of it will go to charities. So if Rachel makes $20,000, she may donate $200–$400 each year; if Ross makes $100,000, he may give $1,000–$2,000 a year. If you are asking for only $25 once a year for membership dues, you are asking for too little. Also remember that most larger gifts are made from a donor's assets, rather than annual income.

If you want to find the most generous prospects, here is what the Independent Sector survey revealed about American donors who give the most to charities:

- They worship weekly. Eighty percent of Americans active in religious organizations made gifts, compared with only 55 percent of people who did not belong to a church, synagogue, mosque, or temple. People who regularly attend religious services made 70 percent of all contributions to charity and gave more to nonsectarian causes than those who do not worship.

- They join. Good donors are members in other organizations, including unions, sports organizations, and political parties.

- They vote. Americans who vote give more money and volunteer more often.

- They have the option to give through their company. The most generous donors have access to payroll deduction at their workplace; they also volunteer more often when the opportunity is offered at work.

- They itemize. Taxpayers who claim their deductions on their federal income tax returns give four times as much as people who do not claim a deduction for charity.

- They volunteer. American households with a volunteer contributed an average of $1,135; households without a volunteer gave an average of $275. More than ninety-three million Americans volunteer, and the number is growing.[1]

The most common mistake fundraisers make is to exclude their own volunteers. Volunteers are your best prospects. Who knows better how wonderful your group is? Who sees the results? Who knows the real people who benefit? Your volunteers!

Individual Gifts—from the First Gift to the Final Gift

Now that you know that 85 percent of the money in America comes from individuals, focus 85 percent of your efforts on getting individual gifts and bequests. Of course, the temptation here is to say, "Great. We can get money from individuals. Let's get Oprah Winfrey to give us a million dollars. Then we'll never need to ask again!"

This strategy has an elegant simplicity, but it probably will not succeed unless the person proposing it is Ms. Winfrey's best friend. Even if it did succeed, the organization would become totally dependent on one person's money, which makes it very fragile (she can change her mind at any time) and very weak (the group has no political power).

At the other extreme, someone will want to say, "We're poor and everyone I know is poor. Let's sell one million raffles at one dollar each. Everyone can buy one."

This is true, but it is not the truth. Everyone can buy a one-dollar raffle chance. But will your volunteers burn out before they have completed one million sales? (Or before one hundred sales?) Even worse, at the end of one million transactions, you will have identified everyone who wants to win a new car. You will not know who wants to support the mission of your organization.

Your fundraisers can devise a strategy that will balance getting the most money per transaction with the real skills and enthusiasm of your leaders and volunteers. You can continue all the fundraising techniques you already know and like. Plus you can add new sources of dependable income for today and the future.

The ideal plan will be built on a broad base of small, renewable gifts and include several different ways for your best donors to give larger amounts. In addition to soliciting the individuals who support your mission, you can use several other techniques to raise unrestricted dollars from the general public. Then your challenge is to change the customers who buy your products or services and the guests who come to your parties into true donors who give money to accomplish the mission of the organization.

The Fundraising Pyramid

The pyramid in Figure 1.3 is a planning tool to help your volunteers and staff to visualize their overall strategy for raising money from individuals. What are the choices available to you, how do they build on each other, and what is the best strategy for your group for each step?

The bottom layer represents the most people. They will give the least money, have the least commitment to the organization, and take the least time to cultivate. The top of the pyramid has the fewest people, who give the most money, are the most committed to the mission of the group, and need the most time to cultivate. There is a direct relationship between time and money: the more money, the more time it takes to get. For example, the average $100,000 gift to a university required at least seven personal visits over eighteen months. The United Negro College Fund needed twelve years to negotiate a $50 million challenge grant from Ambassador Walter H. Annenberg, retired CEO of Triangle Publications, Inc., publisher of *Seventeen*, *TV Guide*, and the *Daily Racing Form*.

Let's look at each level of the fundraising pyramid. Veteran fundraisers will note that although most samples of the fundraising pyramid look like the great pyramids in Egypt, I prefer a model based on the Mayan pyramids like Chichen Itza. The advantage is that the top level is much broader in the Mayan shape. In the best of all possible worlds, all

FIGURE 1.3 **Individual Donor Development**

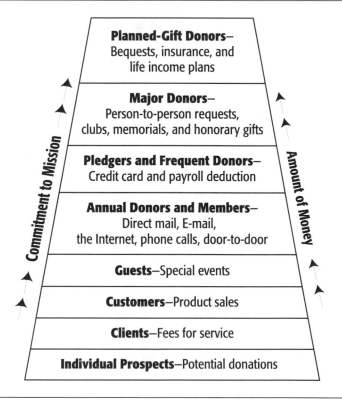

of your prospects would become annual donors, then major donors, then leave your organization a bequest. In the real world, the number of donors gets smaller as each level goes up. Our job as fundraisers is to remember and to remind our team that *every* prospect is a prospect for major gifts and planned gifts as much as dues, donations, and dinner tickets.

Each level of individual donor development is discussed in more detail in Chapters 3 to 10. Raising money from corporations, foundations, and other grant makers is discussed in Chapters 11 to 14. This introduction is to show you how each strategy for raising money from your best prospects—individuals—fits together with the others.

Individual Prospects

The very bottom represents all the people who could donate. I wish I could tell you that everyone in your community will donate to your group. (Of course, they should.) But no matter how wonderful your organization is, you will never get 100 percent of the possible donors to give to you. However, you can always get more than you have now.

Clients, Customers, and Guests

The first income for your organization can come from fees for service, sales, and special events. These are the easiest transactions, because the donors get something tangible in return, and they are the quickest transactions, because it is a yes/no question, unlike negotiating larger gifts. You must value and track all the people who pay a fee, buy a product, or go to your event because they are sources of renewable, nonrestricted money. However, you must also be clear that these people are not giving because they share your vision or your values. They are giving to get something they want. When they do not need or want your service, product, or event anymore they will not continue giving. So the next step is to use your sales and special events to introduce your mission, then attempt to convert your customers into donors.

Annual Donors and Members

Once you begin asking for money for the mission of the organization, you have moved beyond selling to fundraising. Instead of looking for customers to buy cookies or come to the carnival, you are looking for people who share your values and vision. You want them to give money to get the results of your work. The most efficient way to find your supporters is a well-organized annual campaign.

Membership dues are the ideal form for annual fundraising, because they are the most democratic, dependable, and renewable form of fundraising. The members pay a set amount of money for one year. Some publicly funded institutions do not directly have members but create membership organizations such as Friends of the Library to get unrestricted money.

For smaller organizations, your current members can sell memberships in person or via E-mail, letters, or phone calls. If your cause has a broader appeal, especially if it is very popular or very controversial, you can hire professional fundraisers to mass-market memberships through the Internet, E-mail, direct mail, telemarketing, or a door-to-door canvass.

For your organizing, advocacy, and public policy work, it is vital that you have a large group of people who have proved they want your organization. If people give to you every year, they want what your organization does. They are also vital for your long-term fundraising, because 80 to 90 percent of planned gifts and major gifts come from people who have been members or annual donors for three to five years.

Pledgers

The next step up in terms of commitment and money consists of people who pay a pledge. This is the system most religious congregations use, and it triples the amount of money given. A pledge is just a promise to give a certain amount more often than once a year, usually every week, month, or paycheck. The most common forms of pledges are the weekly pledge to a congregation, a pledge through payroll deduction, or a monthly pledge through a bank credit card or electronic funds transfer.

Major Donors—Clubs

The next step up the pyramid is for major donors. Clubs are a strategy used to get these people to increase their annual gift. You simply create the Silver Buckeye Club for $1,000 donors, the Golden Buckeye Club for $5,000 donors, and the Platinum Buckeye Club for $10,000 donors, and then urge generous people in Ohio to give at the higher amount. Clubs work very well because they make it easier for the fundraisers to ask for a larger dollar amount, and they give donors an ego reward.

Major Donors—Memorials and Honorary Gifts

Some of your major donors will want to make a gift in memory of a loved one or in honor of someone they admire. More and more obituaries now include requests that gifts go to the local hospital or hospice, or an association for a specific disease, rather than for flowers. Honorary gifts to a worthwhile nonprofit may be preferred as a retirement gift, gifts for a second or third wedding, or in lieu of presents for certain anniversaries.

Major Donors—Major Gifts

Major gifts are the largest contributions your organization solicits. Most major gifts take much more time, often years, and require more person-to-person collaboration between your current annual donor and your institution in developing the gift. Since major gifts usually come from the donor's assets rather than annual income, the amounts can be much higher. Fundraisers often set a target of ten times the donor's largest annual gift or five times the donor's annual giving for the first major gift request. If the solicitation is successful, the next request is higher.

Planned Gift Donors—Bequests, Life Insurance, and Life Income Plans

Planned gifts used to be called "deferred gifts," but fundraisers changed the name because the donor's temptation is to defer forever. The most common planned gift is a bequest that will go to the organization at the time of the donor's death. Bequests are the most volatile form of fundraising, since there is no accurate way to predict when specific people will die. In the past twenty years, bequests have accounted for 3 to 13 percent of total giving.

The typical American donates to eleven to fourteen charities every year. Americans with a will remember two to five charities with bequests. So two to five charities that get annual gifts from a donor also get a gift in his or her will, and nine are left out. Usually, the charities that get bequests are the ones that asked for bequests.

The second most-common planned gift is the proceeds from a life insurance policy. This is especially popular with younger donors. In its simplest form, the donor buys a life insurance policy and makes the annual payments, which are deductible from his or her taxable income. The organization is the beneficiary, so it will receive a large amount of money at the time of the donor's death.

Planned gifts also can include appreciated stocks, bonds, or other financial instruments, works of art, and real estate. In a well-planned program, donating appreciated property to a charity can mean that the donor saves money on income and estate taxes, may receive a higher annual income, can provide better for his or her children and grandchildren, and supports a good organization, all at the same time.

Planning Chart

The following work sheet on page 19 will help you plan your fundraising strategy for the next year and beyond. First, discuss what your own group already does well. Continue that and increase it if you can.

Second, ruthlessly evaluate your fundraisers that are not producing what you want from them. If they can be fixed, fix them. For example, perhaps your thrift shop is not doing as well as it used to because you are having trouble finding daytime volunteers. If so, open it in the evening when you can get more volunteers and more shoppers.

If something cannot be fixed, prune it out of your plan. For example, many groups do fundraising dinners because they have always done dinners. Today's high prices make it very difficult to make money on a dinner unless you can get corporate underwriting. If it is too much work for too little money, take it out of the plan and replace it with another strategy that can make more money with less work.

Then add on new strategies you want to test this year. Not every group will want to use every strategy, but every group can ask for major contributions face-to-face and ask for bequests.

Talk to other local groups that shine at fundraising, and ask your national organization for ideas on what is working best for similar groups. Then make your long-range plan to intentionally recruit a big base of small donors. Finally, systematically ask them for larger gifts and bequests.

Fundraising Strategy Planning Work Sheet

Source of Funds	Results Last Year	Results This Year	Goal for Next Year	Goal in Five Years
Earned income				
Product sales	_____	_____	_____	_____
Fees for service	_____	_____	_____	_____
Smaller donations				
Special events	_____	_____	_____	_____
E-mail	_____	_____	_____	_____
Direct mail	_____	_____	_____	_____
Phone canvass	_____	_____	_____	_____
Door-to-door canvass	_____	_____	_____	_____
Web page	_____	_____	_____	_____
Workplace solicitation	_____	_____	_____	_____
Annual campaign				
Membership dues	_____	_____	_____	_____
Annual gifts	_____	_____	_____	_____
Weekly/monthly pledges	_____	_____	_____	_____
Major gifts				
Clubs	_____	_____	_____	_____
Memorials/ honorary gifts	_____	_____	_____	_____
Personal visits	_____	_____	_____	_____

Source of Funds	Results Last Year	Results This Year	Goal for Next Year	Goal in Five Years
Planned gifts				
Bequests	_____	_____	_____	_____
Life insurance	_____	_____	_____	_____
Retirement plans	_____	_____	_____	_____
Appreciated property	_____	_____	_____	_____
Life income gifts	_____	_____	_____	_____
Annuities and trusts	_____	_____	_____	_____
Institutional donors				
Foundation grants	_____	_____	_____	_____
Corporate contributions	_____	_____	_____	_____
Religious congregations	_____	_____	_____	_____
Civic organizations	_____	_____	_____	_____
United Ways	_____	_____	_____	_____
Bank trusts	_____	_____	_____	_____
Investment company charitable gift funds	_____	_____	_____	_____
Supporting organizations	_____	_____	_____	_____
Business partnerships				
Corporate sponsorships	_____	_____	_____	_____
Other strategies	_____	_____	_____	_____

How to Use This Book

Now that you have an understanding that the big money comes from individual donors—dead or alive—and lots of other funds come from foundations and corporations, the rest of this book will help you create an effective, ethical fundraising strategy to raise dependable, renewable, internally controlled money from several sources.

Because effective fundraising is a team sport, Chapter 2 tells you how to find the best volunteers and how to turn them into leaders. Chapters 3 and 4 share ideas on how to do the easiest transactions that your own people already know how to do; Chapter 3 discusses selling products and services, and Chapter 4 covers special events.

Starting with Chapter 5 we cover how you ask for money and how you motivate other people to ask for money. In Chapters 6 and 7 we discuss the annual campaign to get first-time gifts and renewals, in memberships or pledges, either completely in-house run by your own staff and volunteers, or with professional help for bigger campaigns.

Once your organization has built a broad base of loyal donors, it is time to organize a campaign to deepen the commitment of the donors. Chapters 8, 9, and 10 discuss how to find the best prospects for major gifts, how to ask for bigger contributions, and then the biggest challenge for new fundraisers—how to ask for bequests and other planned gifts. All of these come from the donor's assets rather than annual income.

The last four chapters of the book cover your other funding opportunities beyond individuals: how to win grants from foundations, corporations, and other grant makers, and how to negotiate corporate marketing partnerships. In all, you will get proven ideas on how to choose the best combination of fundraising techniques for your organization, how to avoid the pitfalls, how to adapt an idea to fit your constituents, and how to increase your revenue each year. Not every technique will work for every organization (with the exception of the give-ask-thank triad that is *always* infallible), but every fundraiser can find several ideas that will work today.

Best of all, if you still want more, there is a Resource Guide at the end of this book that will refer you to the best books, magazines, newsletters, professional associations, and websites. There are also instructions on how to access a list of almost two hundred free Foundation Center cooperating collection libraries, as well as good catalogs and websites that will refer you to yet more good books and other materials. The recommended resources are all easy to find and written at such a level that you can share them with new staff as well as experienced volunteers.

The Fundraising Team 2

There is no "I" in "team". There is no "I" in "success".
—Sheryl Swoopes, Olympic Gold Medalist
and Women's National Basketball
Association star,
Chicago Foundation for Women
1998 annual luncheon keynote address

RUTH ANDREA SEELER, M.D., IS A MEMBER of the national foundation board for her college sorority, the founder of a summer camp for boys with hemophilia, and a no-nonsense type from New York. When she realized how much money her sorority sisters spent each December at their alumnae holiday party, she put an end to the restaurant extravagance by hosting the dinner at her home instead. She threw a ham into the oven, sprinkled tinsel over the tree, and asked each woman to write a check to the foundation for what they would have spent on drinks and dinner out. In only three years their little chapter's year-end gift grew from a token amount to almost $1,000. When I told Ruth I was writing a book on fundraising, she exclaimed, "Fundraising! Ask for money—send thank-you notes. What else is there?"

Actually, she's right. Successful fundraising can be condensed into one sentence: Give a gift (she underwrites the cost of the party), ask for money, and send thank-you notes. If you, your staff, and your volunteers did those three things every day, you would have all the money you need.

But what if there is only "you" and not "your staff" or "your volunteers" yet? Fundraising is a team sport and you need a team of caring people to make it fun and profitable. Both paid professionals and volunteers have an important role to play in successful fundraising. If your daily mantra is "I could do this more easily myself . . . ," read, mark, learn, and inwardly digest every bit of this chapter.

Why Use Volunteers?

You're right—it is easier to do it yourself. Especially if you are a good proposal writer and foundation charmer, you may be able to get along for quite some time without having to find, train, and motivate volunteers. So why all this work?

1. Volunteers enable your agency to tell its story to many different networks where they live, work, play, and worship.

2. Today's volunteers are tomorrow's leaders. Whether we want our own people to go on to become the chair of the festival or governor of the state, we need to begin testing them today with small challenges so they will be ready tomorrow for the big challenges.

3. It is easier only for the first year. If you do not take the time now to find and train good volunteers, you will have to do all the work every year. On the other hand, if you develop good volunteers, the first year is a lot of work, the second year is a little supervision, and the third year you put your hat on your head and go to the party.

Where Do I Get Good Fundraising Volunteers?

The best way to get volunteers is to ask for them. According to a Gallup survey on volunteering, the most common reason Americans gave for becoming involved as a volunteer was that someone asked them. Who did the asking? Most common responses were a friend (51 percent), someone at their church or synagogue (31 percent), a family member (18 percent), and someone at work (8 percent). What is your organization doing to make it easy for your active members to ask the people they know?[1]

The same poll asked Americans why they first volunteered with a nonprofit organization. By far the most important motivators were the idea that it is "important to help others" (56 percent) and "compassion toward people in need" (49 percent). Do your volunteers feel helpful and needed?

Most people will join the organization because they care heart and soul about the cause. In addition to the true believers, you may want to recruit specific kinds of people who will make successful fundraisers.

Newcomers

The days when workers commonly received twenty-five-year pins for faithful service to the same company are over. Today the average American worker has held eight jobs by the age of forty, and often this requires several moves. For people who want to get involved in their new communities, fundraising gives them the chance to meet good people quickly. New people can offer tested ideas that worked elsewhere to complement your own fundraising plans.

Daytimers

In the 1950s and 1960s, the typical daytime volunteer was a housewife raising kids at home. While their husbands rebuilt the world after World War II, these formidable women built the community centers, libraries, youth programs, and nature centers in every kind of neighborhood. There are still full-time homemakers who are terrific fundraisers and the envy of every organization. But most women now work outside the home, because only one job in five in the United States pays enough to support a family of four. So where else can we find good volunteers for daytime fundraising?

There are still people available to volunteer during the day. These include people who are not working now, such as pensioners; and people with inherited wealth, good investments, or generous early retirement packages. Also, there are people who do not work during the day (people with night jobs comprise 18 percent of all American workers), seasonal workers such as schoolteachers and professional athletes, and people in retail—nearly any salesperson on commission wants to work on the weekend and get weekdays off. In addition there were more than 7 million people who were telecommuters in 1999. That means they did not "go" to an office or store, but did their work over the phone, fax, or Internet. More and more consultants, entrepreneurs, and creative people can set their own schedules as long as they meet their goals. Ask at your local coffee shop or post office—they will know who's free in the day. Recruit two and they can connect you to others.

Celebrities

Celebrities can add sparkle and sex appeal to your parties, increase media coverage for advocacy events, and provide inspiration to your leaders. They can attract more volunteers for your hard-to-recruit activities. For example, more people show up to donate blood in Chicago when they know they will be next to the fullback from the Chicago Bears or first violin from the Chicago Symphony Orchestra.

Political fundraisers use their candidates, especially incumbents, most effectively as money magnets. Although the media scolded President Clinton for rewarding his best donors with overnights in the Lincoln bedroom at the White House, presidential fundraising is actually an old practice. In fact, if a president ever invites *you* to visit the Lincoln bedroom, you will see a signed copy of the Gettysburg Address, handwritten by Abraham Lincoln as a fundraiser for a charity for Civil War soldiers. I know this because President George Bush's dog put it in her bestseller, *Millie's Book*, proving that even a celebrity's pet can raise money for a good cause (more than $600,000 for the Barbara Bush Foundation for Family Literacy).

The ideal celebrity is someone who has a personal understanding of your cause. He or she will be more believable to the media, lawmakers, and your own people. For example, TV star Mary Tyler Moore serves as the international chairman for the Juvenile Diabetes Foundation (JDF) because she has lived with juvenile diabetes since the 1960s. Thanks to her televised public service announcements and testimony before Congress, JDF's contributions to research have grown from $3 million a year to $50 million a year.

Celebrities can be even more compelling when they get involved because of a family member. Former Minnesota Twins All-Star first baseman Kent Hrbek supports the ALS Association by spearheading a one-day celebrity golf tournament, dinner, and auction. Since 1985 his event has raised almost a million dollars for research on ALS, also known as Lou Gehrig's disease, that claimed his father.

Shelley Fabares, star of the TV show "Coach," got involved with the Alzheimer's Association because the Los Angeles chapter came to her aid when her mother was diagnosed with the disease. True to the association's motto "Someone to stand by you," their volunteers offered both Shelley and her sister advice and support to care for their mother. Because the disease robs a patient of her memory, Shelley's mother was physically present but could not recognize her daughter. As Shelley says, "My mother could not say 'Hello' to me, and I could not say 'Good-bye' to her."

By utilizing her celebrity status, Shelley has been able to assist the Alzheimer's Association in recruiting fellow actors such as David Hyde Pierce and Kelsey Grammar, the stars of "Frasier," to help put on a black-tie gala called "A Night at Sardi's." She also takes her show on the road, literally going the extra mile for the Alzheimer's Association, to launch the Memory Walk fundraising events around the country.

She has become an articulate spokesperson for the Alzheimer's Association and has testified before congressional panels on five different occasions. Relating her story as the daughter of a person with Alzheimer's disease and backed by hundreds of advocates from around

Actresss Shelley Fabares, national honorary chair of the Alzheimer's Association Memory Walk, speaks to a group of supporters to generate excitement at the 1998 Memory Walk Kick-off event at Planet Hollywood in Los Angeles.

Grateful acknowledgment is made to the Alzheimer's Association and Shelley Fabares for permission to print photo.

the country, Shelley has helped to persuade Congress to increase funding for research.

Shelley Fabares offers these three suggestions for working with celebrities:

1. Set clear goals and share them with the star. For example, say you want him or her to speak to the walkers for fifteen minutes, do three radio interviews, and have lunch with two major donor prospects. Then it is easy for the celebrity to do his or her best for each assignment.

2. Have your information well organized and cohesive. This means clear bullet points, not your ten-page proposal. Tell your celebrity exactly what to expect and what to do. For instance, what should be said? Not said? Who will the audience be? What is the charity's greatest need? What, exactly, should he or she ask for? More volunteers, more pledges, more letters to Congress?

3. Let him or her get to know you and your leaders. Shelley said the best part of volunteering for the Alzheimer's Association is that she has met "the most heroic people you can imagine." All volunteers and leaders get involved and stay involved because they are personally connected to the other people. Make this happen for your celebrity volunteers, too.

Women

Remember when your mother used to tell you to wear clean underwear in case you were hit by a truck? Today, writer Letty Cottin Pogrebin asks, "Suppose you get hit by a truck and someone finds your checkbook? What would the check stubs reveal about your giving habits? How recently did you make your last contribution, and how generous was it relative to your means?"[2]

She suggests that the acid test for giving among modern women is, "Will this money empower women and children or will it just reinforce dependence? I want to fund change, not charity. I want to enable, not just help." These priorities can also be a good test for recruiting women volunteers. To get the best women today, offer the challenge of changing the world.

Low-Income People

If you want low-income people to respect your organization, ask them to give and to raise funds. Poor people, better than anyone else, know that if you want something, you have to pay for it. Writer Nicholas von Hoffman was a community organizer on Chicago's South Side in the 1960s. His team of organizers and leaders filled forty-six buses with poor people from The Woodlawn Organization (TWO) to register to vote at City Hall. There was no free ride. As von Hoffman said, "We had these endless fundraisers for buses. One apartment house after another . . . TWO never put up any money for [this] because you knew that you'd never fill a bus unless the people who are going to ride in the bus pay for it."[3]

Low-income households in America are proportionately more generous than wealthier households. In 1995, households earning between $50,000 and $75,000 a year gave an average of 1.7 percent of their income, while households that made less than $10,000 donated 3.6 percent of their income.[4] Especially if you give them a chance to pledge, low-income households can make generous contributions to the causes they care about. For example, even in households with incomes of less than $12,000, 12 percent of black families and 15 percent of white families gave more than $500 a year.[5]

Senior Citizens

In some parts of the world it is normal for people to live to be more than a hundred years old. When scientists studied these people, they found several reasons for long lives: little pollution, no smoking, no guns, and a good diet. But the most important predictor for long lives is their not retiring: the farmers farm, the shoemakers make shoes, the homemakers make happy homes, forever.

Although more Americans are choosing to retire earlier, their life expectancy is increasing. In the armed forces and some unionized jobs you can retire after twenty years—so you could be retired at forty-two and live to be a hundred. What do you do with the other fifty-eight years? Ideally, you volunteer.

When your organization recruits retirees and gives them responsible work to do, you not only get their knowledge and know-how (and a roster of strong relationships) but you also literally keep people alive. More and more people are looking at volunteering, including fundraising, as a second career.

According to the U.S. Census Bureau, there were 34 million Americans over sixty-five years old in 1997. On a per capita basis this group has the highest discretionary income of any age group. Retirees are by far the most generous givers, donating 4 percent of their household income. Surveys show volunteers give twice as much as nonvolunteers, so senior volunteers are also great prospects for both current and planned gifts.

Generation X and Generation Y

At the other extreme are the young adults in their twenties and thirties, dubbed by demographers as Generation X (born 1964–75) and Generation Y (born after 1976). Especially Generation Y offers great promise for fundraisers. Even as teenagers they spent more than any other generation before, so we know they will spend money to get what they want.

Actually, these groups are pretty easy to work with. By definition you know they are young (mostly healthy), computer-literate (reachable by E-mail), and probably employed (have a paycheck). If you can recruit the right leadership, young adults will participate actively and give generously. (The same applies to other high-income clusters that are hard to reach, such as doctors, dentists, and lawyers.)

What do they want? A challenge. Belonging. To meet nice people with dating potential.

For example, the Children's Memorial Hospital in Chicago wanted to recruit young adult leadership to improve community relations and to raise money. Their plan has been very successful and could be copied by other urban groups.

The hospital interviewed the longtime members from their boards and asked which of their sons and daughters might like to get involved. This yielded the perfect set of leadership prospects. All had parents who had volunteered for the hospital for decades. Many had been patients at the hospital or had siblings who had been patients. All were single and wanted to meet other singles with family values. Best of all, they all were committed to the mission of the hospital.

The hospital formed a new coed auxiliary of young professionals and gave them a challenging goal: raise $100,000 for the pediatric AIDS patients. The group accepted. Although the older auxiliaries always meet at the hospital, the younger adults sometimes meet at a nearby pub. They have organized a variety of events, including the Snow Ball in January, an informal beer bash in a parking lot, a party for the kids at the hospital on St. Patrick's Day (a high holiday in Chicago regardless of your ethnic background), and more. They made their goal of $100,000.

Children's Memorial Hospital's formula for success is one that your organization can copy:

- Make the group coed.
- Give a challenging dollar goal.
- Connect the dollar goal to an urgent need not funded by any other source.
- Recruit bold leadership and assign trained staff.
- Allow the committee to run itself.
- Connect it to the mission of your organization.

Demographers predict that by 2008, Generation Y will make up 41 percent of the U.S. population, surpassing the middle-aged Baby Boomers, who will make up 28 percent of the population. Successful fundraisers can develop Gen Y leaders to attract the largest group with the highest energy and newest ideas.[6]

Rural Residents

Finding and keeping good rural volunteers is the most difficult challenge for fundraising recruiters. There are fewer people, so the same handful of leaders are asked to do everything; there are fewer prospects, so fundraisers feel as though they are asking the same people again and again; and there are fewer organizations, so there are fewer places to test the youngest and newest volunteers.

To get good rural volunteers, first ask the landed gentry who have owned a farm or a ranch for generations. Someone from that family will have the best access to local people. Second, look for someone who has a self-interest in being accepted in the community. Who needs to build goodwill to do his or her job? This may be a member of the clergy, the editor of the paper, or the owner of the largest store. These people need to be known in the community and to help the community grow. Third, who has access to and knowledge of the latest technology? If volunteers are burnt out on meetings because they need to drive for hours each way, could some of the meetings be eliminated through E-mail, teleconferencing, or faxing? Is there a local merchant, student, librarian, or expert who could help save time and energy through technology? Then the people who do get involved can focus on raising money and getting results.

Corporations

Corporations can give you more than money. They can also offer valuable goods, special services, and a terrific source of volunteers. For example, at the Mellon Bank in Pittsburgh, management trainer Dennis McCarthy first learned American Sign Language in order to give a fair and legal job interview to a deaf woman. Then he started a voluntary lunchtime class that has taught more than three hundred Mellon employees to sign, for their own use and to serve deaf customers. With three alumni of the Mellon class he formed "The Signing Friends" to raise awareness of deaf people at hospitals and schools. At Christmas time Dennis volunteered as the "Signing Santa" so deaf kids could tell Santa what they wanted. He learned sign language to do his job better; now he uses it in many ways to make his community better. There are hundreds of employees in the businesses in your town with special skills. They can help your group, too, if you ask them.

Developing New Fundraising Leaders

There are two ways to get great volunteer fundraisers. You can intentionally recruit great talent from the outside or you can develop your own leaders from the inside.

Recruiting Talent from Outside

If you are asking for leadership from the outside, build a team with the "Four Ws":

- Work

- Wealth

- Weight

- Wisdom

In this system, the nominating committee intentionally works to recruit leaders who can give your board a balance of *work*—people willing to ask for money, organize events, and recruit new fundraisers; *wealth*—

people willing and able to give big money; *weight*—people with power in the community whose names can open doors, such as the mayor, the owner of the most successful business, or the hottest local celebrity; and *wisdom*—people who are experts in your field.

Asking for all four kinds of skills on the same board works best when the group is new. Then you get the most diversity and everyone learns new skills. Also, frankly, unless the founder is a celebrity, a new group is limited to the people who are willing to gamble on a new idea. Once the organization has achieved some results, it will be able to attract more prestigious people and bigger donors.

Honorary Board

Some organizations prefer to take the volunteers from the "Weight" category and put them on a separate honorary board. Although these people have great prestige, they probably will not actually ask for money for your organization. Most honorary board members simply lend their names to the organization, which is fine—the mere name of a celebrity will open doors. Honorary board members may send a check once a year or attend an occasional special event; unless the cause really matters to them, they may never attend a meeting. There is no reason an honorary board needs to meet as a group—what you want is their endorsement.

Your honorary board is a great place to put celebrities, sports idols, and politicians. Some of the sparkle of celebrities will rub off on your group and make it easier to recruit workers and givers. The most dazzling stars can give you their own money and use their fame to raise money for their favorite causes.

Advisory Board

An advisory board is just that—a board of people who give advice. Some organizations have more than one advisory board. For example, Horizon Hospice has a medical advisory board, a financial advisory board, and an advisory board of volunteers with assorted skills—such as a journalist, a television producer, an architect, a funeral director, a lawyer, and a social worker.

Look at your current board members and then consider the skills that your organization will need to meet its fundraising goals for the next three years. For example, if you intend to begin or expand a campaign to ask for planned gifts, you will need people who know the most about current tax laws and investment opportunities. If you do not already have these kinds of people in your leadership, recruit a tax lawyer, a banker, and an estate planner for your advisory board. Almost any organization can benefit from a specialist in E-mail and the Internet. Historic properties could benefit from people with expertise in the decorative arts, genealogy, and real estate.

Especially if you set measurable goals, hold your volunteers accountable, and keep good records, after a few years it will be apparent which people are asking for money in the community and which people are just talking at meetings. An advisory board gives your organization a good place to put the volunteers who only want to talk. An advisory board may meet if it wants, or the members may just be available when their expertise is needed.

If your organization chooses to set up an honorary board for people with prestige and an advisory board for people who want to give advice, then the real board of directors can be limited to the two sets of people you want most: the work people and the wealth people. The more the workers, givers, and askers see similar people on a board, the more they will work, give, and ask.

Other Fundraising Committees

In addition to the board of directors, an honorary board, and one or more advisory boards, your organization may want to create other volunteer groups with a specific fundraising goal. These may be called committees, guilds, auxiliaries, or another board.

For example, some organizations working in low-income communities limit the board of directors to people who live and work in the community. This requirement functionally eliminates the possibility of business leaders to serve on the board. So a low-income group can create a "corporate fundraising committee" made up of business and professional leaders who give management advice and raise money from the business community for the organization.

Performing arts groups that attract audiences from beyond their own community may set up guilds of fans to raise money and build audiences for them. For example, the Santa Fe Opera has fundraising committees in California, Colorado, and New York. The Stratford Festival in Ontario has an active group of Shakespeare fans raising money in Chicago.

Communities with a large number of people who own second homes can double their fundraising forces. For example, Manhattanites who spend summers in the Catskills can work on the summer concert series for the arts association in July, then ask for major gifts in Manhattan in the winter. Many organizations in Florida, Arizona, and Texas schedule their events to use the talents of the "snowbirds," folks who move in from Thanksgiving to spring.

Some hospitals have as many as twenty auxiliaries, each of which is focused on a special fundraiser such as operating the gift shop or the 5K run, is focused on a special need such as raising money for cancer patients or pediatrics, or was founded in memory of a specific patient. Churches may have separate committees to run the bingo, carnival, and product sales. Some art museums and symphonies have created "junior boards" to test the best young talent and provide volunteers for special events.

Put It in Writing

Be explicit about what you want from your volunteers and leaders. Many groups find it helpful to write out the benefits and responsibilities of serving on the board. It is clearest if you are explicit about the amount of money you want people to give or raise. For example, Hull House in Chicago asks its board members to donate $1,000. When the nominating committee shares this with prospective board members, they simply select in or select out, depending on whether or not they want to raise the money. The volunteers are going to make this choice anyway, but it is much better for you and fairer to the other members of the board, if people announce their choice *before* they are on the board.

Some charities set a high dollar figure intentionally to get only big donors on the board. Other charities will set a specific figure but then give board members a way to raise the money if they cannot donate it personally. For example, the Illinois Citizens for Better Care, which advocates for nursing home reform, asks each board member to donate $50 and raise $1,000. Since they want some nursing home residents to serve on the board, they always do an event and a raffle with a low ticket price so nursing home residents can raise their quotas.

On the other hand, some charities want to challenge the board members to be generous, but do not want to name a dollar amount. For example, the Rape Victims Advocates of Chicago asks each nominee for the board to commit to "make your own stretch gift annually." Then each candidate for the board must commit to make what is, for the candidate, a major gift, but not a specific dollar amount.

If your nominating committee asks candidates for the board to commit to giving money and raising money before they agree to serve on the board, more people will decline to serve on the board and will participate in other ways. That's just fine. You will simply need to ask more people this way, but the people you get will be enthusiastic givers and askers.

Developing Talent from the Inside

The key to developing new leaders inside your organization is upward mobility. New people must see that volunteers are welcome, good work is rewarded, and there is room at the top. This way the volunteer who recruits the most members this year can chair the membership committee next year and serve on the board the year after that. Everyone sees that hard work is rewarded and that it is the doers, not the talkers, who get promoted.

This system is especially good for organizations that want diverse leadership because it is a good way to overcome prejudice. In big cities prejudice may be manifested in ethnic or racial terms; in small towns it may be focused on who did or did not graduate from the local high school. In either case, one of the beauties of fundraising is that every campaign has measurable results, so you can quantify each volunteer's contribution to the organization.

If members are promoted because of what they do rather than who they are, everyone gets the same chance at leadership. So if someone says, "I don't want any short Irish people on the board—let's not nominate Joan," it is easy to reply, "She sold twice as many platinum memberships as anyone else on the committee. She has the commitment and the energy we want. She deserves to be nominated."

To make upward mobility work, there must be terms of office for the board of directors, and they must be enforced. It will not work if half the board are in their tenth consecutive two-year term of office. After two terms of office, *every* member of the board has to rotate off the board and make room for new people. Every member rotating off of the board can serve on the nominating committee with three or four other people to pick great candidates for the next board. The best leaders can move up to serve at a state, national, or international level of your own organization or go on to use their skills in electoral politics. Or create an alumni council for former board members to keep their names on your materials and their expertise on call.

Professional Staff

Professional fundraisers are the unsung heroes of democracy. Money is power. The professionals who teach community leaders how to raise money are also empowering citizens to control their own destinies.

In most organizations, the executive director or CEO is de facto the professional fundraiser until you hire someone to work as the director of development. Part of the boss's job description is always raising money and helping the elected leaders to raise money. Once an organization grows its budget and programs beyond what the executive director and board can manage alone, it is time to hire professional staff. Although it can be tough to raise the first salary for a director of development, the full-time attention to long-range strategy should pay off in a year or two.

How to Hire a Fundraiser

Although the CEO and board members need to keep asking for money, if you want full-time, in-house professional help doing this work, hire a director of development. Ask similar charities for advice to write up a job description. Agree on your dollar goals before you advertise the job. Any stooge can help you raise "some money" or "more money," but a good professional can help you run an annual campaign for $900,000 or a capital campaign for $9 million.

As for any job, the best recruits come through the grapevine. Tell all your volunteers, employees, allies, funders, and friends that you are hiring a full-time fundraiser. Then advertise through the local chapter newsletters and the national journals of the professional associations, the fundraising trade press, and philanthropy websites (see the Resource Guide), your network's press, and the local newspapers. Be explicit about what you want and do not want, and budget enough money to hire a skilled person.

The National Society of Fund Raising Executives (NSFRE) publishes current salary and benefit data for professional fundraisers. Ask the chamber of commerce what the local for-profits pay their sales and marketing staff. If you are looking for a good professional fundraiser, the best people want more than money. In an NSFRE survey, only 6 percent of the fundraisers surveyed said they would change jobs for more money; almost 41 percent said they would change jobs because they want more challenge. So do not despair if you have a controversial organization or work in a tough neighborhood and need to hire a professional fundraiser. There may be people out there who think this job is just the challenge they want.

Unfortunately, at this time there are more good jobs than there are good professional fundraisers. If you cannot hire an experienced fundraiser, look at your current employees for talented people who would like the job. They already know the organization; now they can learn fundraising skills, too. If someone on the staff has impeccable integrity, a positive attitude, and good verbal and math skills, he or she could become a full-time fundraiser. New fundraisers can learn the ropes through membership in a professional association; being adopted by a mentor; cross-training with a similar organization; attending fundraising workshops and conventions; and reading fundraising, sales, and marketing books and magazines.

If you cannot hire a professional fundraiser or promote a current employee, consider putting an experienced volunteer on the payroll. Many volunteers do almost everything a professional fundraiser does, and they already have a network of contacts in your community. If the organization puts a volunteer on the payroll, that volunteer must resign any elected or appointed offices, including membership on the board of directors.

The last possibility for hiring a fundraiser is hiring someone with sales, marketing, or organizing experience and then retraining him or her to do fundraising. Most of the skills are transferable, and all the fundraising skills can be learned.

The Role of the CEO

Money is the oxygen that keeps the organization alive. With or without a professional fundraiser on the staff, money must be the top-priority item in the CEO's work plan and at every staff meeting. Every nonprofit CEO must commit at least one-half of his or her time to fundraising. More is better but probably not realistic unless it is a crisis or a special opportunity. If the boss is not spending at least twenty hours a week on fundraising, you should reassign work or reduce the programs. No matter how great your professional and volunteer fundraisers are, your top prospects, media, and elected officials will want to meet face-to-face with the boss.

To make sure that the CEO focuses on fundraising first, ask him or her to fundraise every day from 9:00 A.M. until noon. Is this realistic? Yes—if you choose to make fundraising your priority.

Fundraiser John Pruehs tells about when he was working for the Rockford, Illinois, YMCA. Every time he came in the morning to see CEO George Brening, Brening was out with a prospect. He used breakfast, lunch, and special events to tell the key people in town about the organization and its plans. Of course, Brening did not ask for money at every meeting. But the end result was that when the Y needed money for a special campaign, the right people were not strangers to the Y and its plans. At a time that the Rockford economy was in trouble, Brening built up the Y to be one of the largest YMCA facilities in the country; in a town with a population of 100,000, some 25,000 people were members.

As John Pruehs says, "Brening was a genius at time management. He was always out of the building by 4:30 P.M. and virtually never had to work nights or weekends. Because he focused on fundraising and cultivation the first thing every day, he had the funds he needed to get the best staff, facilities, and programs."

If you are the CEO and you are tired of cranking out proposals by the light of the moon, discipline yourself to put fundraising first every day. Put it first on every agenda. Include money, or at least what the money will buy, somewhere in every conversation with the key players in your community.

Consultants

Your organization may also want to hire a consultant to work on a special assignment, such as designing your website or organizing a capital campaign. For more information on hiring a consultant, see Chapter 7.

How to Get the Best from Both Professionals and Volunteers

Discuss frankly how the organization can maximize the strengths and minimize the weaknesses of the people you have. For example, if the professionals have more fundraising know-how than the volunteers, could they offer some training for the volunteers? Or can they take a volunteer every time they go fundraising until the volunteer is ready to go alone? On the other hand, if the volunteers know community and business leaders with power and money, can they introduce them to the professionals? Or bring the prospects out to the next event so they can see the organization?

Annual Planning

The annual plan is the best tool to guarantee a harmonious relationship between the volunteers and the professionals. If you plan your year in advance, everyone will get more results and feel better about the work, too.

If your organization is predominantly families with school-age children, make the plan in September when your members know the dates for school holidays and vacations. If your organization is active only part of the year, like the snowmobile club in the winter or Little League in the summer, plan your fundraising work two months before the busy season. For other organizations, plan the calendar the week after you elect new officers, so each leader has a say in the plan, or else in October for the next calendar year.

Holding Volunteers and Staff Accountable

First, review the fundraising strategies you chose on the work sheet on page 19. Put the names of specific staff or volunteers by each part of your strategy. For example, let us say that your group plans to make $100,000 next year using these techniques and supervised by these people:

FIGURE 2.1 **Sample Work Plan—Goal: $100,000**

Source of Funds	Amount	Person Responsible
Dues	$30,000	Betty
Four mailings	$15,000	Maria
Corporate gifts	$10,000	Tom
Foundation grants	$10,000	Carlos
Major gifts	$10,000	Hassan
Spring event	$10,000	Jane
Fall event	$10,000	Wally
Local congregations	$3,000	Frank
Sales	$2,000	Viola
Total	$100,000	

One Job, One Person

In every case, one person has to be accountable for making the goal amount. "We" may all agree on the strategy, but one person makes each piece happen. Some things, like proposal writing, may be done more easily by the professionals. Others, like special events, may be done better by the volunteers. As long as each volunteer and professional knows his or her goal, the plan can move forward.

Remember, real life goes on while you are making your plans, so the leaders will need to revise the plans based on what happens to their people. For example, in November Jane agreed to chair next year's spring event. Then her daughter got engaged at Christmas to be married in June, so Jane wants to spend next spring making dresses and resigns as the spring event chair.

Now the planners face several possible courses. They may:

1. Find a new spring event chair and leave the plan as it is with a new person accountable for the goal.

2. Discover no one will volunteer to chair the spring event, but three people say they could work on the fall event. Then cancel the spring event and double the goal for the fall event to $20,000.

3. Learn no one wants to lead the spring event, but two people want to start a new chapter in the next county. Cancel the spring event and raise the goal for dues to $40,000. Dues are the only piece of the plan that is totally elastic. You can sell as many memberships as you want.

4. Discover no one wants to lead the spring event, and every other person is already stretching to make his or her projected goals. Take $10,000 out of the plan and meet with the officers and CEO to discuss which programs will need to be cut.

A fundraising plan never exists in a vacuum. Unless you can name a person responsible for each dollar amount, you do not have a plan. The CEO and the director of development cannot (and should not) raise the entire amount in the budget. It is their job to be sure that each person is clear on his or her goal and deadlines and that each person succeeds.

Making Your Calendar

This is where the actual calendar comes in. Make copies of next year's calendar from your scheduling software, buy them at an office-supply shop, or get them donated by your banker or insurance agent. Hand them out at a fundraising meeting and ask each leader and staff member to think about what he or she wants to do next year. Discuss personal goals and ask them to discuss next year's calendar with their families. At the following meeting ask for commitments from volunteers and professionals. This way no one will feel pressured into taking a job, and people can clear their assignments with their families. If Wally discovers that his son will be the starting quarterback for the football team next year, he will not volunteer to chair the fall event. If the son is going out for track in the spring, fall will be a good time for Wally.

This is also a good time to ask the leaders to commit to a gift. How much are they going to give and in what form—weekly cash gifts, a monthly pledge, or one check? Ask the leaders what kind of help each one wants from the staff and exactly when that will be needed. This will save the paid staff from those nightmare days when twelve board members call with an emergency that needs to be handled first.

Schedule vacations. Time off is mandatory for stressful jobs, and asking for money every day is stressful. Depending on your organization, try to plan for at least one month with no fundraising meetings at all. August is ideal for most groups, since the corporate and foundation people are unreachable, volunteers are on vacation and getting the kids ready for school, and the professionals want a vacation, too. In December schedule a holiday party, but skip meetings except important major donor visits to get year-end gifts.

Make fundraising a priority for the board. If you want the board to be enthusiastic about fundraising, put it first on the calendar and first on every agenda. If you put on a major fundraising event, cancel the board meeting that month and ask every board member to attend the fundraiser instead. Your board can certainly make all its decisions in four to six meetings a year. Major corporations handling multibillion-dollar responsibilities meet four times a year—so can you. Plus you want to attract the kind of people who like action and results more than arguing and rhetoric. Do not forget to allocate at least one month for evaluation and planning, one or two months for parties that are just for fun (no one has to sell the tickets), and at least one month with nothing at all scheduled for the organization. Figure 2.2 is a sample calendar to show these ideas at work. You can adapt them to fit your leaders' and your community's calendar.

FIGURE 2.2 **Sample Fundraising Calendar**

Month	*Fundraising Focus*	*Board Meeting*	*Direct Mail and E-Mail*
January	Membership sales	Yes	Newsletter: corporate donor story
February	Business & corporate solicitation	No	Spring event invitations
March	Major gift solicitation	Yes	E-mail promotion of on-line auction
April	Spring fundraising event	No, attend event instead	Newsletter: life income gift story
May	Evaluation and planning	Yes	–
June	Membership sales	Yes	Fall event, save the date cards

Month	Fundraising Focus	Board Meeting	Direct Mail and E-Mail
July	Picnic just for fun. Awards for staff and volunteers.	No, attend picnic instead	Annual report: individual major donor stories
August	Nothing	No	–
September	Major gift solicitation	Yes	Fall event invitations
October	Fall fundraising event	No, attend fall event	Newsletter: program results
November	Personal letters, calls, E-mail for year-end gifts	Yes	Year-end direct mail and E-mail
December	Party just for fun	No, attend holiday party	–

Plan Ahead

The calendar can make your life easier by giving you the lead time you need. For example, Gina Spagnola is the director of marketing and special events for the Galveston (Texas) Historical Foundation. Its festival "Dickens on the Strand" grosses $300,000 for the foundation and produces more than $3 million for the city's economy. After twenty-five years of experience, the staff at Galveston have learned how to master the time line to get the most volunteers, the most visitors, and the most profit.

Dickens on the Strand is always the first weekend in December. Ninety-five percent of the cooperating groups and financial sponsors sign on by April. This enables the foundation staff to write the brochure in May and have it ready in June, because they have learned it is a whole lot easier to wholesale than to retail. If her brochure is out in June, she can market to tour directors and sell blocks of tickets rather than individual tickets. In the same way, Gina uses great volunteer leadership to wholesale the volunteer participation. The Galveston Historical Foundation uses more than 1,000 volunteers to staff the gates, the beer pub, the Dr. Pepper pub, and the information pubs, and perform other tasks. Seventy committee chairs each recruit, train, inspire, and reward dozens of volunteers so that they have fun and keep coming back every year.

Gina says her goal is to have everything completed four weeks before the event, so the last month can be spent "putting out fires." Anyone who has organized major events knows you spend most of the last week fixing things you thought were already taken care of. By working with a time line, you give yourself, the staff, and all your volunteers the time to do everything well.

Even better, you can create a cushion to allow for crisis. When you are working with a lot of volunteers, you know that something always happens. Even the most dedicated people may have some misfortune befall them at a bad time. Gina Spagnola's ideal is to always be one month ahead on the annual time line—and it pays off. One year she had a family emergency that required her to take a five-week leave. Because she had well-trained staff, experienced volunteers, and a very clear time line, the entire weekend event went off as planned. Especially if your organization depends on one event or mailing for part of your budget, be sure you have a yearlong time line to enable all the staff and volunteers to do the best they can.

The Fundraising Team

Volunteering or working for a worthwhile nonprofit organization will give you many tangible rewards. One reason people like to do fundraising is that they can see measurable results quickly. In addition, you and everyone on the team will know that your hard work asking for money is what makes everything else possible.

But even more than the money raised, or all the good things the money can buy, is the reward of working with fine people who care deeply about their community. The qualities you seek in your fundraising team—integrity, sincerity, courage, and persistence—are the qualities that make the fundraisers such a pleasure to work with. Beyond the cold hard cash is the warm feeling of doing good work with people who can see beyond the bottom line.

Selling Products and Services

Raising Money from Customers and Clients 3

My first real, thrilling job was filling balloons with gas, then tying strings around them and making people buy them. They all said, VOTES FOR WOMEN.

—Katharine Hepburn
Ladies Home Journal

MY FIRST REAL, THRILLING FUNDRAISING experience was selling Girl Scout cookies. Unlike the girls whose fathers sold their daughters' quotas at the office, I was the daughter of a dentist, so I had to get my own orders. By going door-to-door in my suburban neighborhood, I sold the most cookies in my troop.

For assorted charities over the years, I have also sold baseball caps, books, bumper stickers, candles, catnip toys, coffee mugs, cookbooks, cutting boards shaped like pigs, designer scarves, golf shirts, grapefruits, greeting cards, herbed vinegars, mouse pads, photographs, personalized letters from Santa, poodles crafted out of golf balls, salted nuts, tote bags, water bottles, wrapping paper, and enough T-shirts to outfit an army of teenagers. What I learned from all this is: (1) it is easy to sell a good product for a good cause, and (2) it is easiest to sell a good product that is chocolate.

Because even little children like to play store, almost anyone can start raising money by selling products. Even better, literally anyone can buy your products, whether or not they care about your organization. Shoppers may buy candy for a dollar from a child at the Near North Health Services Corporation in one of Chicago's worst public housing projects, or a case of wine for $140 from a volunteer at the Lyric Opera in one of Chicago's loveliest buildings. In either case, the shopper might not care about where the money goes (scholarships or sopranos), but they know they like chocolate and chardonnay. Once you capture the name, then you can use the techniques in Chapter 5 to ask the customers to become donors.

Besides selling products, many nonprofit organizations also sell their services. Raising money from fees is most common in schools and universities, but it can be used by any organization. Because both selling products and selling services raise money from many small customers and clients, they make up the bottom of the fundraising pyramid (see Figure 3.1). You can ask the most prospects very quickly to make purchases. Each transaction is very fast and the buyer's commitment very low. The great advantage is the wide number of names that are swept into your net for upgrading into donors.

FIGURE 3.1 **Individual Donor Development**

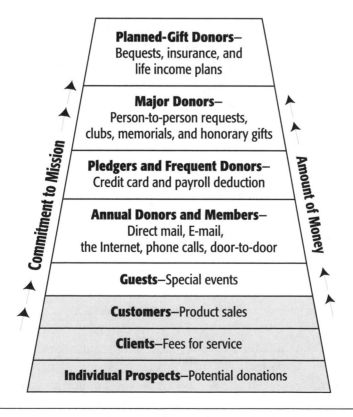

Selling Products

Selling products is one of the easiest ways for nonprofits to earn income. Most Americans already have experience as nonprofit salespeople selling band candy, lightbulbs, or pizzas in their youth. As with other fundraising strategies, creative groups find ways to connect product sales to their mission.

Probably the most familiar example is Girl Scout cookies. Girl Scouts began selling homemade cookies in the 1920s and went to commercial bakeries in 1938. In 1998, the 318 Girl Scout Councils of America and 81 locations overseas (many near military bases) organized cookie sales to make money and teach sales skills. One million girls and adults sold 182 million boxes of cookies to fund their local council's programs.

The Scouts use the cookie sales as more than a moneymaker; selling cookies is considered a program activity to teach girls goal setting, decision making, and responsibility. Some troops learn telemarketing and advertising skills. For most of the girls, it is their first exposure to the business world—an important experience, since the majority of American women will work outside the home. Thus, the Scouts have fun and learn useful skills while they are also making money for their troop. If you want to add sales to your fundraising strategy, see if you can also use the activity to advance your mission.

Advantages of Selling Products

The main advantage of selling is that your customers are going to get something they want anyway. Ideally, your product will be connected to the work you do, so you can discuss your issues at the same time you make sales. For example, environmental groups sell trees, biodegradable diapers, and cloth lunch bags to make money for their causes.

You can connect the sales to your mission. For example, one-third of UNICEF's revenue comes from fundraising, much from the sale of their holiday cards, calendars, and children's games. The UNICEF 1998 holiday-card catalog advertises how much even the smallest purchase can do and what the cumulative benefits are from all of its sales.[1]

- $5 helps a family improve water quality by providing basic sanitation in that home. From 1990 to 1995, programs assisted by UNICEF helped almost 800 million people gain access to safe drinking water.

- $2.35 provides basic educational supplies for one child. In 1996 UNICEF spent $94.4 million fighting illiteracy.

- 7¢ provides three vitamin A capsules for protection against blindness . . . for one year. Vitamin A supplementation saves the lives of one million to three million children a year worldwide.

Sales can involve lots of different types of people. The outgoing extroverts can handle the selling; the shy, well-organized people can handle the order forms and bookkeeping. This is a good place to put the people who are too timid to ask for donations in person. They can fill orders from advertisements or your website.

A business can start small and grow a lot. Almost any group can hold a bake sale or a rummage sale and bring in $500 to $1,000 in a weekend. In 1998, the Junior Leagues of America made more than $2 million from their cookbooks and more than $5 million from their thrift shops and sales, such as the League's Washington, D.C., spring rummage sale, "Tossed and Found."

Nonprofit businesses can also appeal to their customers' good intentions. Buying products from nonprofits can be an act of socially responsible consumerism. Why buy a T-shirt with rude remarks when you could look just as good and at the same time benefit a local charity by buying the charity's T-shirt? As long as you plan to splurge on expensive furniture, why not buy one of the outstanding licensed reproductions from the National Trust for Historic Preservation and benefit the historic properties it manages?

Set a Goal—and Achieve It

In 1998 a group of young teens in the Cabrini-Green public housing project in Chicago decided they wanted to go to Disney World in Florida. Some kids said Disney World was "only for rich people," but led by Rochelle Satchell, coordinator of group activities for the Near North Health Services Corporation, forty-one kids decided they could go, too. So they sold candy, wrote a book about their community and sold it for $20 per copy, and cooked breakfasts for people working in the neighborhood (in time to clean up and get to school). In four months these children from ages six to seventeen in one of the poorest neighborhoods in America raised $10,314 by selling things.

The purpose of the Health Services program is to help the younger siblings of pregnant teenagers avoid pregnancy, drugs, and gangs. Coordinator Satchell used the fundraising and the trip to build up good work habits, positive attitudes, and high hopes in the teenagers. What they learned from her was how to make their own rules to set a high goal and achieve it. What she learned from them was how much children help each other. Each child had an individual dollar goal. Once the child accomplished his or her own goal, that child would help another child make his or her goal so that *every* child was able to go on the trip.

On the trip home, Satchell, the parents, and the bus driver from Atlanta shared with the children one of the great historical sites in America. They stopped to visit the Sweet Auburn national historic district in Atlanta, where they could see the birthplace and childhood surroundings of civil rights leader Dr. Martin Luther King, Jr., and visit his grave site at the Martin Luther King, Jr., Center for Nonviolent Social Change. Satchell wanted the children to know their own history. She told them how former mayor Maynard Jackson of Atlanta said the Sweet Auburn community offered freed slaves "the three Bs—bucks, ballots, and books!" Since these children had been learning how to be good fundraisers, good citizens, and good scholars, they would benefit from the examples of other Americans who learned how to set goals and achieve them.

More than Merchandise

On a much grander scale, the Lyric Opera of Chicago sells merchandise each year from August to October through a catalog and through a volunteer-run kiosk. Both methods raise funds for Operathon, an all-day radio marathon on WFMT, a classical radio station. The event's 1998 goal was $250,000; they made nearly $262,000.

Over the years, Operathon has combined excellent merchandise sales with additional event support, including corporate sponsorships, individual gifts, foundation grants, and great in-kind donations. American Airlines has been one of the corporate sponsors for eleven years, giving cash as well as both domestic and international trip packages. Twenty-one chapters of volunteers raise seed money and challenge grants, and more than 250 members work the day of the event. Two hundred thirty-three premiums are auctioned off, such as CDs, posters, and libretti signed by the opera stars, backstage tours, meals at the best restaurants, stays at great hotels, services, trips, and gourmet treats such as a twenty-five-pound box of Marshall Field's Frango Mints. Each year the cover of the catalog features a prominent celebrity, and among them is Chicago's most famous athlete, Michael Jordan of the world champion Chicago Bulls (see Figure 3.2). Sports fans may not know Der Rosenkavalier from Dennis Rodman, but they certainly know how to shop.

FIGURE 3.2 **Operathon Catalog Cover**

Courtesy of Lyric Opera of Chicago. Photo by Dan Best.

Challenges

There are always some people who will not want your product although they think your group and its work are just wonderful. For example, dieters, diabetics, and health nuts may not buy Girl Scout cookies, although they probably want girls to learn Girl Scout values such as loyalty, courtesy, and cleanliness in thought, word, and deed.

So every time you sell merchandise in person, on your website, or from a catalog, also include a written request for memberships, donations, and bequests. Even if people do not want your product, they may want your mission and will contribute if you give them the option.

The other challenge facing smaller groups is that once everyone you know has your product, then whom do you sell to? One solution is to combine your sales with a special event that will bring in fresh people. The Christmas and Hanukkah season is especially good for combining events and selling products. For example, the Hinsdale (Illinois) Humane Society runs "Santa Paws," a chance to have your pet's photo taken with Santa Claus for $15. At the same time, they sell holiday cards in sets of thirteen (a "barker's dozen") for $10.

Can you "take a ride" on some other activity that brings out lots of new people? Minnesota Clean Water Action Project has planned sales to take advantage of the miles of gridlocked cars going to the best lakes on the first day of the fishing season. One Methodist church in Pittsburgh does its bake sale on Election Day, because the church is a polling site and all the patriotic citizens smell the brownies baking while they vote. What else takes place in your town that can deliver new customers to you?

Growing Sales into a Business

Selling a good product can be the first step to developing a permanent, successful business operation for your nonprofit organization. Earned-income enterprises are becoming more and more popular and profitable for all kinds of charities. They can range from selling quality products such as UNICEF cards or Girl Scout cookies to operating an entire store. Universities and libraries run bookstores, hospitals and museums run gift shops, international relief organizations sell crafts from around the world, historical houses license reproductions of their furniture, hospitals operate pharmacies, and zoos organize photographic safaris—all to make money for their missions. In addition to these in-house ventures, today nonprofits are running bigger ventures, often in partnership with a for-profit. Thus, a museum may work with a developer to build condominiums in the airspace above the museum, or universities may work with drug companies to patent their research.

Using sales to make money for a nonprofit is not a new idea. Medieval churches made money by selling ales brewed in the church house and by renting out vestments to other churches for funerals and festivals. In Cornwall, England, the parish accounts from 1526 show that gypsies stayed in the Stratton church house several times, and the "keepers of the bear" paid one pence rent for it.[1] Today churches near popular sports stadiums, such as Fenway Park in Boston and Wrigley Field in Chicago, can make money selling parking to sports fans.

These days more and more charities test their volunteers and staff in selling products and services so as to form a highly skilled staff that can develop sales into a full-time business.

What is the role of earned-income ventures for nonprofits today? Especially in low-income neighborhoods, business ventures generate income as well as serve as an agency's overall strategy for improving a community. Ventures serve useful social goals such as getting people off welfare, teaching work skills, giving incentives to stay in or go back to school, and providing better goods and services at fair prices. They can add another source of income, which may be vital in times of uncertain cash flow. It is not uncommon for community agencies to pay the phone bill with cash from the recycling center while they wait for some state official to approve $50,000 in long-overdue vouchers.

Taxes

If your nonprofit organization sells products or runs a business, will it have to pay taxes on the profits? Maybe.

If your business is related to your mission for "exempt purposes" according to the IRS, your organization should not have to pay taxes. If your business is staffed by volunteers or operates only once in a while (such as an annual book and CD sale), you are probably not liable for taxes. Also, passive income, such as royalties from use of affinity credit cards or licensing historic designs, is generally not taxed. However, your organization may be liable on any income the IRS can prove is not "substantially related" to your exempt purposes under the Unrelated Business Income Tax.

The IRS is getting tougher on nonprofits that run businesses, and associations of small businesses are going to keep up the pressure to reduce what they consider as unfair competition from nonprofits. Because the laws and court rulings on these questions change quickly, you need to get good up-to-date legal advice.

Start by reading IRS Publication 598, *Tax on Unrelated Business Income of Exempt Organizations*, which defines "unrelated trade or business" and explains the exceptions. To get it free, call (800) TAX-FORM or visit www.irs.gov. Then hire or recruit a lawyer with experience in this area of the law. If your proposed business will owe any local, state, or federal taxes, of course the business manager must pay all taxes on time. Do not dismiss the possibility of establishing a moneymaking business just because it may have to pay taxes. If necessary, consider taxes a cost of doing business and add them to the expenses in your plan.

Fees and Tuitions

Fees charged for services account for about 42 to 45 percent of the total budgets of nonprofits other than religious congregations, although this is set higher for some fields like education and health services, and lower for others like advocacy and community organizing. With ongoing government cutbacks and a strong economy, almost every organization has looked at initiating fees for service or increasing the fees they already have. Instead of selling a product, by setting fees you sell the work your organization does. Most schools call their fees "tuitions."

Fees are good for a nonprofit because the people who want what you do are the ones who pay for it. If you believe in the value of your work and price it so that you will make a profit, fees and tuitions can help support your group.

Some organizations are reluctant to set fees for fear of discovering that their clients do not want the services enough to pay for them. If your clients do not want what you do, why are you doing it? Even worse, why should the taxpayers or grant makers pay for services local people do not want?

Since many fundraisers began their professional careers not as fundraisers, but as program staff, it is often difficult for them to overcome what Rona Smyth Henry of the Robert Wood Johnson Foundation calls "pricing guilt." There are several solutions to this. Here are a few Rona Rules for Fees:

- Do the math! Determine the cost on all of your programs and use the most conservative measures. For example, calculate your unit cost when the agency has its lowest census, not when it is full.

- Never charge less than your true per-unit costs.

- For people who can pay more, charge more.

- It is all right to offer discounts, especially quantity discounts for more use or prepayment, just as a for-profit company would do. If you do give a discount, be sure your clients know it.

- Never apologize—explain the value. Many respite service programs that offer day care for people with Alzheimer's disease have applied Rona Smyth Henry's suggestion, and found they not only developed a dependable income stream, but also had more participants, and best of all, a greater feeling of dignity in the families using the services.

Fees Can Help You Grow

If you are providing a quality service, fees allow your organization to grow as the market for your services grows. For example, in 1978 Bill Draves was the only staff person for the Free University Network. With a budget of $20,000, the Free U Network provided free technical assistance and organized a very low-cost national conference for anyone offering noncredit adult education courses. Half of the budget came from foundation grants because, as Draves says, "I thought that was where the money was."

Today the organization, based in Kansas, is called the Learning Resources Network (LERN). It has a $2 million budget raised entirely from fees for its technical assistance, its national conference, and sales of its publications. LERN receives no foundation grants. The organization now serves more than 5,000 adult education programs in twelve countries.

Fees for Low-Income Markets

The obvious difficulty with fees or tuitions is that some people will not be able to pay. Your organization can choose from several strategies to solve this problem.

You can charge more for some services to subsidize other services. Measure the popularity of everything you do and charge more where you can. For example, when Bill Draves founded LERN he was opposed to charging fees for adult education classes, because he wanted low-income people to be able to take classes in survival skills such as home canning and auto repair. However, an analysis revealed that the most popular adult education courses in Kansas were "Rodeo History" and "French Hair Braiding," neither of which could be considered survival skills. Then he realized he could charge the rodeo fans and beauty queens more for their courses and use those profits to subsidize the classes for low-income people.

LERN uses the same policy today. It makes enough of a surplus on its most popular services to give free scholarships to programs offering classes for low-income people. This helps programs like "English as a Second Language (ESL)" and "ESL Keyboarding" (which teaches immigrants how to use the English-language keyboard so they can get jobs). As Draves says, "We should be doing some things for people who cannot pay." (For more on LERN, call (800) 678-5376 or visit www.lern.org.)

Other nonprofits look at what they can and should do for free and what they can charge a fee for. For example, most libraries let patrons borrow books for free, but charge a small fee for using commercial databases such as DIALOG or LEXIS-NEXIS.

Consider other strategies for setting fees. Some counseling programs charge fees based on a sliding scale keyed to income. Everyone pays something, so they are more likely to continue and benefit from the counseling, but the people with little or no income pay less while the people with high incomes pay more.

Some groups provide sweat-equity opportunities so people can earn the fee. Habitat for Humanity helps low-income people earn a down payment for a home by having them work a specified number of hours building their own home and then volunteer a certain number of hours to help another family build a home.

Most people can and will pay when asked. If you want your agency to be perceived as a permanent, powerful organization accountable to the people it serves, always ask those people to pay a fee for the services they use.

Building the Base

Both selling products and charging fees for service are easy ways to make money from people who want something you can sell. Be sure your telephone number, E-mail address, and website locator (URL) are printed on every item you sell, every invoice, and every bag or box. Include a simple one-page brochure with every sale, telling your customers who you are and how to join.

For every transaction, ask for the buyer's preferred mail and E-mail addresses. At least once a year, do a mailing to all of your customers and clients asking them for donations and volunteer time. Also include local customers and clients on the invitation list for parties, and include everyone on your E-mail advocacy alert list.

Then do your best to turn your customers and clients into donors giving to the mission of your organization.

Special Events 4

Memory Walk sounded like it would be fun.
> —Jason Piette, age 14
> Planning committee member
> Vermont Alzheimer's Association
> Memory Walk

SPECIAL EVENTS ARE THE DR. JEKYLL and Mr. Hyde of fundraising. If you have people who like to have fun, organize events, and focus on the bottom line, events are a dream. On the other hand, if most of the work falls on the already overworked staff and if there is no clear relationship to the mission of the organization, special events can be an energy-draining nightmare.

If your *only* goal is making money, do not even consider doing a special event. If all you want is money, you know the drill: give a gift, ask for money, send a thank-you note. Cancel the luau and go directly to the next chapter to learn how to ask for money. However, if you want to raise some money, have fun, and find new leaders at the same time—it is time for a party!

Personally, I adore special events. Especially if you look at fundraising as organizing—that is, as training and motivating *other* people to ask for money—then events are indispensable for testing leaders and building solidarity. More than any other kind of fundraiser, events raise money and raise awareness about your organization at the same time.

Special events are toward the bottom of the fundraising pyramid because you will entertain lots of people and a few of them will also go on
to be major donors (see Figure 4.1). For example, the foundation that
raises money for the public school in Chickasha, Oklahoma, holds a pancake supper at the local McDonald's restaurant the Tuesday before spring
break. Their board members wear red aprons with the schoolhouse on
them when serving the orange drink, coffee, and unlimited pancakes.
All this at only $5 for adults and $3 for kids. The short-term goal is to
host a fundraising event that every member of the school district can afford and enjoy. The long-range payoff from this event has been to raise
the visibility of the Foundation for Excellence. Although it is only ten
years old, it has already received a gift of $107,000 from a trust and a
bequest of $275,000, because those donors and their bankers learned of
the foundation through the pancake supper.

This chapter will show you how special events can do much more
than raise money: they can raise awareness for the most serious issues

FIGURE 4.1 **Individual Donor Development**

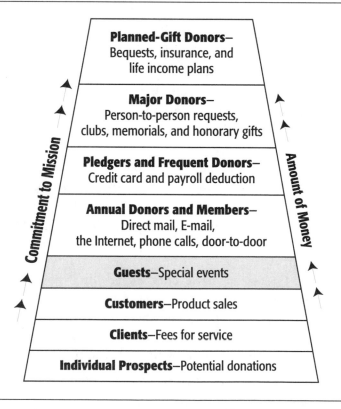

and participation in the most challenging communities. We will explore what is new on the Internet and compare doing a silent auction at a real event versus on-line. You will learn how to choose the best date and the right price, and attract celebrities and corporate support. Last is a checklist to help you choose the best event for your organization year after year.

Make Your Special Event Mean More than Money

What makes a special event special? Many things: the people, the place, or the theme. But what makes a special event truly special—different from a normal party—is the cause.

Most Important: Connect to Your Mission

The best special events link the event to the mission of the organization. It is not enough to have a novel party. It must also harmonize with the mission of the organization. If your community organization is concerned about neighborhood safety, sponsor a Halloween party in a safe place with good supervision. If you want to promote your ethnic heritage, throw a Cinco de Mayo Mexican Independence Day fiesta or a Chinese New Year's Day parade. The Audubon Society sells birdseed and celebrates the bird feeder season at their party called the "Suet Ball."

Even the most serious cause can use an event to raise money and awareness at the same time. In 1996 two Burmese comedians were sentenced to seven years breaking rocks in a labor camp for singing a comic song about the Burmese generals and making a joke about Burmese government officials. Ros Skipper, the Scottish fundraising officer for Amnesty International, organized a fundraising event featuring seven popular stand-up comics to perform at the Edinburgh Festival Fringe in 1997. The midnight show called "Just a Tickle" raised £7,500 (more than $11,000), collected scores of new signatures on petitions for the release of the comedians, raised awareness among the thousands of visitors to the Fringe, and attracted great press coverage on Amnesty International's work to free these and other political prisoners.

Build a Real Community

Good events serve as an antidote to "cocooning," the term that trend gurus like Faith Popcorn use for the growing trend of Americans to spend more time at home. Between the Internet and the Home Shopping Network, some people never see anyone but the delivery truck driver. Non-profits can use ingenious special events to lure lonely people away from staring at their televisions and computers and out into meeting real people.

More important, some experts say cocooning helps explain why people do not even bother to vote. Special events are one effective way to introduce people to your issues. In a *Rolling Stone* poll that asked what it would take to get them involved in public affairs, eighteen- to forty-four-year-olds listed local personal events, not general issues. One-third said they could be mobilized to battle drunk drivers, and another third said they would join a neighborhood crime watch.

In the same poll of eighteen- to forty-four-year-olds, only one-half of this group said they vote regularly, and only one-third said they follow the news. Since these are the people you need to be tomorrow's leaders and donors, get them out of the house and into your organization. The first step can be unique special events.

Overcome Barriers

Much more serious than the challenges of shy people using technology to stay home alone are the divisions of race and class that we still face as a nation. No one is going to explore the inner city at www.ghetto.com. But for people organizing for social and economic justice in the toughest neighborhoods, one of the greatest challenges is getting people out to see and feel what the organization does.

One success story is Sarah's Circle, a program for homeless women in the Uptown community in Chicago. They sponsor a "Winter Walk" each February. Unlike most walkathons, where walkers meander through the park enjoying the fresh lake breezes on a summer day, Winter Walk takes place in the bitter cold, under the elevated train tracks, and through a rough area. This route looks intimidating even in the daytime. Naturally, people say, "This is terrible. Can we go back to the shelter?" This gives the volunteers a chance to say, "Now imagine if you were a woman on these streets—alone—every day."

Sarah's Winter Walk raises about $10,000 each year. But more than money, it brings in hundreds of people from more affluent neighborhoods and suburbs who would never see the Uptown area on their own. The people who have seen what Sarah's Circle does have become the shelter's

most stalwart supporters. When the shelter was burnt out of its building, the Winter Walk donors were among the first who came through for
the capital campaign that enabled Sarah's Circle to move into bigger and
better quarters.

Caveat: A Guest Is a Guest, Not a Member

Special events, also known as benefits or galas, are among the most popular fundraising strategies. The organization sells tickets, priced to make
a profit, for a party, concert, or dinner dance. Unlike asking for donations to support the mission of your organization, selling benefit tickets
requires only that you sell the event itself. Just remember that almost all
of the people who buy a ticket are guests—they are there to eat, drink,
dance, and flirt. If you want them to give to your mission, the next step
is to turn them into annual donors (see Chapters 5 to 7).

For example, my city church attracts new people throughout the year
at the Antiques Fair, a fancy Mardi Gras party, and an amateur play such
as Agatha Christie's *Murder at the Vicarage*. Although the amount raised
at each event is small, the events give us a way to attract new members
in a community where there are always a lot of people moving in and
moving out. Once people join, their average annual pledge is now more
than $1,600. Many give generously to the capital campaigns and some
leave a bequest, so the long-range payoff is much higher. Statistics show
that 70 to 80 percent of a church's members join because somebody asks
them; only 7 to 8 percent wander in on their own. This will also hold for
other kinds of nonprofit organizations. Special events give people an easy
way to check you out before they join.

Ethically, you must always separate your guests and your members.
It is dishonest to claim that your group speaks for one thousand people
just because one thousand people came to an event. You can claim only
to represent the people who say they share your goals—not the customers who eat your dinners or buy your crafts.

Ethics: Gambling

The most controversial kind of special event is gambling, in any form.
It is a great temptation to put on gambling events, because they can raise
immense amounts of money. Americans bet more than $7 billion on
charitable gambling in forty-six states and D.C. An average of 11 per-

cent of the gross goes to the charities. In the United Kingdom, they run a National Lottery with proceeds going to subsidize the arts and historic preservation.

Since it is inevitable that people are going to gamble anyway, why not get a piece of the pie? Some charities do decide to use gambling as part of their fundraising strategy. Depending on the state laws, charities can choose to make money from bingo, pull tabs, card games, raffles, or sweepstakes.

What are the negatives? Gambling, more than any other choice of fundraising strategy, attracts people who may be unaware, indifferent, or even hostile to your mission. Gamblers come to gamble. Period. I am convinced you could run a bingo for "Friends of Dust" and fill the hall with bingo players.

Many religious congregations oppose gambling because it brings out the worst in people. The only way I can win is if everyone else loses. Then it is a very short step from hoping I win to hoping that you lose. This is not in the best spiritual traditions of promoting cooperation and mutual aid.

Progressives oppose gambling as a racist tax and a regressive tax because poor people and people of color gamble more than rich white people. Conservatives oppose gambling because urging people to get something for nothing violates the work ethic. Gambling can be an addiction and lead to criminal behavior.

If your organization wants to raise money from healthy, hardworking people committed to economic justice and racial equality, do not choose gambling.

Advantages of Special Events

Here are some of the things that a well-organized special event can do for your organization:

Advantages for Your Current Members

- People have fun. Never underestimate the importance of fun. Proposals are not fun; parties are fun. Especially if your organization is controversial, special events help form the bonds that hold the group together during the rocky times.

- Parties are not meetings. Any volunteer knows that social time at meetings usually ends with those Seven Last Words: "We have to get through the agenda." Special parties give you a chance to dish about what is *not* on the agenda. You get to meet the families and friends of colleagues. I've seen a lot of romances bloom and babies grow up year to year at the great special events in town.

- Fundraising events offer the people who may not be able to write a large check for the organization an opportunity to raise a large amount of money through their time and talent.

- Your own people already know how to put on parties. If they organized the high school prom or the office Christmas party, they can do a special event for your organization.

- It often seems easier to sell tickets to an event than to ask for money for your cause. Events can be a good place for the new people to start.

- Events can work for anyone. Even children in very low-income communities can do events and make money.

Advantages for the Organization

- Sales can be traced, so you get an accurate way to measure who has networks. You get an objective way to separate the doers from the talkers.

- Events can have lots of volunteer jobs, so you can test your newest leaders to discover who has people skills (and who does not) on the barbecue committee rather than on the board.

- Annual events provide an easy way for your institutional funders to see the organization in action. Foundation staff can feel the vitality of the organization and meet more people beyond the person who is the fundraiser. (No matter how terrific you are, their knowing ten more of your group's leaders is better.) Since most foundation grants are for only one or two years, you have to wait that long before you can go back to them about fundraising issues; an annual event keeps the good grant makers in touch with your people until it is time to ask them again.

- You can get favorable press, radio, and TV coverage. You do not need a big ad budget, just bright ideas.

  The Maritime Center at Norwalk, Connecticut, got free press for its special exhibit called *Sharks!* by promoting a free admission for any lawyer (see Figure 4.2). This was written up in the local newspaper, then picked up by the *Wall Street Journal* in an article about the lack of respect for lawyers. Then the bond traders on Wall Street called to demand free admission, since *they* were sharks too, which the clever Maritime Center staff turned into a second *Wall Street Journal* story. None of this cost an extra cent: only moxie and imagination.

- You can create an event to counter a criticism of your agency. For example, a health counseling center for teenagers in rural Minnesota wanted to raise money and raise the community's awareness of the need for its services. Despite the county's soaring teenage pregnancy rate, some people objected to the program because the counselors discussed sex and contraceptives with the teenagers. The critics said that only families should tell their own children about safe sex; no outsider should interfere.

  So the organization decided to turn a negative into a positive. They designed an annual walkathon called "Walking and Talking." As in any walkathon, the money was raised from pledges per mile walked. The special twist was that the walkers were mother-daughter or father-son teams, who could discuss the problems of dating, peer pressures, and safe sex while they raised money for the counseling service.

- You can attract fresh money. Benefits enable you to reach beyond your own people for support. Especially in low- and middle-income communities, there are only so many times you can ask your own people to give.

- Parties can meet a social need. Especially in rural communities, the nonprofit groups may provide the best dances, art shows, movies, lectures, sports events, and parties. Your group can get the reputation as the one that makes things happen in your county.

- The economic benefits can multiply beyond the dollars that go to the sponsor. A successful special event can bring in new people with fresh money for antiques, art, crafts, food, lodging, gasoline, services, and souvenirs in the short run, for new homes and businesses in the long run.

FIGURE 4.2 **Exhibit Invitation**

What Do Lawyers and Sharks Have in Common?

☐ Appear in the same jokes   ☐ Are often misunderstood
☐ Inspire unreasonable fear in people   ☒ All of these

THE MARITIME CENTER
AT NORWALK

cordially and carefully invites all lawyers
to attend the new exhibit

SHARKS!

From opening day June 27th through August 31,
all lawyers will be admitted **FREE** with proof of profession
Required Proof - Drivers License **AND** Framed Law Degree or Business Card

This offer is good for one free general admission ticket to the aquarium/museum
It **does not** include admission to the IMAX theater
Offer is not valid after August 31, 1992

Grateful acknowledgment is made to the Maritime Aquarium for permission to reprint the 1992 Sharks! exhibit lawyers invitation.

As noted in Chapter 2, every December the Galveston Historical Foundation sponsors a Victorian Christmas celebration called "Dickens on the Strand" (both Galveston and London have a street named the Strand). In 1998 the two-day festival grossed $300,000 for the foundation itself from tickets, house tours, the Victorian Costume Ball, and other moneymakers. The event also provided a great opportunity for other Galveston charities to participate, from fundraising events like the County Historical Museum Forest of Christmas Trees to educational events like the Civil War reenactment and the petting zoo enjoyed by eight hundred schoolchildren the Friday before the celebration. (Guess where they took their parents on Saturday?) Every hotel, motel, and bed-and-breakfast room for miles around was sold out, and one street was devoted just to art and antique sales. The economic impact for the city of Galveston (both for-profits and nonprofits) was projected at more than $3 million; the result for the entire county would be three or four times as much.

Also, seize the opportunity to use what is special about your community to attract home buyers and investors. Some entire urban neighborhoods, like Old Town in Chicago or the German Village in Columbus, Ohio, were turned from dilapidated areas into the darlings of the real estate agents through savvy marketing at their annual events. For example, the Slavic Village Harvest Festival in Cleveland gets celebrities out to the southeast side to judge the annual Kielbasa Cook-Off sponsored by First-Merit First National Bank. Then everyone dances the night away to great polka bands like the Button Box Players and the Toledo Polka Motions. Everyone has fun, local bars and businesses make a bundle, the Slavic Village Broadway Development Corps makes more than $15,000, and best of all, they have found new businesses to fill their storefronts and new families to buy homes in the neighborhood.

Disadvantages of Special Events

On the downside, special events are not perfect. Here are some of the pitfalls:

- They can lose money. Never depend on money from the day of the event. Either have 90 percent of the tickets sold two weeks before the event or get corporate underwriting and "angels" (major donors) to cover the expenses.

- They can leech staff time away from programs. Keep a strict time log for every paid employee working on an event, and include the real cost of their time into the expenses. As much as possible, find or train volunteers to run the events.

- They can take fundraisers' time away from asking for individual gifts. One reason volunteers love to do events is that they can put off asking for contributions face-to-face. Put both in your fundraising strategy.

- They always exclude someone. High-priced events exclude poor people. Dances exclude people who do not like to dance. Casino nights exclude people who disapprove of gambling. The only way to include everyone is simply to ask for money. Not everyone can play golf, shoot turkeys, or run five kilometers, but anyone can give you money.

Fundraising Past

Special events have been around since George Frideric Handel composed the oratorio *Messiah* for a fundraiser in Dublin in 1742. It was a smashing success—so crowded that the organizers had to ask the ladies not to wear their hoopskirts and the officers not to wear their swords. They raised enough money to release 142 prisoners from the Irish jails and to subsidize care for indigents at the Dublin hospital. *Messiah* was always produced as a fundraiser when Handel was alive, including the performance in London where they claim King George II got so swept away by the "Hallelujah Chorus" that he stood up, thus launching a fad that lives on in sing-along versions every Christmas. As happens in any fundraising event, a few evaluations came back saying it was too dull, so they hired Mozart to punch it up a little bit for Handel's centennial, then hired Swedish superstar Jenny Lind to add some sizzle to the soprano part.[1]

Fundraising Future

So what's new in your fundraising plan? No matter what you are doing well now, it can be improved with new ideas. Many fundraisers are testing ways to improve their fundraising events via E-mail and the Internet. Every organization can build a list of people who prefer to get notices on-line, and then E-mail the "save the date," the invitation, the volunteer opportunities, and the request for auction or raffle prizes. Frequent short updates from the committee chairs—great place, exciting celebrity, best band—can build excitement. If you have leaders who travel a lot for their jobs, or split their time between different residences, it is much more reliable to keep them up-to-date via E-mail. Also, E-mail can help you recruit more students and young adults as volunteers and guests. The advantage for the staff is you can reach more people more quickly with less work and less expense.

Silent Auctions: In Person and On-Line

Any event with people and tables can include a silent auction. A silent auction involves a committee asking for unique items signed by sports, TV, or movie stars, gift certificates for meals or services, vacations to exotic locales, and unusual or luxury merchandise. Instead of having a live auctioneer, guests write a dollar amount on sheets of paper, and the person with the highest bid at the designated time gets to buy the prize. Some items will sell for less than their fair market value, some exactly at their regular price, and some for much more, such as tickets to the winning sports team's games. All of the money is 99 percent profit for you the sponsor.

The advantages of a silent auction at a real event with live people are:

- It is fun. Some people love to compete, and everybody loves a bargain.

- It may be easier to get donated products and services than a cash contribution from some merchants, because they want visibility for their products.

- It creates a way for people to mingle and is an automatic conversation starter.

- It gives you an extra way to get more money from the people who can pay more.

- It adds the glamour of celebrities' stuff, even if you do not have the stars themselves there live and in person.

The auction items that move the easiest are vacations and celebrity items, because these items are not available in any store. The hardest things to auction off are works of art, because taste is so subjective and your party crowd is probably not the same as the gallery crowd. It is often hard to get the starting price for works of art, let alone what the artist considers the work's fair market value.

So how can we take all this and put it on the Internet? First, your organization has to have a website where the cyber-auction can take place. Second, you need to develop a long list of E-mail addresses for your own people and other likely bidders. Start asking for E-mail addresses on every piece of correspondence, every agenda, and every newsletter. Once you have people on-line, encourage them to share your website with their friends. Third, you need a secure way to accept credit card payments.

Actually, some auctions are run entirely on-line, without a real incarnation anywhere, and some vendors will run the auction for your organization for a fee. If you have access to many celebrity items with very high and wide appeal, this may be a good route for you. Otherwise, you can test the cyber-auction by continuing to run your regular silent auction at a special event and at the same time put part or all of the prizes on-line.

If you are running real and on-line auctions at the same time, decide which pieces should go on the Internet. Some generous donors will offer their vacation homes, ski lodge, or flat in London for a real event where every guest is a friend or a friend of a friend. Since these are their personal homes, they want some limits as to who can win. On the other hand, airline tickets and hotel packages are open to the public. For artwork, unless your site and web-master are sophisticated enough to show art well, or the artist has international name recognition, you would be smart to leave it out of the Internet auction. Veterans also advise against listing anything too heavy or fragile, such as wine, because it causes so many headaches with shipping. Limit the Internet prizes to celebrity items, unique opportunities, or great bargains that are easy to ship.

Now shop the competition. Browse the Internet for-profit auctions such as eBay at www.ebay.com and find a few nonprofit auctions to see how they make you feel welcome, how easy it is to become a bidder, and how they keep you involved. Usually there is a way for you to register, get a credit card approved (to prove you are a real person with purchasing power and not an adolescent prankster), then choose a password so you can continue raising your bids. As you bid, you will see when you have the top bid, or your E-mail will get a message when you've been outbid to encourage you to raise your bid. Most Internet auctions open two weeks before the event, and most bids are made on the last day—usually in the last hour. Then you get instant feedback on what you've won and an E-mail thank-you for your contribution, followed by a real letter and delivery of the item.

The advantages of the Internet auction are:

- Anyone can play. You can be in Budapest and still bid on an autographed copy of Stephen King's *Bag of Bones* in the auction for the Bangor Public Library.

- Everyone can play. Sometimes you get great auction items, but no one in your group has the disposable income or interest to turn them into money. If you have memorabilia from sports stars or trendy stuff from current TV shows, the Internet gives you a worldwide market that will turn these donations into gold for you.

- You never close. Your Internet auction is open twenty-four hours a day, seven days a week for anyone with access to the Net.

- Bidders may come for the bargains but stay to learn about your organization and your cause. Even if they are outbid for Mark McGwire's mitt or Sammy Sosa's scorecard, they will have found your website. Ideally, a few will come back to the site to get involved in your issues and, better yet, your organization.

The negatives are:

- Internet auctions attract bargain hunters and dealers in collectibles. At a silent auction with real people, guests can razz each other into going over the fair market value or intentionally give a higher amount because they care about the cause. On the Net, fundraisers find that once the item hits the market value, bidders drop out.

- In real life, higher bids can be encouraged by flirtatious committee members and intoxicating beverages. On the Internet, your prospects can be just as sullen and sober as they want. Just like shopping in a store, a real auction benefits from the "suggestive sell"—such as prodding an English teacher, "Did you see the first edition of *Great Gatsby* on table 3?" On the Internet, your allure depends instead on your sales copy and graphics.

- Except for your own members who are out of town and bidding on-line, 99 percent of the audience are looking for deals. They do not know who you are or what you do. At the real auction, fans of the leader may run up the bids for lunch with the founder, but on the Web the reaction will be "Mary who?" Do not expect the same response from the souls out in cyberspace as from the people at your party.

Clearly the uses for the Internet will continue to grow and offer you more new opportunities every year. Share your results with other fundraisers, "go" to on-line auctions and other events, and track every expense to get a useful evaluation.

How to Choose the Right Special Event

The right event is the one your organization's people want to do. Your own leaders already have some ideas from other parties they have attended for other charities. Recruit new people and bring in their fresh ideas. If your delegates hear about a terrific idea at the national convention, budget money to send two people to train with the other chapter, and then produce a similar event in your community. Some national organizations publish helpful how-to manuals, such as the American Red Cross's booklet *Be Special—In Any Event*, which tells its chapters how to do a Swim-A-Cross and other events.

As your group members consider possible benefit ideas, ask them to think about the best dates, prices, and people.

How to Choose the Best Date

Try to plan your special events at least a year in advance to get the most ideas and the best volunteers. What are the holidays and events that people celebrate anyway, and how can you use them to spice up your fundraising calendar?

For example, the Zoo Society of the Lincoln Park Zoo in Chicago sponsors an elegant ball in July that is called "Zoo La La" when it falls close to Bastille Day and "Red, White, and Zoo" when it is closer to the Fourth of July. Also in the summer the society puts on a gigantic member picnic; in the fall it offers the SpookyZoo Spectacular so 30,000 kids can show off their costumes and have safe fun; in December it sponsors caroling to the animals; and in January it hosts a few hundred football fans at a ZooperBowl. (Go to www.lpzoo.com to see more.)

What date fits best with your group's mission? The Illinois Committee for Control of Handguns sponsors its big dinner every year on

Abraham Lincoln's birthday, February 12, because it is a state holiday anyway and the Great Emancipator was assassinated with a handgun. Volunteer fire departments schedule the Fireman's Ball during Fire Prevention Week in October. A project for disabled children used Groundhog Day and asked people to "bring light to the lives of disabled children."

Use people's normal party patterns. Thirty-nine percent of families eat out on Mother's Day; 24 percent eat out on Father's Day. If you schedule a breakfast or dinner on one of those Sundays, you know you can draw a crowd. Any group can find an occasion for a party in *Chase's Calendar of Events*, the world's greatest collection of special days, weeks, months, historical anniversaries, and celebrities' birthdays, published annually. Even better, once your event is a success, get it listed in *Chase's*. For order information, see the Resource Guide.

Competition for a good date can make you crazy. In some communities multiple fundraisers take place every Saturday night of the year. In New York City there are often competing black-tie galas on weeknights, and this trend is spreading to other large cities. Some charities "own" certain holidays. It is futile to try to do an event on Valentine's Day if the local Heart Association has done its Sweetheart Ball on February 14 for the past fifty years.

Call around and find out when the major competition will be. Big hospitals, cultural institutions, and associations for diseases may plan their events a year or two in advance. Many communities have some central clearinghouse for benefit dates; it may be the newspaper, the Junior League, another organization, or the nonprofit website such as www.npo.net in Chicago. Also check with the local and state arts councils, the convention and tourism bureau, organizers of the county fair, and the major political parties. Ask a sports fan for important national and international sporting events, and never underestimate the zeal of sports fans.

Ask your leaders for dates of school vacations, graduation, and significant events in their own lives, such as weddings and anniversaries. Do not schedule your biggest event in June if the event chair is planning her daughter's wedding that month, or a New Year's Eve party if your president's son will be the quarterback at this year's Rose Bowl game.

There is a great advantage to choosing a date that connects to your mission and making it your "own" through repetition, enthusiastic sales, and skillful public relations. Then the rest of the community can plan around your date, rather than vice versa.

However, any negative can be a positive. When the benefit committee of the St. Mary of the Plains Hospital Foundation in Lubbock, Texas, tried to find a date for a gala, the committee members discovered that all the Saturday nights were taken by bigger charities and every Saturday afternoon was devoted to college football, an activity that in Texas reaches the heights of a religious experience. So they got creative and decided to use Saturday morning. They sent out a poster-size invitation, decorated in the spirit of New Orleans jazz, inviting people to a "Breakfast at Brennan's with the Preservation Hall Jazz Band."

The breakfast was novel and made just as much profit as the nighttime parties. It also allowed everyone to support a good cause and still get to the football game on time. St. Mary of the Plains attracted the usual benefit crowd who wanted to be part of a unique event, as well as all the morning people who had never attended an evening socializer. All in all, it was a great way to turn a negative into a positive.

Repeat, Repeat, Repeat

As long as an event is making money, it is best to keep repeating it so it becomes an important part of the members', organization's, and community's calendar. There is a learning curve to starting a new event, so it is best to repeat the event for at least three years.

The first year is a learning year; your profits will be lower because your expenses are higher as you learn which vendors and volunteers are the most dependable. Consider the higher expenses as tuition to learn how to do the best event. Keep meticulous records and ruthlessly evaluate every piece of your event, every vendor, and every idea (especially your own). It can be unnerving for the fundraiser the first and second years, but keep smiling and asking for new ideas. Honest evaluation can turn a mediocre event into a masterpiece. Prune out the losers, and pump up the profit makers.

For example, although I love the name, the Galveston Ronald McDonald House discontinued their 5K race called "Run Like the Dickens," which had been part of Dickens on the Strand. Apparently the Texans kicked back enough at the Costume Ball the night before that no one wanted to get up and run on Sunday morning. On the other hand, some events will surprise you. Who would expect the handbell concert to sell out? It did, so they scheduled two concerts, and both sold out. They also doubled the High Tea and the Feast but still had a waiting list, so they added an Irish breakfast complete with Irish band, and that sold out too.

Be sure everyone on the fundraising team knows that it will take more than a year to develop a great fundraising event. Otherwise it is easy to get discouraged and give in to the people who say, often correctly from a one-year sample, "This is too much work for too little money." As Clifford Swick, the Sage of Saratoga Springs, says, "Fools and children judge half-done work." Give every event at least three years to become an efficient moneymaker. The second year, you can expect to double your profits; then the growth of the event will mirror the growth of the organization.

Solving your first-year problems will often be the key to future success. An arts group in New Hampshire scheduled a concert series in December and January, but every concert was snowed out. The intrepid fundraisers scheduled a new series for February and March and billed them as the "Cabin-Fever Concerts." Their market was eager for any diversion after spending the bleak midwinter indoors, so the concert series has become a dependable moneymaker.

The ideal system for a big event is to have selected next year's date and chairs before this year's event. That way the 2002 people can intern under the 2001 chairs and learn the ropes. At the big event you can announce the chairs for next year and put their names in the program. Then the new chairs can get right to work the day after this year's party, and everyone knows whom to call with any good ideas. This system also creates people with a self-interest to do the nagging to get this year's reports written and turned in.

Some organizations also announce how much money they made at the event itself. You can do this if it fits in with the style of your audience. Other groups do not mention the event total at the party itself but will include it in the newsletter article and all the "you did a fabulous job!" thank-you notes to the workers and big donors.

How to Price the Tickets

No matter what price you set, several people will tell you it is too high. Be sure to test this. First, ask everyone on the committee to buy four tickets. If none of your own people will buy tickets at this price, they are not going to sell them either. Change to a less fancy, less expensive event.

In most cases, take complaints about money with a grain of salt. Often a higher-priced ticket is easier to sell. Because people have a consumer mentality, most people think that the more something costs, the better it will be.

Set a basic price for tickets and a special higher price to find major donor prospects. If you ask for more, you will get more. Let's say you've planned a picnic and softball game in the park for a low-priced family event. Basic tickets are $10. Your categories could be:

Category	Price
Rookie	$10
Designated Hitter	$20
All-Star	$50
Free Agent	$100
MVP	$500
Hall of Famer	$1,000

Most people will still pay you $10 or $20, but you will always get one or two pleasant surprises in the larger categories. Then you can begin to cultivate those people for larger gifts, too.

Make up names for different price categories that reflect your mission (see Figure 4.3). The public-interest law firm BPI uses a knight as its logo to represent the firm's tradition of fighting for forgotten and defenseless people in the courts. At BPI's 1999 30th Anniversary Law Day dinner, which netted more than $150,000, donors could support BPI at one of the following:

Category	Price	Tickets
Saint	$10,000	includes 30 guests
Knight	$5,000	includes 20 guests
Hero	$3,000	includes 10 guests
Good Samaritan	$1,500	includes 6 guests
Squire	$1,000	includes 4 guests
True Friend	$500	includes 2 guests

Any group can use the tried-and-true category names such as benefactor, contributor, sustainer, patron, and donor.

FIGURE 4.3 **Front of Reply Card**

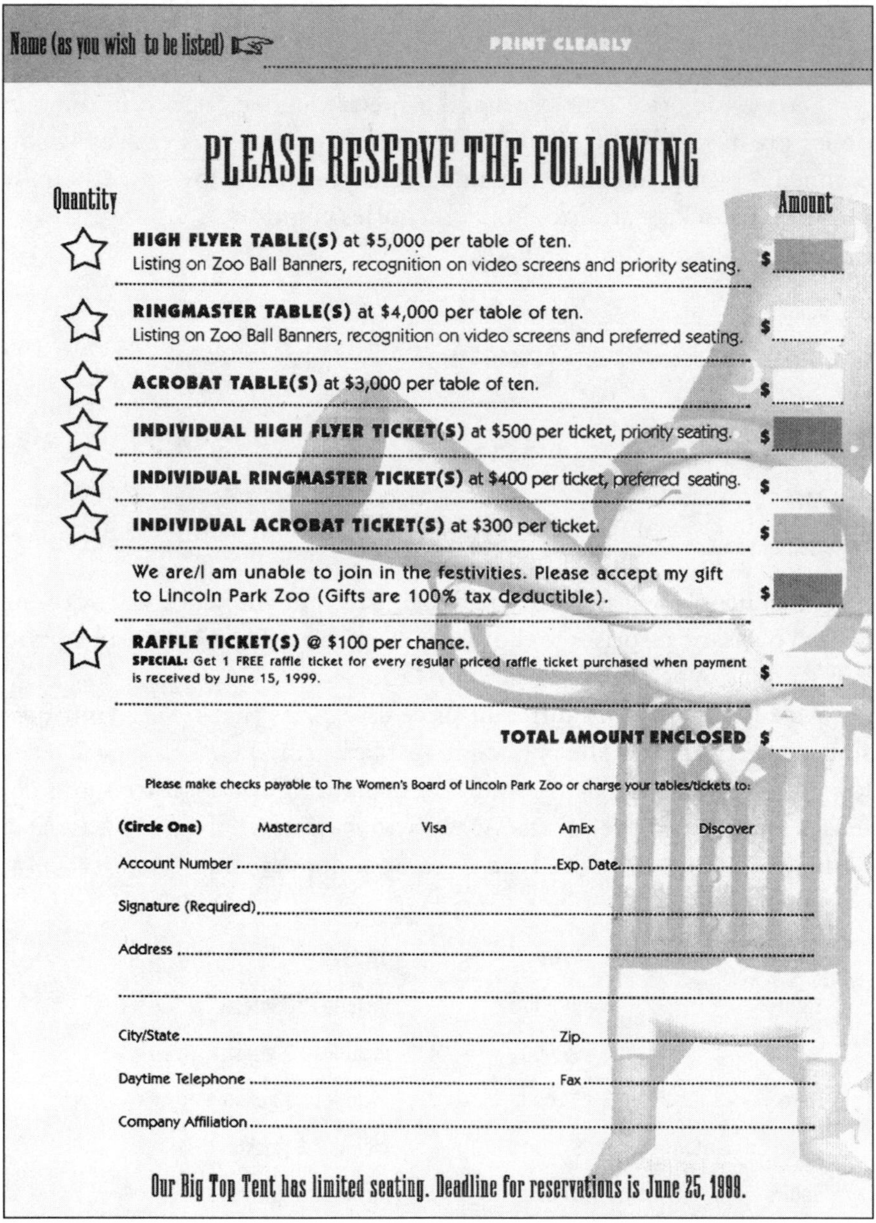

Name (as you wish to be listed) ☞   PRINT CLEARLY

PLEASE RESERVE THE FOLLOWING

Quantity   **Amount**

☆ **HIGH FLYER TABLE(S)** at $5,000 per table of ten.
   Listing on Zoo Ball Banners, recognition on video screens and priority seating. $ _____

☆ **RINGMASTER TABLE(S)** at $4,000 per table of ten.
   Listing on Zoo Ball Banners, recognition on video screens and preferred seating. $ _____

☆ **ACROBAT TABLE(S)** at $3,000 per table of ten. $ _____

☆ **INDIVIDUAL HIGH FLYER TICKET(S)** at $500 per ticket, priority seating. $ _____

☆ **INDIVIDUAL RINGMASTER TICKET(S)** at $400 per ticket, preferred seating. $ _____

☆ **INDIVIDUAL ACROBAT TICKET(S)** at $300 per ticket. $ _____

   We are/I am unable to join in the festivities. Please accept my gift
   to Lincoln Park Zoo (Gifts are 100% tax deductible). $ _____

☆ **RAFFLE TICKET(S)** @ $100 per chance.
   SPECIAL: Get 1 FREE raffle ticket for every regular priced raffle ticket purchased when payment
   is received by June 15, 1999. $ _____

                                        TOTAL AMOUNT ENCLOSED $ _____

Please make checks payable to The Women's Board of Lincoln Park Zoo or charge your tables/tickets to:

(Circle One)   Mastercard   Visa   AmEx   Discover

Account Number ....Exp. Date..............................

Signature (Required)..

Address ....

....

City/State.. Zip...

Daytime Telephone .... Fax ....

Company Affiliation ....

Our Big Top Tent has limited seating. Deadline for reservations is June 25, 1999.

Grateful acknowledgment is made to the Women's Board of the Lincoln Park Zoological Society for permission to reprint the 1999 Zoo Ball Cirque du Zooleil invitation reply card designed by Laughing Dog/Chicago.

FIGURE 4.4 **Back of Reply Card**

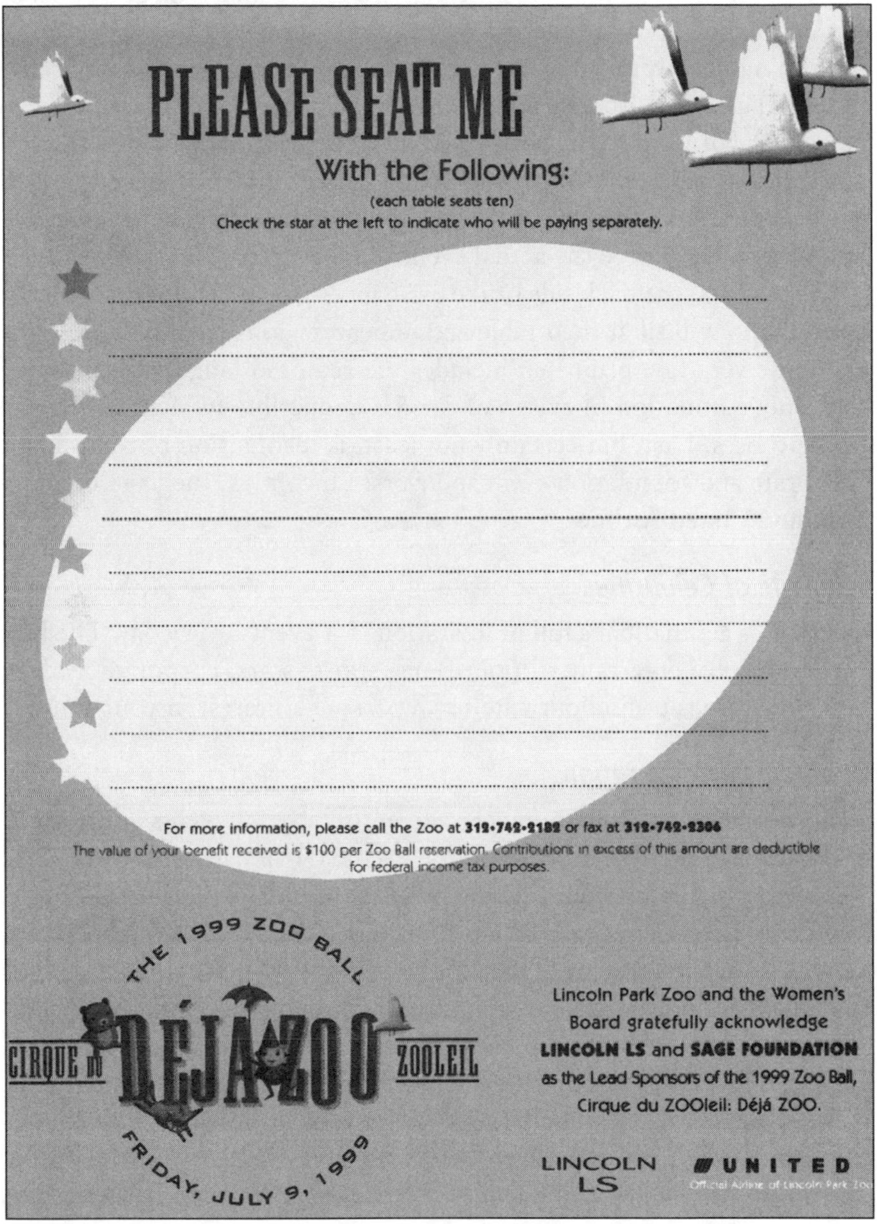

PLEASE SEAT ME

With the Following:

(each table seats ten)

Check the star at the left to indicate who will be paying separately.

For more information, please call the Zoo at **312-742-2182** or fax at **312-742-2306**

The value of your benefit received is $100 per Zoo Ball reservation. Contributions in excess of this amount are deductible for federal income tax purposes.

THE 1999 ZOO BALL

CIRQUE DU DÉJÁ ZOO ZOOLEIL

FRIDAY, JULY 9, 1999

Lincoln Park Zoo and the Women's Board gratefully acknowledge **LINCOLN LS** and **SAGE FOUNDATION** as the Lead Sponsors of the 1999 Zoo Ball, Cirque du ZOOleil: Déjá ZOO.

LINCOLN LS

UNITED
Official Airline of Lincoln Park Zoo

Grateful acknowledgment is made to the Women's Board of the Lincoln Park Zoological Society for permission to reprint the 1999 Zoo Ball Cirque du Zooleil invitation reply card designed by Laughing Dog/Chicago.

Figure 4.3 is the front of an actual reply card for the 1999 Zoo Ball of the Women's Board of the Lincoln Park Zoo called "Cirque du Zooleil." Note how it offers guests a range of donation fees, the opportunity to send money even if they do not attend, and the chance to buy raffle tickets. The card also gives guests different payment options: they can pay on one of four credit cards or write a check. It also asks for a company affiliation to find prospects for matching gifts. Because this ball has become one of the "hot tickets" in town, the board can make a deadline two weeks before the actual event.

Figure 4.4, the back side of the card, gives guests the space to list the people who will sit at their table and indicate who is paying. Note especially the very fine print that includes the required language specifying that only a donation in excess of $100 is deductible for federal income tax purposes. Last, but certainly not least, is recognition of their major corporate and foundation event sponsors: Lincoln LS, the Sage Foundation, and United Airlines.

The Role of Celebrities

Celebrities get mailbags full of invitations for events every day. The best way to involve entertainers, politicians, sports stars, corporate leaders, and socialites is to find out who has a personal interest in your cause.

The Role of Corporations

Some corporations like to underwrite entire special events so they can reach the people who will attend the event. Obviously, this works best for events with very high visibility and thousands of guests. However, you can still get support from corporations if they care about your mission. The headquarters for the Dr. Pepper soft drink company moved from Galveston to Houston, and most of the company's major sponsorship now goes for a rodeo in Houston that attracts thousands of people for a month of shows. But they are still the soft drink sponsor for the Galveston Historical Foundation's Dickens on the Strand festival, because they care about education and historic restoration in Galveston.

Other companies will buy a block of tickets and distribute them as incentives for top employees. Large companies can use a participatory event, such as the March of Dimes walkathon called "WalkAmerica," in place of the old company picnic as a way to get everyone together for a good cause. The 1998 WalkAmerica made more than $75 million. Some large companies will budget for the entry fees for their runners clubs to promote team spirit among their runners, but leave it up to the teams to choose which charities' events to enter.

Unfortunately, some corporate donors really hate getting asked to sponsor or attend special events. Business leaders get deluged with invitations; they could easily attend a dozen events every night in a big city. What we think is a fun event, they see as work.

So be careful. If you are asking corporate leaders to support your benefit, make the event truly special, relate it to your mission, and make it more fun than work. No long programs, no guilt, and no preaching. Start on time and finish early. Even better, for corporate donors, skip the event and simply ask for money.

Taxes

The IRS has issued very explicit rules for the language and arithmetic that charities must use to inform donors of how much money they may legally deduct from their taxable income. Now the charity is responsible for informing the donor exactly what amount goes for the party and what amount goes to the cause itself. So, for example, if the value of the party is $50 a head and the ticket is $150, then the donor may legally deduct $100. The charity needs to indicate that on the invitation (see Figure 4.4).

For more information on your organization's responsibilities for informing its donors, order IRS Publication 1391, *Deductibility of Payments Made to Charities Conducting Fund Raising Events*, from the IRS at (800) TAX-FORM or www.irs.gov.

Conclusion

The key to successful special events is attention to detail. For more details on the details, attend as many events as you can, observe the staff and volunteers in action, and then interview the people who run the best benefits. For more advice on special events, get *The Grass Roots Fundraising Book*, which is listed in the Resource Guide.

Special events give you more ways to have more fun, meet more prospects, and test more leaders than any other form of fundraising. You can meet your social needs and your organizational needs at the same time. For fun and profit, always include at least one or two special events in your fundraising strategy.

Checklist for Success

This checklist as an easy way to ensure the success of your events. If you can check each of these off by the date of your event, your organization will make money and everyone will have fun.

_____ Leadership as a group is personally committed to a specific dollar goal.

_____ Each leader commits to buy ten tickets and personally attend the event.

_____ One cochair and several committee chairs are veterans of the event.

_____ You have written contracts for sponsors for all fixed costs six months before the event.

_____ One hundred percent of the tickets are sold two weeks before the event. All sales at the event are gravy.

_____ An enthusiastic fundraiser or organizer is assigned to staff the committee.

_____ Your organization has a tradition of doing a great event on the same date every year. You may add or subtract pieces of the event (line dancing one year, tango lessons the next), but use the same date so the community knows it is yours.

_____ You collect a list of guests' preferred mail and E-mail addresses at every event through the silent auction, door prizes, and charming board members working the crowd.

_____ You have set measurable goals for what you want to achieve in addition to the dollar profit.

_____ Next year's cochairs are announced at this year's event.

_____ You have a system in place to evaluate this year's event.

_____ Your organization has high visibility. Controversal issues are especially helpful, but anything involving celebrities, children, and/or animals is excellent.

Getting Started
How to Ask for Money

5

Money will not come in and surrender.
>   —Roy L. Williams
>   Narragansett Council
>   Boy Scouts of America

FROM TIME TO TIME, VETERAN FUNDRAISERS will tell you a story about some old geezer who just wandered into the office, left a shopping bag full of cash (or the deed to the ranch, or a diamond bracelet . . .), and then wandered out. However, purely spontaneous contributions are so rare as to be ranked as miracles. The reason these stories get repeated is that they are so unusual.

You are not serving your organization by waiting for money to come in and surrender. To guarantee a dependable income, you need to ask for money and ask your volunteers to ask for money.

If you want to raise money and identify the citizens who care about your cause, you have to ask people to give money to your organization because they want what it does. Good people will want to pay for the good work your group does, just as they want to pay for good products or good parties. The fastest, easiest, most accurate way to find the people who share your values is to ask them for money.

The biggest advantage to asking for money (as opposed to selling anything) is that you can get more money per transaction. If Darryl bought everything at the bake sale, he might spend $1,000. Then if you want him to give again, you have to bake some more. On the other hand, if you ask him to support the worthwhile work your group does, he can give you a small donation the first year, pledge a larger amount the second year, and put your organization in his will the third year. The only limit is your enthusiasm.

Asking for money for your programs identifies the most interested donors, the most committed leaders, and the most desirable issues. Remember, this is building the broad base of small givers, many of whom are also voters (a list of voters is available from the county board of elections), and some of whom will later make larger gifts and bequests.

This chapter will show you an easy way to help any group find good prospects who will donate money. In Chapter 1 you learned that 85 percent of the philanthropic dollars came from individuals. Now you can learn how to help your volunteers translate that into names of specific people they can ask. Then you will learn how to train your people to actually ask for money in person from people they know. But before we look at finding good prospects or making a persuasive sale, let's begin with a review of your organization's mission.

Begin with Your Mission

Very few people are natural fundraisers, because we all have deep-seated phobias of talking about money. Money is the last great taboo subject in America, much more so than sex. (The media's coverage of President Clinton's sex scandal virtually eliminated anybody's chance to remain a prude about sex.) However, even if your staff and volunteers feel awkward about asking for money, they do feel passionate about the mission of the organization. So start with a discussion of the mission, then discuss the programs that will enable you to achieve your mission, then what kinds of things (staff, office, computers) you need to make the programs work, then the costs, and only then, fundraising. Your people will see that fundraising is not even a means to an end, it is the means to the means to the end.

Once your people are clear that fundraising is the way to make money to hire staff to run programs to achieve the organization's goals, then you can talk with them about how to actually make that happen. The best way to raise money and find political support is to ask people you know for money. Since 85 percent of charity dollars come from individuals, find which individuals your volunteers know and are willing to ask.

How to Find the Best Prospects

The best prospects for your organization are the people your own leaders know from their jobs, their neighborhoods, and their clubs. Ask your fundraising committee to make a list of the names of people they personally can ask for a donation. There may be a volunteer who recommends that "we" ought to ask "everyone." Smile pleasantly and translate every suggestion like this into second person singular. Then transactions can be traced so volunteers and staff can be held accountable.

You can get started by asking each person to make a list of ten individuals he or she can personally ask for $20 each. (Adapt the dollar amount up or down to fit your constituents.) Remember that this exercise is to help all of your committee think about all the kinds of people they can ask to donate. In Chapter 8 we will discuss how to find the people who'll make larger gifts. This chapter will help you uncover every possible prospect your own people already know.

Ask for ten names so that your volunteers must stretch a little. These ten should be individuals who are not already donors to your group. For right now, do not worry about duplications; just get each volunteer to write down the names of ten people he or she can ask for money.

If some people on your committee object that it is not worth their time to ask for small gifts, remind them that this is the first, entry-level donation for all new donors. Even the wealthiest people often give a modest first gift, then increase their giving as they see results from the organization. For example, wealthy publisher Ambassador Walter Annenberg's first gift, in 1961, to the Colonial Williamsburg Foundation was $50. His most recent pledge, in 1993, was $25 million. When you start your annual campaign asking for smaller amounts, you make it easy for everyone to ask and to give. Do not worry about aiming too low on the dollar amount. If you get prospects who should be asked for more, you can simply move them onto the list of major donor prospects, whom you will learn how to find in Chapter 8 and how to ask in Chapter 9.

Then the volunteers who are eager to ask at a higher level can take their enthusiasm to the major gifts campaign described in those chapters.

Yourself

The first gift must be your gift. Salespeople say, "You can't sell something you won't buy." That is why people use the products they promote. If you sell Fords, you drive a Ford; if you sell Chanel, you wear Chanel. In the same way, you need to practice what you preach.

The most persuasive fact is always, "I've made a gift; now I'm giving my time to ask you to make a gift."

Family and Friends

Whether for or against, volunteers often feel strongly about asking their family and friends for money. Many people hate asking their own family members and friends. Volunteers may not want to feel indebted to their family or friends, or they may be afraid that their loved ones will feel unable to say no. So some of your volunteers will flatly refuse to ask their own circle.

In that case, simply ask them to trade their "refusals" with other volunteers who feel the same way. Clifford can ask Molly's family and friends, and Molly can ask Clifford's family and friends. No contact is left out, and your volunteers still feel good about the process.

On the other hand, many people like to ask their family and friends. If you feel strongly about this cause, if this group has given you joy and strength, and if the group has made real improvements in your life, of course you are eager to include your family and friends.

In fact, consider it the other way. What if you do not ask them? Your brother and your best friend are going to wonder, "Don't you think I have the same values? Don't you think I want the same things you do? Why did you ask everyone else, and not ask me?"

Some charities intentionally market to families. The Shelburne Museum in Vermont offers a membership for individuals at $20, adult couples at $30, or families at $40. They also offer a "Grandparents Membership"—$25 for an individual or $35 for a couple—that offers all of the benefits of the other memberships plus free admission for all grandchildren under eighteen.

Neighbors

If you have lived in the community for a while, you probably know many of your neighbors already. If you are active, you may already be part of a block club, condo association, or civic group. In that case, begin working through the existing structures in the community.

If you are new to the community, one easy way to start recruiting your neighbors is with the list of registered voters, usually free from the county board of elections. The list gives the names of the registered voters for each precinct or township, organized numerically by address or alphabetically by name. In some communities, this list also tells the political party and the age of the voters, so you can easily recruit Generation X Republicans or senior citizen Democrats.

If you are fundraising in a community with many unregistered voters, you will need to make your own list. In neighborhoods with many immigrants, try working through the local clubs, such as the Sons of Norway or the 18th Street Soccer League. Or you can simply go door-to-door and ask everyone to get involved. Many churches and political campaigns were built this way, and door knocking can work for you, too.

In rural areas, raise funds from your neighbors when they come to you. One group in Tennessee signed up members when people came out of the hills and hollers to vote on Election Day. In Montana the Northern Plains Resource Council began when Bill Mitchell set up his card table in the general store and sold memberships to all the ranchers who came in to buy supplies.

Coworkers

There are many advantages to raising funds from the people you work with. First, you know they have a job and hence at least *some* income. Second, you may know something more about their interests. If Joy started the recycling collection system in the lunchroom, she is a good prospect for an environmental group. If Bob spends every lunch discussing box scores, he is a good prospect for the Little League.

Ask the chamber of commerce for the names of the largest employers in your community. These usually include the school system, labor-intensive sites such as hospitals, and large manufacturing plants. In the county seat or state capital, it will include all the branches of the county or state governments. Recruit a volunteer for the fundraising committee from each of the top ten largest employers.

Asking coworkers is an area where your own staff are really limited. How many people do they know at their jobs? How much money do those people make? Recruiting volunteers from the largest employers gives you people with bigger networks and more variety of talents and income levels.

Students and Teachers

If you go to school or live in a college town, ask the students to raise money for your cause. Fraternities and sororities often need to organize fundraising events to get their parties approved. Most students and teachers get three to four months of vacation, so they can be great summertime volunteers. Also, students are often the most knowledgeable and the most enthusiastic about finding ways to use the new technologies. A few sophomores from the Tech Club can send the entire fundraising committee speeding down the information highway.

Merchants

As the anonymous Washington-insider snitch "Deep Throat" told Watergate reporter Bob Woodward, "Follow the money." Where do your own constituents spend their money? Track where your own dollars go, and then ask those merchants for support.

Also ask the vendors who sell to the organization itself. Every group buys office supplies, insurance, printing, computers, and food. Be sure to ask the merchants who sell to the organization to donate; if they say no, shop the competition.

Even if your community is experiencing hard times, there are still merchants making money. If people are not buying new cars, they are getting their old cars repaired and buying new batteries, parts, and tires. If people are not buying new clothes, they are buying new hats, earrings, or neckties. Accessory sales always go up in hard times. If times are good, even better reason to ask the businesses that benefit.

In smaller communities it is vital to recruit a few insiders for the fundraising committee so you are not misled by the owners' modesty and underestimate the profits of local businesses. Unlike big city showoffs, successful people in small towns usually do not flaunt their wealth through conspicuous consumption. Instead, they try hard to blend into the crowd. One committee from a small town in Kansas laughed about the local bank president who always drove a Chevrolet when he was working; the day he retired, he bought a Cadillac.

Professionals

Ask your own doctor, dentist, pediatrician, barber, stockbroker, veterinarian, lawyer, accountant, or insurance agent. You have to contact these people anyway. They never have any problem taking your money; you can simply ask for some of it back.

In smaller communities, compare your lists to avoid duplications. If everyone in your group goes to the same dentist, nominate the person with the largest recent bill to ask. If Jack never had a cavity, do not assign the dentist to him; if Rose just had root canal work, she is the one to ask the dentist.

In larger communities, first ask two or three professionals to give to your group, and then ask them to ask other people in the same profession. Structure the campaign so the Realtors can be competing with the lawyers and the accountants.

Some charities are having great success asking professionals through videotapes. Because doctors are very busy and ethically have to respond to their patients when called, it is often difficult to see them in person to ask for money. The Lakeland, Florida, United Way made a videotape asking for donations and stressing how the money would be used locally. Each doctor could play the tape at his or her convenience. The videotapes produced a 54 percent increase in giving from doctors, almost $20,000 more than the year before.[1]

Other Organizations

Sometimes volunteers will try to weasel out of fundraising by saying, "I can't ask for money—I don't have the time!" When you ask for more information, you find out that Monday they drive the carpool, Tuesday is the volunteer fire department practice, Thursday they tutor at the library, Saturday is a birthday party, and Sunday they go to church. Now the same volunteers who just claimed to have no time to fundraise have given you five possibilities for asking for money. Make it easy for them to ask everyone they see. In five minutes anyone can sell a membership, if prepared with all the materials.

Other organizations may be able to help you if they see a connection with your cause—even a whimsical one. In 1987, the Vancouver Aquarium lost many of its fish through a terrible act of vandalism. In the spontaneous outpouring of generosity to help replace the fish, the police department paid for a fish called a sergeant major, the carpenters' union donated for the sawfish, and parochial schoolchildren contributed for the angel fish.

Religious Congregations

Every year almost half of the money given in the United States goes to religious institutions, including churches, synagogues, mosques, temples, and every religious denomination. About a third of this money is donated back to the community for peace and justice causes.

Your Organization's People

Last, but certainly not least, are your own people. Always ask your own constituents, patients, and clients for money, and ask them to ask for money.

Getting Started

Once the committee has a list of prospects, review the list and develop a strategy for who would be the best person to ask each person on the list. It is often much easier to ask volunteers to go in pairs. For example, if two people belong to the same temple, they can work together to ask their friends. These small gifts are building the base for your overall fundraising strategy. Over the next few years, you can begin asking some of the donors to make larger gifts and consider a bequest, but you need to start with many small givers. Make your own contribution, and then start asking these people for money.

Before You Ask

There are three things you can do before you ask for money that make it easier for you to ask and easier for the prospect to say yes:

1. Give a gift yourself.

2. Research your prospects.

3. Educate your prospects.

Let's look at each of these.

Actions Speak Louder than Words

First, give a gift of money yourself. If you are asking for big gifts, give a big gift. If you are asking for planned gifts, name the group in your own will, trust, IRA, or insurance policy.

Giving a gift yourself will guarantee your success as a fundraiser. You may be tempted to say that you can wait till the end of the campaign and then give your gift, but that will not work.

Givers become better askers, and askers become better givers. In the best campaigns the leadership gives at the beginning and then becomes even more committed through the process of asking for money. Often your fundraisers may be surprised and delighted when their prospects give larger amounts than they themselves gave. Then the fundraisers may want to give more to keep up.

If you are asking your mother or your best friend, she may simply reply, "Well, dear, how much did you give?" If you just mumble about your good intentions, she will know this cause is not important to you. You may say very eloquently that this is urgent, but if people do not see you giving your own money, they will not believe you mean it.

Many charities now videotape sessions in which their volunteers practice asking for money. Videotapes show that if the asker has not made a donation of his or her own money, the asker's eyes will drop when he or she gets to the "close," the part that involves actually asking for the donation. So people can tell from your body language whether or not you have given money yourself.

Should the Fundraising Staff Also Contribute?

Giving to the organization is indispensable for the fundraising staff. If your paid staff is working on a major gifts campaign, they should make major gifts, too, according to their means. If they are working on the planned-gifts campaign, they should put this organization in their own will, IRA, or insurance plan. In fact, ask ten of the most successful professional fundraisers you can find, and I will bet the ranch that all of them have made a serious gift to the place where they work.

The boss can set a good example and make a meaningful gift first. Then make it easy for the fundraising staff to give through payroll deduction, a credit union, credit card pledges, or electronic funds transfers at their bank.

When your organization runs its first fundraising campaign, do your best to get every volunteer and staff person who is working on the campaign to make a gift before the campaign. You may get 100 percent participation, and if you do, that is great. More likely, a few people will make excuses and "wait" to make their gift. Do the best you can to persuade everyone to give, but do not hold up the campaign because of a few stingy people. Launch your campaign and keep track very carefully of who gives at the beginning and who does not. Then keep track of who gets the most donations. After a year or two you will have enough data from your own people to show that the best fundraisers give their own gifts first. After five or ten years the connection between giving first and getting the most will be so glaring that you can simply make it a criterion for serving on the fundraising committee.

Most of all, do not wait to start the campaign because you do not have 100 percent of the board behind you. If you have the majority, step out in faith and just accept that some people will always be more timid. We cannot let the negative people stop a worthwhile effort. Remember, not even the American Constitution was signed by all the members of the Constitutional Convention or ratified by all the states (Rhode Island held out). So get the majority of the positive people behind the campaign, then move ahead.

Research Your Prospects

After making your own gift, you can further facilitate asking for gifts by learning more about your prospects. If you are asking your brother, you probably already know his commitments and his financial status. If you are asking the stranger who moved in next door yesterday, you will need to do more research.

You want to find out two things:

1. The prospect's commitment to your cause

2. The prospect's ability to give

Of these two, commitment is more important. This is why volunteers are such good prospects for donations. You know they care about your cause.

To get started, work with the people you already know. After you have built a base of believers, you can begin to research people based on their wealth. Of course, the ideal thing is to find someone who loves the group and has a lot of money.

To find people with wealth, see the advice in Chapter 8. Use this information to look for new prospects to ask for money. But always begin with your own volunteers, board, and current donors before you ask strangers, no matter how much money you're aiming to raise.

The last thing to research about your prospect is when that person has money. When is payday? Senior citizens in the United States get their social security checks on the third of the month. Most other government checks, such as welfare or disability, arrive on the first of the month.

If your prospects are on a payroll, when do they get paid? Most workers get paid either twice a month—for example, on the fifteenth and at the end of the month (twenty-four checks a year), or every other Friday (twenty-six checks a year). It is easier for them to say yes if you ask at the time they get their middle-of-the-month paycheck.

If your constituents live paycheck to paycheck, with the check spent before they get it, try to arrange for payroll deduction where they work so you get the money first. This gives them twenty-four or twenty-six opportunities to give you small amounts that will add up to a large gift. This can be collected for your group through the accounting department, the credit union, an alternative payroll deduction plan, or a donor option handled through the local United Way or Combined Federal Campaign.

Some executives are paid once a month, usually on a day other than Friday to even out the work for accounting. Since these people have to plan ahead more, ask them to make a monthly pledge. Again, try to arrange for a regular deduction from the payroll or a monthly pledge on their credit card.

For students, when do they get their scholarships? Most students get scholarship checks at the beginning of each semester. Ask very early in the semester.

Many salespeople are paid a commission on their sales, so they get the most money when they sell the most. Eighty percent of toys are sold during the six weeks before Christmas and Hanukkah; most chocolate is sold before Easter; most houses sell in the summer. Know when salespeople are likely to do best.

Similarly, some professions give big bonuses at the end of the year. Lawyers, brokers, and executives may have big chunks of cash at year's end. Ranchers and farmers make money when they sell their crops. Learn the timetable for harvest and sales in your area. (Note: Annual timing is more important for annual gifts from annual income. For major gifts, which usually come from donors' assets, the right time is when the prospect wants to meet with you.)

Educate Your Prospects

The last step before you ask for money is to educate your prospects. Sometimes people are already sold on your cause because their children participate in the program, or their parents have the disease, or they personally have interest in your cause. If so, asking is easy. If you have a brand-new cause, you may need to educate your prospects.

In 1978 I was part of a group of nine people who started the first hospice in Chicago, a special program of care for people who are dying and their caregivers. The first question in every new group was always "What is a hospice?" Some of those early, curious people have been our most stalwart supporters for more than twenty years.

If you are brand-new, get an older group to host your first presentations. When Horizon Hospice was still operating from a card table in the president's bedroom, we hosted events at a local university, at a hospital, and in volunteers' living rooms.

If your program is already up and running, get people to witness the work you do, meet the staff, and hear success stories from your constituents. Throw a party in your office so people can see the neighborhood and meet the leadership. Special events are a great way to attract new people for a fun time while you sneak in a little program on your cause, too.

Always share any third-party endorsement of your work, such as newspaper clippings or letters from leaders in your field. Keep your written handouts simple and easy to read. If possible, refer people who want more details to your website or provide more in-depth position papers or research to the people who ask. A videotape of even the briefest report from the TV news can be very effective for starting a conversation about the issue covered.

How to Ask for Money

Building the Base: How to Ask for Gifts from People You Know

1. Make a gift yourself.

2. Research your prospects.
   —How much do they care about your work?
   —How much money can they give?

3. Educate your prospects.

4. Practice.

5. Make the appointment. Ask in person.

6. Smile. Make eye contact. Listen.

7. Ask for a specific dollar amount.

8. Answer questions. Think.

9. Ask for the dollar amount again.

10. If you get a gift, send a note the same day, thanking the donor for the donation.

11. If you do not get a gift, send a note the same day, thanking the donor for his or her time and helpful suggestions.

To ask for money, begin with your list of ten prospects for small gifts. Then use the following system, which I have copied from sales training. Try out these steps yourself, and then ask your fundraising committee to try them. Most people find it easier than they thought.

Expect Success

Decide you will succeed. Before you do anything else, tell yourself that you are going to raise the money so this great group can do terrific things.

Smile

Trial lawyers teach witnesses to smile at the jury, because research shows that juries believe a witness who smiles more than a witness who does not smile, regardless of whether or not this person is telling the truth. (Of course, your fundraisers will have the advantage of telling the truth, the whole truth, and nothing but the truth at all times.)

As fundraisers, it is especially important for you to smile and to train your volunteers to smile. You cannot control your emotions; you can control your actions. You may feel apprehensive about asking for money, especially if you are new or if you are asking for a large amount. But if you smile, make eye contact, and act as though you are enjoying this transaction, the prospects will think you are great—and you will too.

Identify Yourself

Say your name, the name of your group, and what it does. Never assume that your prospect has read or will remember your literature. Always tell the prospect right at the beginning who you are, who you are representing, and what that group does.

Explain Your Need

Yes, you should say you are there to talk about money. Explain your fundraising strategy and why you need this contribution now.

The Close

The hardest part to learn is the close. The preceding part comes naturally, because people tend to like to talk about the groups they like, anyway. Actually saying, "I want $20 from you now" can seem a lot harder. Here is how to close:

1. Say the dollar amount you want.

2. Say what it is for.

3. Say why you want this amount now.

4. Engage your prospect in discussion.

5. Repeat the dollar amount.

6. Stop talking, smile, and wait for the prospect to say yes.

Let's look at each of these steps.

Specify an Amount

First, you do need to ask for a specific dollar amount. People cannot respond unless you tell them what you want (assuming this is your first request for their first gift). If the prospects want to give less, they will say so. If they want to give more, you can ask again and ask for more next time. But you have to begin your conversation with a specific amount. No one can write a check for "some" money.

Explain the Use

Say what the money is for. For your first request, it is easiest to ask the prospect to pay dues and become a member. Then you are building the size and political strength of the organization at the same time that you raise money.

If your organization does not have members who pay dues, simply define what the money will buy. You can put a menu of choices on any reply card, return envelope, or brochure. See the reply form in Chapter 6 (page 110) for a sample of several different levels of giving.

Be prepared with such a menu of what the members' money can buy. If you have researched your prospect, you may be able to guess what he or she will like the most. But people can always surprise you, so have two or three choices ready. Include one choice that seems like a financial stretch, because some donors will always choose the top category because "it's the best."

Create a Deadline

Say why you need the money now. It is always easier for people to say "not now" rather than "no." If there is a real urgent need or a real deadline, it will be easier for your fundraisers to get the gift now. Schools create artificial deadlines through homecomings and reunions. If your class is having its twenty-fifth or fiftieth reunion, then the school can create an artificial deadline and ego rewards for you to give a gift now. Any organization can celebrate a tenth, twenty-fifth, fiftieth, or one hundredth anniversary and use the same tactic.

Another strategy for creating a deadline is a matching grant or challenge gift. A major donor, corporation, or foundation agrees to match whatever donations come in by a certain date. Then the fundraisers can urge prospects to make a gift now because the money will be doubled by the match. You can hear this strategy used every hour during your public radio station's fundraising campaign on the air.

Involve the Other Person

Engage the prospect in discussion about your cause. What, if anything, does Mr. Jones already know about it? Has he used any of your services? Does he recognize the problem you are trying to solve? Does he have any questions?

Repeat Your Request

Ask for the dollar amount again. Bring the discussion back to the need for money and, more important, what the money will buy. Say the dollar amount at the beginning, the purpose, the urgency, then the dollar amount again.

Wait for an Answer

Finally, stop talking and wait for your prospect to say yes. For those of us who love to talk, this is the hardest part. But it is the clearest message you can send that you are serious, you want the money, and you want it now. If you are not talking, the prospect has to talk, and probably will say yes.

Yes or No

If the prospect says yes, get the cash, check, credit card information, or completed pledge card. Thank the new donor and give him or her any recognition materials, such as a membership card, button, or decal. Emphasize how the gift will help the group achieve its goals.

Ask for all the data needed for a new donor's record: name, mail and E-mail addresses, phone numbers, dollar amount, and special interests. Pass this on to the fundraising office (or the secretary if your group does not have an office). If the donor wants to volunteer, pass on the name to the volunteer coordinator, organizer, or committee chair. Then check in a week to be sure they follow up.

Especially if the prospect says no, "kill him with kindness." Thank Mr. Jones for his time and ask to leave your brochure and pledge card. If you leave a good impression it will be easier for another fundraiser to ask again next year. Whether you get a yes or a no, send a thank-you note to the prospect.

Thank-You Notes

The thank-you note is the most important tool in fundraising. If you want small givers to become major donors and new volunteers to develop into active leaders, recognize every contribution with a prompt, sincere thank-you.

Ask your fundraising team to tell about the best thank-you they ever received and how that made them feel. Then ask for examples of times when your people worked hard or made a big gift and felt ignored. Make yourselves a list of dos and don'ts from this discussion.

At the very least, each fundraiser can send a personal handwritten note after every meeting with a prospect, thanking him or her for the time, good suggestions, and new leads. Send another handwritten thank-you note when the person you ask sends in a donation. Remember, you want people to join your organization and give gifts for a lifetime. Every thank-you note makes the next request and the next gift easier.

For major gifts, remember to thank the donor and anyone else who helped, such as the lawyer, accountant, or appraiser. For corporate gifts, thank the secretary who advocated your cause and the bookkeeper who helped you set up your accounting system as well as the executive who arranged the contributions. For foundation grants, send a prompt thank-you note for every check and a progress report at least quarterly. Although you know that foundation grants run out after one to three years, the foundation staff make up a tight fraternity, so one good grant maker can recommend your program to another good grant maker.

Mail each day's thank-you notes before the sun goes down. If you are asking for money from corporations or foundations, write the note ahead of time, add a postscript after the meeting, and drop it in the mailbox before you leave the building. If you are working with dozens of volunteers, write short thank-you notes and address the envelopes for each person as he or she signs up, and then mail them so the notes arrive the day after the event. For extra-special efforts on the day of the event, send a second thank-you. If you are chairing a major festival or telethon with thousands of volunteers, create a pyramid to delegate the notes, but be sure each volunteer gets a handwritten note the day after his or her service.

This can be a real challenge to your creativity. I have a friend who arranged for twenty-six thoughtful older women to bake cookies for a special event. Several of these ladies call each other every morning to ask, "Did you sleep well?" and then call again every afternoon to ask, "Did you get any mail?" Then they read their mail over the phone. So my friend knew she had to find twenty-six different ways to say "Thank-you for baking the cookies." It was not easy, but she did it.

In the same way, your organization may negotiate a major gift such as a piece of property that involves several branches and generations of the same wealthy family. Each person needs to get an equally wonderful and equally sincere but differently worded thank-you note.

No, it is not enough to send a receipt. You may choose to send a form letter and an official receipt from the office (or from the treasurer if your organization does not have an office), but the person who asks for the gift must still send a personal note. If the donation is earmarked to pay or endow the salary of a specific staff person—the first violin, the oncologist, or the professor of Slavic languages—that person could also send a note. Extra notes from the CEO and the top elected officer are great, too.

What If?

Of course, in real life asking for small gifts is never this tidy. Usually, several other questions come up before you get the contribution. Let's look at some of these.

What if they ask a question I can't answer?

Smile, say, "What a good question!" and tell the truth. Never lie and never guess. Remember that this is the first contribution you are asking for, and if this is a good prospect, you (or another fundraiser) can get future gifts from the same donor for a lifetime. So if you do not know an answer, get the answer and then fax or E-mail it by the next day. Then you will be ready for the next person who asks this question.

What if I ask for too much?

The most important quality for fundraising volunteers is the ability to think. They do not need to be rich, or beautiful, or aggressive. But they do need to have the confidence to negotiate on the spot.

Think of your first dollar amount as your opening bid. Once you get any response except "No, thank you" from prospects, use the conversation to learn more about how they want to give. They may want to give a smaller "test" gift to see what results you can get. They may want to spread out their payments over more time. Or they may be financially overcommitted now due to college payments, starting a new business, or providing a challenge grant to a different charity. In that case, accept what they can give now with sincere appreciation, and ask when it would be best to meet again.

What if I ask for too little?

This one is easier to solve. If you ask for $20 and the person says, "Is that all?" you can always ask the prospect, "Would you like to give more?" or, "Would you like to pledge $20 a month? Or a week?" If someone gives very easily, you can always repeat the transaction. Be sure you send a thank-you note the same day, and then follow up the next week with a clipping, brochure, or letter. Ask again the next month.

What about controversy?

Controversy is usually very good for your fundraising, because it will clarify the issue and emphasize the urgency of the need. When the Seattle conservatives forced the United Way to expel Planned Parenthood, they were doing Planned Parenthood a favor. Leaders from that organization went directly to local individuals and businesses for support. Result: their donor list went from three thousand to seventeen thousand people, and they made up more than the $450,000 lost from the United Way.

There is an old union song with the refrain "Which side are you on?" Any controversy will get your organization's name out in the public. Most service delivery organizations lose more people from apathy and boredom than from honest differences of opinion. A good fight will help you define who is on your side (hot prospects), who is on the other side (not prospects), and who is undecided, so you can use a fundraising call to raise money and persuade another voter at the same time.

Can you write out what I should say?

There is always a temptation to say, "Just give me the script. If I know what to say, I can do it." Surprisingly, because Americans are so generous, a scripted request for money will work, for a while, for small amounts of money. However, if your organization wants to build a permanent, powerful institution, if you are approaching the movers and shakers in your community, or if you are already tired of raising the budget from nickels and dimes, simply reading a script will not work.

If you want to get bigger gifts—the farm, the Van Gogh painting, or the balance of someone's estate—then you need to do more than read the script. You need to do the work ahead of time to feel proud and confident about your organization and the entire fundraising process.

Show Time!

Once your committee has lists of names each person will ask, work as a group to decide what you want to say. Actually act out calling on a person to ask for money. Review your lists of prospects, and set up different pairs of people to act out asking a friend, a neighbor, a coworker, your doctor, your grocery store manager. This will give half the committee the chance to see how it feels to ask, and half will see how it feels to give. This process should flush out many questions so your group can brainstorm to find the best answers.

Do It Now

Now the time has come to make all this real—it is time to ask for money. Remember, before you go to ask, give a gift yourself, find out why the prospect would like your organization, and prepare simple materials to share the achievements and needs.

Then it is time to visit the ten people on your list and ask them for money. Like any new activity, it gets easier every call. But even if you are afraid, just do it. There is no other way to find the people who share your values and want to support your group.

No matter how wonderful your organization is, if you do not ask, you will not get. At one of my fundraising workshops, a participant was the executive director of a consumers' organization that had just been featured on the TV show "60 Minutes." This show has 29 million viewers every week. She was waiting for the money to roll in, since the broadcast had been very favorable about her organization. Unfortunately, all the organization did was wait, and all it got was a trivial amount of money.

The organization could have sent an E-mail alert as soon as they knew the date the show would run, a second E-mail the week of the show reminding people about the show and asking them to watch or videotape it, and an E-mail or phone call on Sunday to remind key people to watch. They could run an ad in the local newspaper's TV section alerting viewers to watch the show and contact the office or website to make a pledge. Volunteers could have called the two hundred best prospects right after the show to ask for gifts. The fundraisers could have organized parties to watch the show with their best donors and prospects, then have someone who was in the show give an update on the campaign, and then have a good closer ask them for gifts. Asking in several different ways could have turned this great publicity into great profits.

If your organization does not ask, not even the best publicity will motivate people to give. You have to ask.

Building the Base by Yourself

With Direct Mail, E-Mail, Phones, and Door-to-Door

6

All serious daring starts from within.
—Eudora Welty
One Writer's Beginnings

FUNDRAISING IS CAPTURING NAMES. Once you have the names, it is about engaging prospects' minds and, as they say in Texas, "twanging on their heartstrings," until your prospects choose to become donors. With careful cultivation, your loyal friends and supporters can give to you several times every year for their lifetimes.

Most organizations build their bases of small donors through a systematic campaign using direct mail, E-mail, telephoning, or going door-to-door. Ideally, you will ask your market at least four times a year in three different ways. The best, by far, is simply asking as many people as you can face-to-face. For the rest, use any combination of mail, E-mail, phones, and door canvass that fits your community and your volunteers.

After persuading people to give you a gift at least once a year, the easiest upgrade is to ask them to pledge (see Figure 6.1). Pledgers promise, usually in writing, to give a specific amount either every week (the collection at church), every pay period (the payroll deduction system at work), or every month (electronic deduction or credit card through their bank). Even small givers can become major donors through pledges.

This chapter will look at why you want annual donors and how to get them by using regular mail, E-mail, telephones, and a door-to-door campaign. You can learn to use all of these very profitably. When your organization's appeal is big enough, you can consider hiring skilled professionals to reach a huge audience via a well-run and well-financed campaign using direct mail, telephones, a door-to-door canvass, or the Internet. Using professional expertise to run your larger fundraising campaigns is discussed in Chapter 7. This chapter shows you how to market your message and ask for gifts by yourself.

FIGURE 6.1 **Individual Donor Development**

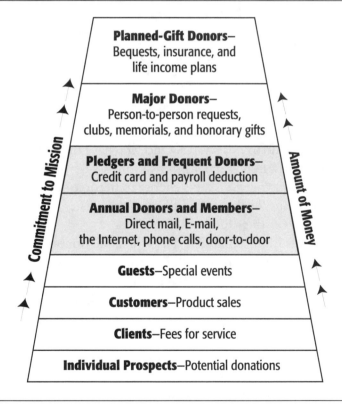

Membership Drives

Membership drives are the reality check for an organization. I could move to Fargo tomorrow, rent an office for the Friends of the Fargo Fe-lines, and say that I represent every cat lover in Fargo. Or in North Dakota. Or in the Red River Valley, including all of Minnesota and Manitoba. However, the way my donors, friends, enemies, and elected officials measure who my organization really represents is by asking, "How many members do you have?"

Members are people who give you money because they want to support the mission of your organization. They are not giving money for a T-shirt or a party. They are giving money because they want the results that only your organization can produce.

Why Do It?

Besides the money itself, there are five advantages to raising money through membership dues. Your organization will get:

- More political power

- More accurate evaluation of your programs and leaders

- More prospects for major gifts and planned gifts

- More loyalty from your donors

- More opportunities to educate your donors and prospects

Your organization gains more political power as it obtains more members. Almost every organization will need to influence public policy. If you can tell your state representative that three thousand members of your museum are voters in her district and they all want the culture trolley to go past your museum, she is more likely to vote to fund it.

The second reason for doing a membership drive is that it will give you a current, accurate, and objective evaluation of your programs and your leadership. Selling memberships separates the fundraisers from the philosophers. Convincing regular people to pay dues keeps you from sinking into a swamp of jargon or taking the easy route of preaching to the converted.

Dues also allow you to "test the turf." Sales tell you which neighborhoods or kinds of people really care about your issues. If they pay, they want it; if they do not pay, they do not want it. You will never waste staff or supplies if they are allocated to the communities that pay dues for your group.

For example, Mike Easter is the star membership salesman of the Roane County chapter of Save Our Cumberland Mountains (SOCM) in rural Tennessee. He says, "Most of the recruiting happened around people working on an issue that they cared a lot about, such as the proposed medical waste incinerators in Roane County, and really, the SOCM organization sold itself. People were saying, 'We couldn't have done this without SOCM,' and it was easy to say, 'SOCM isn't something far off; it's us, we're doing it,' and to ask them to join us."[1]

Selling memberships is the only form of fundraising that gives your organization an incentive to grow. New members are also a source of new volunteers. If you sell one hundred new memberships, you can project twenty new names for the annual event and ten new people to actually volunteer and do some work for you. Out of the ten volunteers, perhaps one or two will have the interest and aptitude to become your future leaders.

Best of all, your own leaders are raising money internally for your own programs. This gives you pride, power, and independence. Your organization can with dignity negotiate with any grant maker outside the community, because you know you have enough internal money to walk away from any deal that does not meet your ethical standards. By asking for money, your own leaders will be locked into the organization itself. As Mary Gonzales, associate director of the United Neighborhood Organization (UNO), says, "If the people are paying for it, the people are going to do two things: number one, they are going to demand accountability, and number two, they are going to stay in their inner circle, where the decisions are being made, because it's their money on the table."[2]

Annual Membership Drives

Many groups sign up all their members once a year. School groups, clubs, and parents' associations sell their memberships in the fall. Summer sports clubs and block clubs sell their memberships in the spring. Professional associations often run on a calendar year, with memberships renewed in the fall for the next year.

Especially when you start, it is easiest if the membership committee does a lot of intense work all at one time. In reality, the committee's effort takes place in about three months. When your campaign is a success and the group is larger, you can spread out the work, doing sales and renewals all year long.

Three months before the membership drive, clean up your lists. Take off the people who have moved out, have died, or no longer want to be involved. Add the new names. Also add the names of people you are not sure about; at least half of them may be interested.

Two months before the drive, prepare your membership materials, such as receipts, membership cards, buttons, and any other materials you want to sell. Recruit the people to sell the memberships, and make any necessary arrangements to reserve rooms or advertising.

One month before the membership campaign, collect prizes for the salespeople. Get the committee together and have a short meeting to practice your sales pitch. Divide up your prospects by geography (Barb and Charlie will recruit everyone west of the river), dues category (Chris and Shannon will sell to the President's Club prospects at $1,000+), or subgroup (Juanita and Hector will be responsible for all the parents of the preschoolers).

Kick off with some unusual event that will get you on the evening news or the local paper. Sell enthusiastically for two to four weeks, and then have a party and stop. Celebrate and announce the chairs for next year's membership drive. They can handle any sales between the campaigns.

Membership Categories

Create membership categories that relate to your mission. The Friends of the Topeka Public Library uses the following membership categories:

Lifetime	$1,000 (or more)
Bibliophile	$100 (or more)
Researcher	$50
Bookworm	$25
Avid Reader	$10
Gentle Reader	$5

Each lifetime member gets his or her name on a plaque by the front desk. The last time I was in the Topeka Public Library, librarian Jeff Imparato pointed out that three of the "lifetime" memberships had been given posthumously in memory of a library patron. This suggests some donors will always choose the largest category, so aim high and make at least one category more expensive than a "lifetime" category.

Figure 6.2 is a reply form used by the Newberry Library in Chicago to recruit new members they call associates. Note the features that make it work. You can adapt these for your next mailing. The reply card highlights what advertisers call the "you get," which stresses the benefits for the new members. The card offers a range of dollar amounts to donate

---

FIGURE 6.2 Reply Form to Recruit New Members

Spring 1999

Dear Newberry Library Friend,

What you can do for us . . .

Join the Newberry Library family of Associates today with a contribution of $50, $75, $100, or more.

What we can do for you . . .

Offer you behind-the-scenes tours exploring our most treasured collections and book conservation lab—September 16 and November 4;

Invite you to exclusive exhibit previews and Associates-only gallery walks. *Signs of Judaism in Portugal opens in October*; and

Give you access to one of the world's major humanities research libraries with your Associates membership card.

Much of our operating budget is raised through people like you. With your annual support, you can ensure that one of the world's great cultural treasures remains free and open to all. Your contribution provides renowned reader services, enhances numerous educational programs, and maintains unique collections.

We look forward to sharing our riches with you. Please join the Associates today at $50, $75, $100, or more.

Sincerely yours,

Charles Cullen   *Kathryne M. Smith*

Charles T. Cullen   Kathryne M. Smith
President and Librarian   Associates Chair

P.S. We would be grateful if you respond by June 30, our fiscal year end.

(vertical text along tear line) Please tear off and return in the enclosed envelope

Yes!
I/We want to join the Newberry Library Associates.

☐ $35 Student (with photocopy of valid student ID)
☐ $50 Individual (one adult)
☐ $75 Joint (two adults in the same household)
☐ $100-$249 Contributors
☐ $250-$499 Leaders
☐ $500-$999 Benefactors
☐ $1,000+ President's Fellows*

For more information about gifts at $2,000 and above, please call (312) 255-3510.

☐ Anonymous

Your Name _____
                                   As you wish to appear in our records/publications

Spouse's/Partner's Name _____

Address _____

City _____ State _____ Zip _____

Daytime Phone _____

Evening Phone _____

We are pleased you have decided to join. Please make your check payable to the Newberry Library, charge by calling (312) 255-3510, or charge your contribution to:

☐ VISA   ☐ MasterCard   ☐ American Express

Credit Card # _____

Expiration Date _____

Signature _____

Please send me more information about:
☐ Gift Memberships   ☐ Memorial and Tribute gifts
☐ Friends of Genealogy   ☐ Friends of the Consort
☐ Public Programs

fy99s

Grateful acknowledgment is made to Newberry Library for permission to reprint reply form FY 1999.

and makes it easy to pay. The form suggests a deadline (the end of the fiscal year) and more ways for associates to give both time and money.

The Amistad Research Center in New Orleans is a manuscript library for the study of ethnic history and culture and race relations in the United States. Ninety percent of its collection pertains to the history and culture of African-American individuals and organizations. The center's membership categories are named for famous African Americans. Here is a sample of what members get at each level:

- Phillis Wheatley Club ($35)—Get the quarterly newsletter, invitations to special events, and discounts on reproductions from the center's art collections. (Seniors and students $20.)

- Sojourner Truth Club ($50)—Get all of the above and a special-edition poster or print.

- Frederick Douglass Club ($100)—Get all of the above and the annual magazine.

- Carter G. Woodson Club ($250)—Get all of the above plus recognition in the annual report.

- Harriet Tubman Club ($500)—Get all of the above and be an honored guest at the annual Heritage Banquet.

- Cinque Club ($1,000)—Get all of the above and receive recognition in the Banquet Program.

Also, businesses and professional partnerships can join as a Sustaining Partner for $250, Curatorial Partner for $500, or Conservator Partner for $1,000. For more information on big money gift clubs, see Chapter 9.

Track Your Turnover

You need to know your net membership—how many members you have left at the end of the year. In every community, people die, move away, or simply lose interest. They may drop out because they change jobs (work nights), get married (had triplets), go back to school (double major), or retire (gone fishing).

Keep track of how many people join and how many quit each year. Then you will know how many new donors you need to recruit. In other words, if you know that 20 percent leave each year and you want 1,000 members each year, you need to start with 1,200 to allow for attrition.

The turnover figure will vary radically depending on your location and constituencies. Most small towns have less turnover than suburbs; age-specific groups, such as the Little League, have more turnover than institutions for all age groups.

Renewals

Most organizations limit their membership sales drive to one or two months, but some organizations get members year-round. The easiest system is to put your membership data on a computer, code it by month and salesperson, then generate letters by month. For example, if Gail sells Morgan a membership in May, the office sends Morgan a letter the next March saying, "Your membership is about to expire; renew now for another exciting year." If Morgan does not respond, send another letter in April. If he still does not respond, in May give his name (and all the others who have not responded to the mail) to Gail, who sold his membership last May. Then she can reach him by phone or in person to ask him to renew.

If the original salesperson is not available, give the renewals to someone else in the same neighborhood or category. Renewals are much easier than new sales, so they are a good way to help timid salespeople get started.

Reward Renewals

The Santa Fe Opera attracts fans from all over New Mexico as well as Texas, California, Colorado, New York, and beyond. To encourage repeat audiences and repeat gifts, the opera created the "Encore Club." Those who give four years in a row get an asterisk by their name in the program. An explanatory note reads, "Santa Fe Opera extends special thanks to those individuals and businesses who have contributed on an annual basis for the past four years. Such dedication and loyalty are deeply appreciated."

The Denver Symphony gave its season subscribers purple buttons that said, "I've renewed—have you?" This way, the people who renewed first could urge everyone else in their row or their box to renew. Think of ways to reward your members who renew.

Fundraising by Mail, E-Mail, Telephone, or Door-to-Door

You can get the most money by asking for it face-to-face. But even the most enthusiastic fundraisers have limits on how many people they can visit in person. Phones, mail, E-mail, and door-to-door canvassing using volunteer solicitors will enable you to reach a large number of people for small gifts. Then you can use other strategies to get them more involved and to give larger gifts.

Mail

In a survey conducted in San Francisco, 71 percent of the respondents said the best part of the day was when they got the mail. This tells us two things:

1. Mail is very important to most people. You can use it to educate and motivate your public.

2. These people need to get out more! Nonprofit organizations can fill that need when you ask people to join up and march, pray, tutor, party, sing, build, organize, serve, clean up, or fundraise with your group.

Volunteer Mailing

When nine volunteers started Horizon Hospice in Chicago in 1978, it was the first hospice in Illinois and one of a handful in the United States. There was nowhere to buy or borrow a list of hospice supporters, so we had to begin to build a base of supporters with the names of the people we knew. The president asked every board member to address an envelope to each name in his or her own personal address book, and then to write a note like, "Hospice is an idea whose time has come. I'm supporting it this year—I hope you will too." She set the standard by bringing in four hundred names she had hand-addressed. That pulled up the standard so that everyone else brought in at least fifty, most about one hundred.

We were careful to get an address for every person who attended our open meetings, speeches, and parties, and then mailed information to these people. Also, we tested small lists from other organizations; these were the least successful. Music lovers and sports fans did not respond to a request to help people die pain-free and alert.

However, our own friends, families, and coworkers responded generously. Over the years, we have collected more names at every meeting, benefit, and speech, and board members are asked for new names at least twice a year. As Table 6.1 shows, the profits grow each year.

Horizon Hospice Do-it-Yourself Mailing

The hospice began using direct mail by mailing a photo of a patient and a volunteer, and an explanation of the services offered. The message: most of our patients are able to have a peaceful death, pain-free and alert, in their own homes if they want. Each letter included a reply card asking for the cost of one day's care, and a reply envelope. As the cost for one day's care went up, so did the amount requested. The office staff computerized the donor list so that they can print out a list of donors coded by the "worker" (that is, the person who asks them), for each board member. All of the envelopes were hand-addressed by board members and volunteers, sent with a live first-class stamp, and included handwritten notes to people they knew.

As you can see, even from a modest beginning, the growth was slow but steady. Increases come from the excellent packages prepared by the director of development, rigorous record keeping by the data-entry staff, and personal notes from board members to their own friends. During the campaign, each worker is notified weekly (daily for really big gifts) of donations from his or her list. Then the hospice board member or volunteer sends a personal handwritten thank-you note to the donor.

TABLE 6.1 **Horizon Hospice In-House Year-End/Holiday Mailing Income: 1980–1993**

1980	$7,000	1987	$49,000
1981	$8,000	1988	$53,000
1982	$13,000	1989	$58,000
1983	$20,000	1990	$65,000
1984	$22,000	1991	$75,000
1985	$29,000	1992	$80,000
1986	$36,000	1993	$91,000

By 1993 the mailing list had grown large enough for Horizon Hospice to get more sophisticated and divide the list. Larger and more loyal donors received the year-end appeal package, still hand-addressed by the committed board members and volunteers. Smaller donors, allies, and prospects received a newsletter twice a year with a reply envelope. Funds from both lists continued to grow, as Table 6.2 shows.

TABLE 6.2 **Horizon Hospice In-House Mailing Income: 1993–1998**

Year	Year-End Letter with Handwritten Note		Newsletter and Reply Envelope	Total
1993	$77,000		$14,000	$91,000
1994	$125,000		$18,000	$143,000
1995	$106,000	$27,000*	$29,000	$162,000
1996	$123,000		$28,000	$151,000
1997	$122,000		$45,000	$167,000
1998	$107,000		$50,000	$157,000

*1995 included a special mailing asking for support for indigent patient expenses not covered because of cutbacks in Medicaid payments.

You can see that with hard work and a good cause, even the smallest effort can grow to significant numbers. Especially with a new cause that was virtually unknown in the United States, mail was an effective way to reach and educate many new donors. With personal care and excellent management, the in-house mail is now both our tool to reach major donors once a year, and new prospects twice a year.

Year-End/Holiday Mailing

Even the smallest group can send at least one mailing a year during the holidays. Statistically, November is the most profitable month for mailers,[3] proving once again the benefits of competition. Ask all the board members and key volunteers to bring in their lists of names in the summer, and get them on a computer.

Meanwhile, ask the staff to compile statistics on the organization's results and recruit volunteers to take photographs, write copy, and design your package. Proofread everything out loud twice. Print the letter and envelopes in early September, and then organize addressing parties in October, so the mailing can go to the post office in November.

Be sure you code each return so you know which lists to use again next year and which ones to replace. The easiest system is to stack the reply cards and run a wide felt marker down the side of the stack. Use a different color for each list. It will leave a faint line of color on one edge of the card; most readers will never notice it. If you do several mailings a year, ask your printer to code the envelopes when they are printed.

As the mail comes in, record the contributions, send a receipt and a thank-you note from the office, and then notify each board member so he or she can also thank the donor. After two months, analyze what worked and send the final results to each volunteer with another thank-you note.

Every group can mail at the end of the year to take advantage of donors who get extra bonus money at that time, such as law partners, executives, and salespeople. Mailing in November will keep your group's name and achievements before the people who wait till the end of the year to make their tax-deductible donations. Remind them about your terrific organization.

How Often to Mail

Most organizations can, and should, mail more than once a year. Some mail-order catalogs and political parties mail as often as fourteen times a year. In the fundraising frenzy that occurs the year before a presidential election, the major political parties have mailed as often as every ten days in order to wring every possible dollar out of their donors. Then that sum will be matched by the federal government in January of the election year.

Obviously, volunteer groups would burn out their donors if they mailed thirty times a year. But you can mail at least four times a year asking for money. Here's the easiest system:

1. Mail in November for the year-end/holiday mailing.

2. Send your annual report in February (the third best month), or two months after the end of your fiscal year.

3. Ask members to renew their memberships or increase their annual gifts ten months after the date they first gave.

4. Mail a letter relating specifically to your issues or to a date connected to your cause. For example, hospices and veterans' organizations mail near Memorial Day; literacy and tutoring groups mail in August to arrive with the "back to school" advertisements.

If you want to mail more than four times a year, simply plan for each mailing to highlight different issues or needs. Fundraising mailings can be planned to add to a regular newsletter or to alternate with the newsletter. If you are asking for a planned gift, add one or two mailings about your planned gift opportunities to the mailing calendar.

Connect to Your Mission

Americans get the most mail near Christmas and Hanukkah, so think about other holidays that fit in naturally with your issue or constituency. For example, the Minnesota Women's Fund sent a letter in May that was connected with Mother's Day. It said, "As we prepare to honor our mothers, and be honored by our children, it is a good time to think about the world in which we live the other days of the year." The letter went on to describe the needs of women and girls in Minnesota and asked for "an investment in the girls and women in Minnesota. When the flowers of Mother's Day have faded, your investment in the future of girls and women will continue to grow."

It is more effective to mail more than once a year, because it is so easy to discard or misplace even a good letter for a good cause during the hectic holidays. If you mail at other times of the year, too, you can take advantage of less competition in the mailboxes, other income patterns (income tax refunds February to May, farm sales at harvest time, scholarships in September and January), and just random luck.

Repetition is good for raising money. Remember, your organization is competing with every other product for the public's money. If people see and hear commercials twenty times every day for beer, hamburgers, and gasoline, how much impact will you have if you ask for support for your group only once a year?

E-Mail

The most widespread change in communication in the last decade has been E-mail. Virtually all college and university students get it and use it all the time. Boomer parents have gone on-line, too, after waiting in vain for snail mail. Many high schools now have E-mail for their students, often run by the Tech Club masters who delight in proving they know more than the teachers. Most large companies run their internal communications on-line to save time, save money, conserve resources, cut down on chitchat about football or fashions, and give supervisors an Orwellian way to check on their subordinates. (Creepy, but very effective.) Especially for large multinational corporations, E-mail is invaluable for grinding out volumes of work. Computer managers in the United States now E-mail their programming jobs to India when they leave for the day, and when they return the next day, an excellent program is waiting because their Indian colleagues worked while the Yankees slept.

Charities are also using E-mail to ask for donations. Obviously, the first step is to build a file of E-mail addresses for your donors and prospects who prefer to get their mail on-line. This works especially well for young adults, workaholics (some executives brag about how they handle 150 E-mails a day), frequent fliers who can answer E-mails at 26,000 feet, and people who work odd hours. Fundraisers have found that most of the techniques that work for direct mail will work for E-mail, too.

The biggest advantages of E-mail are:

- It is quick. If your president is under arrest or going to be on "Nightline," you can contact your E-mail list within ten minutes. With mail, the fastest you can do a letter is ten days.

- It gets there. With some on-line services you can even confirm whether it was read. Especially if you are communicating with people around the world, or in places where the mail service is very unreliable (war zones, Moscow, Chicago), you know your message will get through if they have electricity and phone service.

- It is easy to change from day to day, or even hour to hour. If you are raising money for a very intense organizing or electoral campaign, this can be invaluable.

- It is easy for the donors to respond. Remember that fundraising is now donor driven. On E-mail, your donors can tell you in seconds what they want.

Recruit a committee of four people who use state-of-the-art E-mail on their jobs. They will know the latest products and services and, best of all, think big. These people can set up an E-mail system that will work well for you now, and then help it grow as your organization grows. For example, when Horizon Hospice decided to put its silent auction on-line, we had fewer than thirty E-mail addresses in our database because we had never asked for them. I recruited one of our volunteers, who managed the electronic systems that moved $72 million a day at the First Chicago NBD bank, to help us set up the E-mail and website for the auction. Her skills and enthusiasm changed us from turtles to turbos on the information highway.

Dialing for Dollars

It is most effective and most fun to do fundraising phone calling in a group. First, the planning committee culls through the organization's donor cards, takes out any cards marked "Do not call," and then prepares a duplicate set of cards with name, address, phone number, amount of the last gift, suggested amount for this gift, and issue interest. This can be done easily with a computer or laboriously with a team of volunteers.

With new technologies, telephones are everywhere. Be sensitive to local customs. In Los Angeles and Houston, for example, it is normal to call people on their car phones, because it is normal for people to be in traffic for hours every day. In most other communities, the use of car phones is limited to family emergencies. One Florida organization unfortunately antagonized its best donor when an overeager fundraiser called him on his boat. Use a little common sense and a lot of restraint when making up the cards to call for contributions.

Then recruit a team of callers. Colleges and universities try to recruit alumni from the same age groups. Politicians recruit people from the same precincts or townships. Everyone looks for a few veterans with experience and a few rookies with enthusiasm.

The key to success is making it all fun. Have a lot of production prizes. Ask celebrities to stop by. Keep each night short, and your volunteers will be glad to help again next year. Most groups find that any evening except Friday and Saturday works well, and Sunday afternoon is the best for getting people at home. A few people used to ask to be called at work, but most of those now prefer getting messages on their office E-mail.

My college does a volunteer phone solicitation every year at an advertising agency. We call names from our graduating class and ask for donations, and then we all adjourn to the saloon in the basement to reminisce. It is easy to get volunteers year after year, because the college makes it fun, it is only three hours, you get to see old friends and make new friends, you know the cause so the rap is clear, and the college gives lots of prizes: best amounts per hour, most gifts, largest gifts, rookie of the year, and most valuable player.

Calling has been made tougher by the prevalence of answering machines. If you are calling the people you know, you can target the calls when you know the prospect is home. So you never call John on Tuesday, because you know he is at volunteer fireman's practice, but you always call him on Saturday, right before *Prairie Home Companion*. For strangers, you have to leave a very brief message saying why you are calling and when you will call back, plus a phone and E-mail address where you can be reached. Some gifts, especially renewals, are negotiated by messages back and forth on dueling answering machines. Other times you simply have to leave three messages and then follow up with a letter.

Volunteer phonathons also work very well when your group needs to raise a lot of money quickly. They are a staple of civil disobedience campaigns. Volunteers get on the phone and say, "Henry David Thoreau is in jail because he refused to pay the poll tax. We need to raise bail tonight to get him out!" Once you get the leader out of jail, you can use the phone, regular mail, E-mail, and door-to-door campaigns to ask for money to support your campaign to fight the unfair tax.

Volunteer Canvassing

For decades, door-to-door canvassing by housewives was the backbone of raising money for disease associations in middle-class neighborhoods. As the majority of American women went to work outside the home, "passing the envelope" fell to the minority who were full-time homemakers. In wealthier neighborhoods, residents did not want to bother with a fundraising technique that raised only a few dollars per transaction; in rough neighborhoods, it was not prudent to ask volunteers to walk through gangs with an envelope full of cash. More and more, this valuable fundraising technique has been replaced with special events, direct mail, E-mail, and telemarketing to reach the same households.

However, going door-to-door still can be a very effective way to reach households who do not respond to mail or phone.

Since your volunteers are talking face-to-face with the public, they can find hidden treasures. A canvassing coordinator for the Heart and Stroke Fund in British Columbia, Canada, told me about motivating her newest volunteer to go door-to-door in February, Heart Month. The young volunteer was discouraged after one block with no donations, but the team leader told her to try one more block. On that block, a man greeted her with "The Heart Fund—great! I've been waiting for you to visit: I'm a member of the 'Zipper Club'!" (This is the fellowship of men who have had open-heart surgery; the stitches and staples leave a pattern like a zipper down the middle of the patient's chest.) He gave her $500 at the door.

This man believed he was alive because of heart research; he did not need a hard sell. But the important fact is he was *waiting* for the charity to call on him. He may be one of thousands of people who will not give through the mail or on-line, or come to parties, or buy products. But if you ask him in person, he can tell his story and begin a relationship with the group.

Most volunteer canvassers will get $5 to $50 at about 20 percent of the doors. Obviously if you know more of your own neighbors or have already canvassed the area for a political candidate, your results will be better. But every campaign will have a few pleasant surprises of getting larger gifts or hearing stories of how your organization changed their lives. Those surprises help make door-to-door canvassing worthwhile.

Your fundraisers can plan a safe way to meet your neighbors and ask them for money. Especially for community organizations, it is vital that you make the effort to reach every neighbor. A door-to-door membership drive will build your budget and your political power at the same time.

Door-to-door canvassing by volunteers is especially good in very low-income areas where residents may not have telephones or reliable mail service. There is no cost for phone calls or postage, so even the poorest people can sell memberships with no expenses. It is also the ideal way to sell memberships in a community with a large number of immigrants who do not speak English. Volunteer canvassers who speak the languages and dialects of the community can sell memberships, introduce your organization, and assess current neighborhood needs at the same time.

Putting It All Together

First, ask your volunteers how they want to raise money from the public. Then look at your calendar and plan how to space the campaigns. Adapt this to fit your own community.

For example, you could send a team of volunteers door-to-door once in the spring or the fall; telephone for donations in the summer in the South and the winter in the North, when people more likely are eager to be indoors; use mail two times in between for their membership renewal and one program; and last, try three E-mail requests on urgent issues. This gives you seven ways to ask your prospects for money and find your supporters. It also gives you four different ways for people to volunteer. The shy people can work on the mail, and techies can master the E-mail, while the more outgoing volunteers can telephone and go door-to-door.

Pledges

We mutually pledge to each other our lives, our fortunes, and our sacred honor.
                              —Declaration of Independence
                              Thomas Jefferson et al., 1776

A pledge is a promise to your organization. In a Gallup survey of American donors, 38 percent of the contributors said they wish they could have given more money than they did in the previous year. Pledges are the perfect tool to make this happen. Pledgers promise to pay a specific amount of money each week, month, or quarter for one or more years. During the American Revolution the founders literally pledged their entire fortunes to the cause of liberty, and some of them lost their homes and livelihoods. All you are asking for is a regular donation.

The best explanation of setting up a pledge program is in Mary Harrington's booklet *Guide to the Fabulous Family Pledge System* which describes how her committee created a pledge program for the Harmony Ark Education Foundation. The pledges go to pay for programs and services at two small elementary schools—everything from arts and computers to teacher science training and the wrestling coach. Mary's committee of parents created a pledge system that raised $60,000 a year from a community of 5,000 in rural California. They started the pledge system because they did not want to work on special events and they emphatically did not want the children to sell things. Instead they did want to make the most money with the least work and spread out the participation among as many families as possible. Mary and other parents share how they got started, with unusual frankness, good humor, and energy. Your school or other organization could do the same thing if you want a way to raise money that is "positive, fun, different, interesting, and easy."

The most common pledge is the weekly pledge for a religious congregation. In most congregations, pledges are solicited in a tightly organized "stewardship" campaign in the fall. The most enthusiastic fifth of the parish make their pledges first; then each of those people asks four other families to make their pledges. In a month, the campaign is over, and everyone has been asked in person. The obvious advantage that religious congregations have over other nonprofits is that they see the pledgers fifty-two times a year.

Credit Cards

For most charities, the ideal way to ask for pledges is via the donor's credit card. In this case, your fundraiser can arrange to use the major credit cards issued through your bank. If there is more than one bank in your community, shop around for the best deal. Just like a store, your organization will pay the bank a small percentage, usually about 3 to 5 percent, for servicing the credit card accounts. It is well worth the fee, because you can use the money the next day, rather than waiting weeks for checks to clear. Having a credit card option will also increase sales on all your special events or any other time you sell merchandise.

With credit cards, your fundraisers need to ask only once, and you keep getting the pledged amount every month until the donor tells the company to stop payment. You get the pledge even if the donor moves away. Credit cards are the most popular tool for telephone canvassers to get monthly pledges or to sell season subscriptions. A donor who will give someone $10 to $25 at the door will pledge twelve times as much over the phone via his or her credit card.

For further lessons, watch the next time your public television station does its membership drive. Many stations now offer donors four credit card options and urge viewers to call in because it will take only "one minute to become a member." This is why credit cards are the payment plan of choice for younger professionals.

When I was in Kansas City, I picked up a brochure at the Nelson-Atkins Museum of Art, one of the outstanding art museums in the world. (It owns what is considered the finest collection of Chinese art outside of China.) The brochure is called *An Hour with the Masters* and gives patrons the quickest route to see the top fourteen objects in the museum. I'm sure *An Hour with the Masters* grew out of dozens of people walking in every day and asking, "What can I see in an hour?" The customer is always right. If they want speed, give them speed. So if your donors want to sign up in one minute, give them a credit card option.

While young people like to give via credit cards, older people prefer to use electronic funds transfer (EFT). This is the way the federal government sends out social security checks under the name "direct deposit." Money is sent electronically into bank accounts, so nothing can be lost, stolen, or delayed. In the same way, you can offer your donors the option of making payments directly from their bank to your bank through the magic of electronics. More and more people are paying their utility bills, bank loans, and mortgages this way; they can make payments to good nonprofits this way, too.

Naming Names

All annual campaigns keep a list of all the donors. Some charities publish the names in an annual report that is mailed to every corporation, foundation, donor, and prospect. This can be a wonderful tool to encourage people to give and to impress your institutional donors with the breadth of your support from individuals. They also force the staff to use a system that captures every name and compiles cumulative giving totals for each person. Because ego is a motivator, naming names works well for most groups.

However, the most egalitarian kinds of organizations found they can run very effective annual campaigns without naming names. The Harmony Ark Education Foundation chose not to print a list of the people who pledged, nor to have groups of donors with different levels of appreciation. As they said, "What's a generous gift depends on your resources—$10 from one family might represent a lot 'more' than $1,000 from another." Because they were working in a public school system that included all income levels, they were more concerned about not embarrassing any family or especially any children because their names were not listed.

For performing arts groups, season subscriptions serve the same function as pledges. Rather than depend on fickle single-ticket buyers, you can presell the entire season to subscribers. You get the revenue in March for a season that starts in October. For hundreds of ideas to sell season subscriptions, see Danny Newman's classic book *Subscribe Now!*

Payroll Deduction—Pledging at the Workplace

In 1943 the federal government began withholding social security and federal income taxes from workers' paychecks. Soon fundraisers used the same strategy to collect money directly from workers' paychecks for charities. Today workers give more than $3 billion through their paychecks to the United Way, the Combined Federal Campaign (CFC) for federal employees, and hundreds of smaller alternative campaigns. Your organization can use all three of these to ask for pledges from prospects' paychecks.

The payroll deduction strategy is good for charities because the money is handled for you through the payroll department of the workplace, all of your target market is employed, and a pyramid structure is already in place to run the campaign. It can be very difficult to get accepted into new workplaces, but once you are in, this approach can be a dependable source of money.

United Way Donor Option

Some organizations collect pledges from working people through a donor option program of the local United Way. United Ways raise 90 percent of their money through payroll deduction, so they are the best place to start. Your opportunities will be different for each of the 1,400

United Ways in America. Some allow only their own health and human service agencies to ask for gifts through their payroll deduction plans. Others will allow any 501(c)(3) tax-exempt charity to ask. Ask your local United Way for its rules for donor option, and then ask for the unwritten rules from a charity that uses payroll deduction through donor option.

It is in the self-interest of local United Ways to encourage donor options, because a well-run campaign with real choice will always result in more money raised for both the United Way and for other charities. Most important, real donor choice changes the employees' participation in the United Way campaign from mindless coercion to thoughtful decision making. More charities competing for the donors' dollars means that more significant education has to take place before the campaign launch, rather than just this year's jingle from a pro bono ad agency.

More and more large companies are now using new technologies to run their payroll deduction campaigns. In some large firms, the entire campaign, pledging, record keeping, and reporting are done on their internal intranet E-mail system. As the use of E-mail and the Internet continues to improve, we will see major transformations of the ways employees can be asked to give and volunteer. Other companies are reevaluating the best way to encourage voluntary giving by their employees. For example, for decades the employees at Marshall Field's department store had to spend an hour to watch the promotional film put out by Chicago's United Way. It never varied much year to year, and the employees already knew who they wanted to support. Once the department store allowed donor option, they canceled the mandatory attendance at the film and gave their employees, most of whom are women, that hour to get their annual mammogram taken for free in the store. As one twenty-five-year employee said, "I love the new choice and the free mammogram. It really makes me feel like my store cares about me."

(See Chapter 14 for more on getting allocations and grants from the United Ways.)

Combined Federal Campaign

The CFC is the world's largest employee charity drive. It is how U.S. federal employees—both military and civilian workers—give at the office.

In 1997 more than 4 million employees gave $136 million in more than 300 local campaigns.

To get the rules, application, and calendar for the Combined Federal Campaign, contact the Office of Personnel Management, Office of CFC Operations, Room 6H28, 1900 E Street NW, Washington, D.C. 20415 or www.opm.gov/cfc. National organizations must apply to the national office. The CFC defines a national organization as one that has had programs or provides services in fifteen states during the last three years, and its fundraising and administrative expenses do not exceed 25 percent of its budget. For local campaigns, either ask the national office to send you the address for the Local Federal Coordinating Committee (LFCC) or ask one of your members who is a federal employee to find the name of the LFCC. Ask the LFCC for the rules, applications, and calendar.

These materials are all written in bureaucratic jargon. Get someone involved in your local CFC campaign to help you understand the application process and walk your application through. If you decide your organization should get donations from federal employees, you can apply in the spring. If accepted, you will be included in the campaign in the fall.

Most of these campaigns are managed by the local United Way. But even if you are not a United Way agency, your organization may still ask for employee donations. Since the Combined Federal Campaign was opened up to more agencies in 1987, about 35 percent of the funds go to the United Ways and their member agencies, while the other 65 percent go to non–United Way charities, including more than $20 million for nontraditional social justice and environmental groups

The Combined Federal Campaign is a model of open donor options. Federal employees may give to as many as five charities through payroll deduction, and they are offered a huge list of more than 1,000 national charities, including groups on both sides of issues, such as the gun control groups and the National Rifle Association, pro-life groups and pro-choice groups, and groups that raise money for either Palestine or Israel.

State and Local Government Charity Drives

Forty-nine states and many more cities and counties permit their employees to use payroll deduction to make donations to the charities they want to fund. Some of these are accessible only to the United Ways or other fundraising federations; others are open to all charities in the community.

To learn how to participate, ask one of your members who is a state, county, or city employee to obtain the name of a person who handles the charity campaign from the person who handles payroll deductions. Ask how your organization can apply. Then check with other local charities that get employee contributions to find out the best strategy for getting the most gifts.

Alternative Payroll Deduction Plans

The United Ways and the Combined Federal Campaigns have now been joined by more than two hundred smaller fundraising campaigns that allow donors the choice of giving to programs for the arts, environment, health care, social action, women, children, and minorities. These include federations such as the Black United Funds, National Voluntary Health Agencies, and Earth Share. Plus there are now four alternative payroll deduction campaigns working in Canada.

If your organization cannot get payroll deduction gifts through the United Way, consider working with an alternative plan. The alternative payroll deduction plans are now raising more than $300 million a year and growing at about 10 percent every year. These all use the same strategy of asking workers to designate a specific amount from each paycheck. Since workers will give a little bit twenty-four or twenty-six times a year, even small amounts will add up to major gifts. Big employers like combining alternative funds with the United Way option, because their empoyees respond so favorably. For example, Earth Share reports that Dell Computer ran its first combined campaign in 1995, and pledges doubled; then they doubled again in 1996, then they tripled in 1997 to more than $700,000.

Contact the largest workplaces in your community to find out which campaigns they allow to solicit their workers. Then ask the people who run those campaigns how your organization can be included. If there are no campaigns already organized, meet with the CEO of the workplace and ask him or her to allow employees to give to your organization through payroll deduction.

Money and Power

Building a broad base of donors by marketing memberships and asking for pledges is the only form of raising money that builds your organization's political power at the same time that it builds your budget. If you want more people, more volunteers, and more voters on your side, always begin your fundraising strategy with a well-organized annual campaign.

Mass-Marketing Your Message

How the Professionals Use the Internet, Direct Mail, Telemarketing, and Door Canvassing

7

The Web has its highest value doing what fundraising is supposed to do: building relationships with donors.
— Jeff Hallett, chairman
AppNet Systems, Inc.

THE MOST EXCITING OPPORTUNITY IN fundraising today is the Internet. Instead of marketing to 750 doors a night in one neighborhood, or 25,000 names from a mailing list of like-minded people, the Internet offers your message to 50 million people worldwide. Fundraisers are learning how to find new donors, persuade them to give, and then get them more involved.

Just as in the early development of direct mail for fundraising, a lot of the most successful Internet techniques are copied from retailers who are selling things on-line. Other techniques are discovered by fundraisers who, thankfully, are too young or too inexperienced to "know" that such techniques will not work. One of the greatest benefits of the growth of Internet use for fundraising has been the influx of many young people whose training and work experience have been neither fundraising nor nonprofits. Therefore they are ready, willing, and able to try anything and discover great new techniques that will work for any charity.

Like the older mass-marketing techniques, raising money over the Internet works best as one piece of a diverse fundraising plan. In this chapter we will look at all the ways professionals can help your organization raise money by reaching large numbers of prospects. All of these can be done in-house with your own staff and volunteers. But they will almost always be done better—make more money and find more new donors—under the direction of a professional firm that specializes in this kind of fundraising.

If you have a cause that appeals to the emotions and a very large market, your organization can hire the best professionals to reach the widest possible audience. This strategy is both an art and a science, and it is well worth investigating. Even with a terrific board of directors, great volunteers, and a full-time fundraising staff, your organization would be prudent to hire a special consultant for soliciting through the Internet, direct mail, telemarketing, or door-to-door canvassing. All of these strategies require attention from an expert in the current laws, technologies, and creative trends. If you want to ask a few thousand people in your own state to join or donate, review the techniques in the last

FIGURE 7.1 **Individual Donor Development**

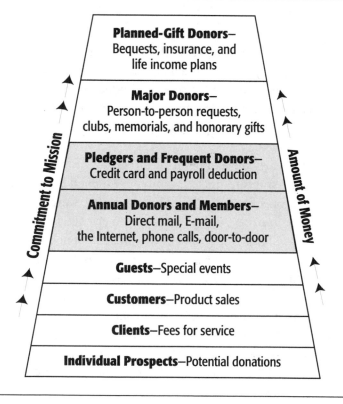

chapter for doing it yourself. If you have a cause that can attract much broader support, such as saving the castles in Poland or the buildings of Frank Lloyd Wright in Wisconsin, or banning strip-mining in Appalachia or land mines worldwide, you can hire a specialized consulting firm to help you.

Fundraising today is donor driven. Using a combination of these mass-marketing techniques enables you to ask people in four different ways so the prospects can choose to respond to the method they like best. Each method requires a substantial investment of money by your organization but no personal involvement from your leaders. These techniques are primarily used for finding new donors and building loyalty through repeat gifts. Once they are working, you and your leaders will get many more good prospects to ask for major and planned gifts (see Figure 7.1).

How to Hire Professional Fundraising Counsel

If your staff and leaders decide they want to launch a new kind of fundraising campaign and want outside advice, first decide exactly what you want. If you need expertise in a new fundraising technique, like raising money from your website, or for a much larger goal, such as a capital campaign that needs to raise five times your annual budget, get your goals in writing and then be sure there is consensus on what the staff and leaders want from a firm. What is your dollar goal, who from your organization will supervise the firm, and who will give written approval for each decision? Make a list of what you want and do not want in working with an outside firm.

Then ask your national network and local allies to recommend good professional experts. Many of the Foundation Center cooperating collections maintain files of consultants who work in your community. (Link to the list of collections from www.fdncenter.org.) Most firms are active members of the local chapters of their professional associations. You can also read the advertisements in the trade press and shop the vendors at conventions.

Interview three to five firms in person. A direct-mail or Internet fundraising program will take three to five years to make money, so be sure you are hiring a firm with similar values, style, and politics. A big capital campaign can take even longer from the first feasibility study to the campaign wrap-up. Most firms send out the charismatic boss to sell you their services; demand to meet the other individuals who will work with your people throughout the campaign.

Satisfied customers are always the best recommendation. Ask for references from the firms' repeat customers. Remember you want a firm that will make money and make your life easier, not more complicated. Ask the references if the consultants deliver their work on time and on budget. Do they handle follow-up? Do they tailor their plans and materials to fit your unique situation, or do they sell the same templates to everyone? Will they go the extra mile when necessary? How much turnover is on their staff? Do the same people remain on your account for the entire campaign? If you want to test a new firm, hire it to do a small project for you and proceed to a bigger campaign only if you're satisfied with its work.

Also ask experienced fundraisers for the right questions to ask. For example, if you hire a direct-mail or telemarketing firm, your organization will need to get a written agreement regarding who owns the names of your donors and members. Who will manage the names? The American Association of Fundraising Council also offers an excellent guide called "Choosing Fund-Raising Council—The 8 Steps," which you can download for free at their website at www.aafrc.org.

Ethics

Never pay a percentage. Pay the consultant a flat fee based on the work you want done.

There is a great deal of turmoil in the fundraising profession over the issue of paying consultants a percentage of what they raise. Because Americans are so generous, any aggressive salesperson can sell a good nonprofit cause. So new people are flocking to fundraising, offering unsuspecting nonprofits "no-risk" deals to raise money on a percentage. This is obviously great for any aggressive fundraiser but probably not great in the long run for your organization.

Fundraising is simply asking for money. If you hire someone on a percentage basis, he or she will say anything to get the largest possible gift. The consultant can burn out your market, get his or her commission, and then move to a new community and do it again. Then, next year when you try to go back to the same donor, your calls will not be returned, because your donor was pressured by the aggressive consultant pushing up his or her percentage.

Most states now regulate professional fundraising firms. Get the current regulations from the attorney general's office, and be sure the firms you interview know and comply with all state and federal rules.

There are professional associations for the experts who specialize in direct mail and direct marketing for nonprofits. See the list of professional associations in the Resource Guide and contact them for the list of members who subscribe to the association's code of ethics. Professional associations also sell inexpensive booklets to help you decide if a new fundraising strategy is right for your group.

The Internet

There are two different ways that your charity can get new donors. Either they find you via your website or 800 or 900 phone number, or else you go to them via direct mail, telephone calls, or knocking on their door. All of these have advantages for you, and all work better in combination with other techniques. Let's start by looking at how to get new prospects to come to you, and then discuss how to go to them.

More than 1 million shoppers spent more than $1 billion on the Internet during the holiday season 1998. On-line retailers are using E-commerce very effectively, and obviously, lots of consumers like to shop this way. Now charities are also learning how to raise money on-line.

The biggest charities have been the pioneers in using the Web for fundraising, because they started with the largest base of donors, they have the widest appeal, and they could raise the seed money to get started. To see what other charities are doing, go to the websites of ten or twenty of the largest international charities and note how they ask for money, how they involve the browsers, and how many different ways they offer for people to give. For example, CARE's Web page not only makes it easy for you to make a gift, but they also introduce their planned-giving options and list job openings, fellowship programs, and merchandise.

Convene a planning committee of four to six people who use the Web daily. Ask each of them to donate on-line to three charities of their choice to experience how it works. Also have the committee try out those charities' other interactive links to see how the targets and the organizations respond. For example, when I sent an E-mail to the president of the United States urging him to ratify the treaty to ban land mines, his system responded before I could take a breath. After three months, I'm still waiting for my member of Congress to respond. Once the committee has tested several other sites, have them interview the web-masters and the fundraisers at the most effective charities to learn the possibilities and the pitfalls. Then the committee can help you request proposals from three firms to put your fundraising efforts on-line. It is important for this committee to have people who use state-of-the-art technology, because they will know what to ask, understand the jargon, get excited about it all, and help you raise the seed money.

As with direct mail, starting to ask for money on your website will usually take three to five years to produce a net result. It is well worth the investment, because it puts your message into a much wider universe than any other fundraising tool can. The advantages of raising money on the Web are:

- People can see and hear what you do, which is how most people want to get their information. Now more than 80 percent of Americans get their news from television; only 18 percent read a newspaper. Any alluring visual is solid gold. Millions of people watched the three African lion cubs grow up on Lincoln Park Zoo's website at www.lpzoo.com and, at the same time, learned about the importance of zoos for the survival of endangered species.

- It is still novel for most people, so it is still perceived as fun.

- You can offer more information for the people who want more. Most direct-mail packages are a letter, one insert, and a reply envelope. Your website, however, can include entire press releases or model legislation, a video of your project, or an interview with someone who has made a bequest to your organization. It can involve your most thoughtful donors in a more respectful way than standard direct-mail packages.

- It is fast. So far, the greatest dollar amounts have come in on very dramatic campaigns linked to natural disasters. For example, care downloaded television reports from cnn directly onto their website after Hurricane Mitch in 1998. They raised $70,000 in a week in response to people seeing the devastation in Central America. You could never do that in a letter.

- It is available anywhere that has telephone service and electricity. The Internet gives us more opportunities to involve new people than any other form of asking, because they select our site on their own.

Figure 7.2 is an example of the fundraising page from the website for the World Wildlife Fund in Canada (www.wwf.ca). See how they ask you for money in several different ways, how they show you what your money is for, and how they ask for more than money.

David Love, who developed this site, also shares a few tips for beginners. He recommends that you get on the Web as soon as you can, even if your site is relatively crude. Your organization needs to have some presence for the people who want to visit you this way. Second, be sure that there are enough staff or volunteers to reply daily to responses and keep your site up-to-date. Last, he warns, "Don't fall in love with the technology. Don't make it too complicated, and most of all, don't forget to ask for money, members, and involvement."

Make it easy for people to find your website. List your URL "www.etc" on everything you print, every agenda, every newsletter, every tote bag, every van, and every T-shirt. Let the world know how to find you, and you will be thrilled by the global response.

Calling In—800 and 900 Numbers

Like the Internet, prospects find *you* on your 800 and 900 phone numbers. Unlike telemarketing, where your fundraisers call your own list of donors and prospects, with an 800 or 900 number you make your market aware of that number. Then the people who want to give call you.

With an 800-area-code number, the charity pays all of the costs. Any print, radio, or TV advertisement can ask for a donation that will be charged to the caller's telephone bill or credit card. (Pledges promised to be mailed in have a much lower receipt rate.) The advantage of using an 800 number is that more donors are familiar with it, and it can reach every U.S. phone. (In the near future, better technology will also allow calling to Canada and Europe.) There is no cost to the caller.

The disadvantage is that all costs are covered by the charity, so partisan causes can be victims of jamming by the opposition. An 800 number is easy for your friends to use and for your enemies to abuse.

FIGURE 7.2 **Website Membership Page**

WWF CANADA MEMBERSHIP

Become a member of World Wildlife Fund Canada and help lengthen the list of conservation success stories...

Every year, WWF Canada funds many hands-on field projects designed to save critically endangered species. with the support of our members, WWF has helped to improve the chance of survival for many species, including: the sea otter, the white pelican, the wood bison, the eastern bluebird and the Arctic peregrine falcon.

Here are a few examples of what your contribution can do for wildlife today:

$25 develops film of northern bottlenose whales for researchers to use in identifying individual animals which inhabit the Gully, off Nova Scotia.

$35 supplies lupine and other nectar seeds to Toronto's High Park in order to restore the natural habitat necessary to reintroduce the Karner Blue Butterfly.

$60 allows researchers to conduct on-site pest analysis to help farmers reduce their use of pesticides.

$100 helps purchase specially designed transmitters to track the highly endangered Vancouver Island marmot.

> Join Now!

Your WWF Membership benefits include:

Value for your money!
At WWF only 11% of the money we raise is spent on fund raising and administration. And since we cover all these costs with income earned from product sales, promotions and investments, we can spend your entire donation where you want it - *on conservation action!*

Your WWF Welcome Package
An informative booklet outlining WWF's Programs and our committment to you. It includes lots of ideas on how you can become more involved.

Working for Wildlife
Your quarterly newsletter full of project updates and the latest conservation results.

You can become active!
Join WWF's *Members in Action* or *Advocates-on-line* and receive up-to-the-minute information about our latest letter - writing campaigns.

WWF's Wildlife Rescue Team!
You can join WWF's 11,000 Canadian WRT partners who provide on-going support for urgent conservation projects through convenient and flexible monthly giving.

WWF's annually updated list of Canadian Species at Risk.

Exclusive product offers.

And most important of all - you get results!

Grateful acknowledgment is made to WWF Canada for permission to reprint website page from www.wwf.ca.

With a 900-area-code number, each caller is charged a fee that is a specific amount per call. After the phone company deducts its charges, the charity gets the balance. The advantage of using a 900 number is that the call is charged directly to the person who calls. Unlike direct mail, start-up costs are very low since the phone company deducts the telephone costs from the caller. Because the phone company handles billing, there are fewer administrative expenses for the charity. Also, because the caller pays, enemies of the agency cannot afford to jam your 900 phone lines.

A great deal of experimentation is going on now with new ways to use 800 and 900 phone numbers, especially in conjunction with television. As homes become wired for fiber optics in the next decade, there will be new fundraising opportunities through telephones and television.

Direct Mail

Direct mail is still the most effective way to tell your organization's story to a very large audience. Experts claim that a mailing on an average draws ten times as many responses as newspaper ads and one hundred times as many as television ads.[1] Current technology allows mailers to target specific markets, whether by location, such as congressional districts, or by demographics, such as forty-year-old Asian-American men.

Mail is the most common way that most middle-class people are asked to donate money. According to a recent Gallup survey, 30 percent of the people who gave to a charity for the first time did so because they received a letter asking them to give. Anyone who is "mail responsive"— that is, buys or gives through the mail—knows that the amount of mail has exploded in the last ten years. If you give to a whale, you will be on the list for the dolphins and the manatees.

It used to be that a nonprofit group could start a mailing on its conference room table for $5,000 and make money in a year, just as entrepreneurs could once start a mail-order business on a kitchen table. Those days are gone. With increasing costs and increasing competition, nonprofits need at least $50,000 of seed money and three years of lead time to get into the mail and see a profit. But it is worse for the mail-order catalog companies. Today it takes $5 million and five years to start to make money from a mail-order catalog.

To survive the competition, most nonprofits cannot run a successful large direct-mail program alone. You need a savvy, experienced, ethical specialist to guide your campaign from year to year. Think of going into the mail as going into business. Just as you do not open a store one or two times a year (and make money), you cannot mail sporadically and make money. Direct mail must be an intentional strategy to mail over and over to a mass audience to find the tiny minority who will support your cause.

If you need cash to spend in the next three years, do not even consider direct mail. To produce cash quickly, choose another strategy, especially asking for money face-to-face. However, if you can budget to wait three years before you see a positive cash stream, look into direct mail.

Also, do not consider direct mail unless you have the seed money to launch the program, probably about $50,000. If your organization does not have the funds to begin this strategy, it will not have the funds to handle success. The members and donors brought in by a good direct-mail campaign will cost even more to effectively serve so they will renew year after year.

Again, do not be tempted by a consultant who offers to begin your organizations' direct-mail campaign by taking a percentage out of future profits and thus requiring no up-front investment from you. Successful direct mail depends on your members and donors giving repeat gifts year after year. A consultant working on a percentage is going to be looking for quick hits rather than loyal donors who can become a dependable funding base. If you do not have the money to start the program, focus on low-overhead fundraising strategies, especially asking for money face-to-face, until you have enough funds. Then hire an experienced firm that will work for a flat fee.

Prospecting

The way to understand direct mail is to think of it as prospecting. It is like looking for gold. Somewhere in all of the lists are a few people who will give to your organization. The purpose of direct mail is to systematically look for such people, then find out what they like best, and find a way to keep them giving to you.

The standard goal for a first mailing is a 1 percent rate of return, but it can be less. It happens this way:

- Ninety-two percent of the people never open the envelope. In other words, 8 percent of the people open the envelope.

- Of these, half, or 4 percent, read past the first paragraph.

- Of these, half, or 2 percent, read to the end of the letter.

- Of these, half, or 1 percent, take the action you want—send money.

Because of increasing costs, when only 1 percent (or less) of the people respond to you the first year, you cannot make money. All the money that comes in has to be reinvested in more prospecting. So if you want to make money in direct mail, you need to fundraise from some other source for venture capital up front to pay for experimenting the first year or two.

The way this turns into gold is through the people who renew. Every year you keep a donor, you get a higher percentage of renewals. According to expert Mal Warwick, only about 40 to 60 percent of direct-mail donors renew the first year, and 60 to 70 percent of donors renew the second year. However, by year five, 83 to 90 percent of donors renew, and by year eight, 87 to 91 percent will renew.[2]

You need a professional direct-mail expert in order to get donors to respond the first time (by opening the envelope, reading the letter, and sending a check) and to keep responding every time you mail to them. Because there are so many factors in keeping costs down and returns up, you need to hire someone who knows the best vendors, the current postal regulations, and what is working now.

Within the mailing itself are several areas of concern. What can you honestly and ethically say your organization will do? How will you say it? For a free lesson on how to write effective letters and compile effective mail packages, save all the begging letters you receive for a month (a week if it is November). Then open them all up and consider the pieces that make up a typical direct-mail appeal:

1. The outside envelope

2. The letter

3. Other copy, such as photos, clippings, brochures, or ballots

4. Premiums, such as decals, membership cards, or address labels

5. Gimmicks, such as balloons you need to inflate to read the message or (my personal favorite) a shower cap with the outline of a

hand on it sent by a preacher; you can wear the cap and pretend he is laying his hand on your head

6. The reply card

7. The return envelope (which can double as the reply device)

One reason mail is so wonderful is that every element of the package and every list can be tested. You never need to guess about anything. Continue using the letters and lists that work, and discontinue the ones that do not work, even if you like them a lot. You can apply this terrific lesson to all your other fundraising strategies.

Give through the mail to all of your competitors so you will know what their letters are saying. Ask family and friends from other cities to send you fundraising letters they like, and ask your board and staff to save all the fundraising mail they get. Note the formats and contents that are working for other fundraisers. For example, fancy packages and gimmicks are a thing of the past; today, simplicity works best.

I used to get mail handed down by my ninety-nine-year-old landlady, who had voted straight-ticket Republican in every election since Harding. Even when I did not agree with Ronald Reagan, I was always dazzled by the brilliance of his fundraising letters. Of course, not everyone can mail from the beaches of Normandy on the anniversary of D-Day, but every group can get million-dollar ideas to think bigger and ask for more.

What Works

To be effective in asking for money through the mail, you need to have an issue that your readers feel strongly about. Controversy is excellent, and any high-profile news campaign will help you a lot. Remember, you do not have committed volunteers and staff asking in person. All you have is a piece of paper to do the asking for your group. The hotter the issue, the easier it is to raise money via mail.

Different causes will get different results. For example, mail does very well for environmental causes, homelessness, and cancer. It is less effective raising money for inner-city youth, hospitals, and little-known diseases. Mail does well marketing memberships for zoos; it is less effective asking for contributions for zoos.

Professional direct mail works best for a controversial cause, an emotional cause, or a project identified with an appealing leader. If you use a do-it-yourself mailing by your own board members, you can get a 10 to 30 percent return, because they are writing personal letters to their own friends. The best direct mail simulates the same kind of person-to-person contact. One of the most effective letters was the Katharine Hepburn letter for Planned Parenthood. She was believable because her own beloved mother had worked shoulder to shoulder with Margaret Sanger, the founder of Planned Parenthood. The Hepburn letter to get new contributors raised almost $5 million from 170,000 new donors.

In the same way, the Bob Hope letter for the Vietnam Veterans Memorial Fund was so successful that it laid the foundation for the entire fundraising campaign to build the wall. Because of his enormous popularity from television and fifty years of valiant efforts for American servicemen and -women, Bob Hope could get the massive response needed. His postscript read, "If you can give $20, it will sponsor the name of one Vietnam War veteran who gave his life in service to our country. We intend to inscribe every single name—57,661, to be precise. A lot of names—a lot of lives. Won't you please help us to begin by sending your tax-deductible gift of $20, $40 or more today?"

Luckily for us, the creative genius who wrote this letter, Kay Partney Lautman, got together with her equally talented colleague Henry Goldstein and blabbed all of the secrets of direct mail. Their book, *Dear Friend: Mastering the Art of Direct Mail Fund Raising*, tells you everything you need to know from the pilot mailing and renewals to computers, the post office, and consultants. In any fundraising business that can be a money drain the first three years, a little knowledge is a dangerous thing. This book will give you the best grounding in the basics to decide whether this is the strategy you want to use to ask for money for your organization. See the Resource Guide for this and other useful books.

Telemarketing

Telemarketing—asking for money by calling your donors and prospects on the telephone—is one of the mysteries of fundraising. I lead fundraising workshops for about two thousand people every year. The vast majority of these people have chosen a career working for a nonprofit. They are people with big hearts and generous habits. When I ask them what type of fundraiser they hate most, their most frequent response is getting called on the phone. They loathe getting called on the phone. At suppertime. By someone obviously reading a script. Or worse, by a computer. Twice in the same night.

Yet telemarketing makes millions of dollars for the groups that use it well. In 1996 the Direct Marketing Association projected that more than $65 billion was raised for charities by telemarketing. Traditionally it has been used extensively by colleges and universities, which use high-energy students with a clear self-interest.

Today telemarketing is used extensively for sales, politicians, performing arts groups, and consumer organizations. It is usually most effective when used in conjunction with television documentaries, direct mail, or a door-to-door canvass. The advantages of the phone over mail are that it is more personal, there is two-way communication, and prospects can be persuaded to give larger amounts, especially by using their credit cards. The advantages over a door-to-door canvass are that it is easier to hire people because telemarketing is an indoor job, callers can make more money, and the skills are more transferable to other jobs.

Successful fundraisers can reach more prospects faster by the phone than by any other fundraising strategy available today. The telephone is terrific for truly urgent causes, prompt response to legislation or court rulings that affect your donors, or taking advantage of a breaking news story.

Some of your prospects and donors will just love being called on the phone. Ask any successful phone canvasser, and he or she can tell you stories of their donors who look forward to their calls every year. When Kim Simmons was a telephone canvasser for the Illinois Public Action Council, she was so popular with the people she called that one woman not only sent in a generous donation each time Kim called but also invited Kim to her daughter's wedding.

The telephone makes it easy for new friends to donate or join. Donors do not have to find an envelope, a stamp, and a check; they simply answer the phone and presto, the deed is done.

Telemarketing enables you to reach younger donors and members who like the speed and ease of using the phone. You get a proven way to expand your base beyond the names you have now.

Door-to-Door Canvassing

Professional door-to-door canvassing has been the backbone of fund-raising for consumer and community organizations for more than twenty-five years. A team of paid professional canvassers knock on doors and ask for money Monday through Friday, all year round. Canvassing is the most personal of the professional mass-marketing strategies and gives your fundraisers the chance for the most two-way communication. Prospects can be asked to do much more than just give money. An effective door-to-door canvass will also get petitions signed, get letters written, and find new volunteers.

The professional canvass has seen the most changes as the politics and economy of America have changed. When the first fundraising canvass began in the early 1960s, it was raising money for environmental organizations and was considered almost radical. Now most people have grown up as environmentalists and there is recycling in every community. It was easy hiring people to go door-to-door during the hard times of the Reagan years. In the boom economy of the Clinton administration, the same labor market became baristas at Starbucks or clerks at the Gap instead of knocking on doors for social justice.

Fortunately, some very savvy people have kept on canvassing and keep adjusting the canvass to fit the current economics. There are still canvasses working in most big cities and larger college towns, because that is where you can hire teams of people to knock on seventy-five doors a night. In most cases the door canvass just breaks even, but it serves as the prospecting tool to feed new names to the phone canvass and direct mail.

However, with good leadership, hot issues, and a clear political analysis, some door canvasses are still good moneymakers. The star in 1998 was the Clean Water Action Project canvass in Lansing, Michigan, which was the first field office to make $1 million.

Weather, surprisingly, is not a factor. That is because door-to-door canvassers are true believers; they believe in their cause heart and soul. Canvassers in the Midwest go out in the summer when it is 100 degrees in the shade and in the winter when it is 30 below.

The door-to-door canvass is a great entry-level job for any young person who wants to consider a job in fundraising. Today canvasses are also attracting older workers who want to do political work and make some money. One of the star canvassers in 1998 was a retired school principal who liked the team, liked to talk, and liked to raise money. You learn to qualify the prospect, get attention, and present your case in less than a minute. Best of all, you learn to get to the close in less than three minutes.

Even the best door-to-door canvass does not work well in very low-income or very high-income neighborhoods, so you need to combine it with other strategies to reach low-income and wealthy donors. Like mail and the phone, door-to-door canvassing needs a "hot" issue with wide popularity, so it works best for emotional issues like stopping a local toxic waste dump.

Complaints

Complaints are inevitable. No matter what fundraising strategy you choose, prospects will complain. However, it seems as though more people complain more often about phone, mail, and door-to-door canvassing.

Some organizations simply take out all their big ($1,000+) donors from the lists for mail and phones. Most of these people are typically exempt from the door-to-door canvass, since wealthy neighborhoods and buildings have not been profitable to canvass. If you are good at using your computers to segment your market, you can specify which strategies to use for each donor.

Since complaints are a part of fundraising, you need to plan to meet them. Let's look at common complaints of each fundraising method.

Internet

The cyber-world has its own code of manners, known as "netiquette." Unlike direct mail where we know that 99 percent of the letters will just get thrown away, sending a message on-line to people who are not interested is considered "spamming" and will really get them riled up. Ask your experts how to focus your communication, and always make it a priority to respond by the end of the day, if not sooner, to anyone who complains on-line.

Make it easy to get on and off of your lists with a clear choice at the end of your E-mails, such as "To leave this list at any time, send a message to:" or "To rejoin this list at any time, send a message to:." Be sure your system is set up to add and delete names as requested, and test your system once a week to verify that it does what you want.

Telemarketing

Ask people to name why they hate fundraisers, and nine out of ten will say, "They call me at dinnertime. I hate it when I have to answer the phone in the middle of dinner!"

Disregard the obvious response, which is "Don't answer the phone." Instead, ask people to tell you the best time to call, and put that information on their donor card. Some jobs will not let employees get calls at work; parents with new babies may not want to have naps interrupted at home; families with teenagers may have no good time to get through on their home phone and prefer to get calls at work.

The customer is always right. Ask each person when and where to call, then follow those instructions rigidly.

Some phone campaigns now head off complaints by mailing their best donors a postcard in advance. The card alerts donors to the call and offers them three ways to avoid the phone call: mail in this year's contribution or call the 800 number or log on the website and pledge via credit card before the fundraiser's call.

Direct Mail

Some of your donors will go berserk over multiple mailings or misspelled names or late mail. In any such case, answer their complaints with a gracious letter and then be sure to meet their wishes.

Ask your donors what mail they want to receive:

1. One mailing a year—only their dues renewal or annual gift.

2. Mail on specific issues. For example, they want to get the mailings on the health clinic but not on the senior citizens; they want the mailings on international missions but not on the local soup kitchen. Or vice versa.

3. Send it all. They are curious about everything, and they will respond when they can.

4. Nothing. Never send anything. They do not want to get any mail ever, about anything.

It does not matter what the donors choose; honor their choice. If they do not want to be asked through the mail, you can choose different ways to ask.

If any members feel strongly about receiving mail, suggest that they register their name and address with the national association that maintains a "Mail Preference Service" used by the largest for-profit and non-profit mailers. Individuals can write to the Mail Preference Service, c/o the Direct Marketing Association, P.O. Box 9008, Farmingdale, NY 11735. The file is updated quarterly, so it will take three to six months to get one's name off mailing lists.

Door Canvassing

For a door-to-door canvass, people will again complain about the time of day, interruptions, or other annoyances, such as frightening their dog. Most people are nicer in person, but someone will still want to complain to the canvasser or to the office. Apologize and mark the card, "Do not canvass at the door."

For any complaint, the president of your organization can send a written apology the next day. Simply say, "Thank you for letting me know of the frustration you experienced. . . . Please accept our personal apologies." Then say what action you have taken, and apologize again: "Again, Mr. Jones, please accept my apologies for the inconvenience caused."

Watchdogs

Two independent organizations have created a set of standards to evaluate charities and advise donors. Conforming to these standards will give you an outsider's endorsement to assure donors and prospects that your organization is well run. For free copies of the standards, write the National Charities Information Bureau, 19 Union Square West, New York, NY 10002 or www.give.org, or the Council of Better Business Bureaus' Philanthropic Advisory Service, 4200 Wilson Boulevard, Arlington, VA 22203 or www.bbb.org.

A charity is regulated by each state where it operates, usually by the attorney general as a charity and by the secretary of state as a corporation doing business in the state. Some cities may also require licensing for door-to-door canvassers or for some special events, such as raffles. Of course, every charity must scrupulously obey all laws. In addition, set your own internal standards for ethical fundraising. A good start is the "Donor's Bill of Rights" that is distributed in English and Spanish from the National Society of Fund Raising Executives. Some charities, such as the School of the Art Institute in Chicago, send this one-page document with every thank-you note as a way of showing they are committed to respecting their donors.

It is important to see the big picture. No matter what you do, someone will complain. Or maybe a dozen people will complain. This is no reason to stop a strategy that enables you to tell your story to tens of thousands of people each year. Respond promptly and courteously to all complaints, but do not stop a big campaign because of a tiny minority of the whole list.

Marketing to Millions

Direct marketing enables your organization to tell its story to millions of people and motivate thousands of them to join you. In addition to raising money, all four of these fundraising strategies can be used to educate the public on your issues, ask them to take action, or get them out to vote.

How to Find the Big Givers 8

You have to keep up the high touch and the high tech.
—Milton Murray
Chair of the Philanthropy Stamp Task Force

EVERY CULTURE HONORS THE PEOPLE who share their wealth to make the community better. For example, in Nigeria novelist Chinua Achebe's great-grandfather represented the old Ibo ideal of the man who was both productive and generous. This was reflected in his name, Osinyi, which means "someone who cooks more than the whole town can eat."[1] In that culture you could gain status, delight your neighbors, taunt your enemies, impress members of the opposite sex, and appease the gods by cooking yams. In America you can do all of that as well as contributing to positive social change by making a major gift to a worthwhile nonprofit organization.

Unfortunately it is more difficult to find out who has valuable assets when the wealth is in stocks, bonds, or real estate rather than farm produce. But we can use our own network of community leaders as well as print and on-line research to find the people with the best potential to give to our organizations. In Chapter 9 we will discuss how to ask for major gifts from the prospect's assets and in Chapter 10 we will discuss how to ask for planned gifts from the prospect's estate. This chapter will focus on how to find the individuals with the highest net worth.

America is more than ever the land of opportunity. There are now more than 170 billionaires in the United States (compared to 13 in 1982).[2] In addition, there are 250,000 decamillionaires and 4.8 million millionaires. Of course, it is easier to find prospects in rich enclaves where they cluster near cutting-edge computer companies, gated retirement communities, or exclusive golf courses. But every community may have residents or alumni who are wealthy now, because 80 percent of America's millionaires are first-generation rich.

It is common sense that rich people are going to first support the politicians who keep them rich and the charities that make their lives nicer. However, do not reject the idea of asking for money from major donors simply because your organization is new, controversial, or unorthodox. Every organization can include an economic mix of prospects in its fundraising strategy. Let wealthy people know how great your group is, and give them a chance to support you, too.

How Do You Define Major Donor?

First of all, define what is, for your organization, a major donor. Some grassroots groups consider any donor who gives more than $100 a major donor. Other groups put the trigger at $5,000. It does not matter what you choose, but your organization must be intentional about the size of gifts it wants to get.

After you set the dollar size of a donor, then do the research to learn where you can find people who can pay that amount and more. Giant charities and universities employ several full-time professional researchers. Smaller charities make donor research one of the jobs of the director of development. Volunteer groups can make donor research a job for two people who are too shy to ask for money.

Give the researchers a specific goal. Let's say your organization wants to get major gifts from fifty donors this year. Assuming one in five says yes, the researchers need to find 250 prospects, or about one every business day.

Respect

Before you get started on prospect research, be sure to review the big picture, especially with your staff and leaders. Prospect research can seem like candy-land, with all these multimillionaires waiting in line to donate to your group. In order that you do not lose all sense of focus, remind yourself and your committee of four important things:

1. We in America begin with a very distorted vision of what being wealthy means. Remember that 55 percent of the world's families earn less than $725 a year. Only 15 percent of the world's population earn more than $9,000 a year. We are all rich, in financial and many other ways, and we need to be reminded of that before we start throwing around million-dollar salaries and billion-dollar net worths as everyday conversation.

2. This kind of research can tempt us to think in stereotypes that are not appropriate. Just as we fight against name-calling and labeling when we work with people with disabilities or other groups, we need to fight labeling when we do our prospect research. It is morally wrong to think of *any* people by stereotypes.

3. It is also unprofitable. Experts in demographics, especially, love to make up catchy names for clusters of similar people. But creating clusters of people from what brand of cars they drive does not encourage you to learn about the people as individuals. Clusters do not give you major gifts; individuals do. Downplay the demographic lingo and spend the time getting to know the people instead.

4. We are called to respect every person's gift. Once we find that Jerry Seinfeld made $225 million a year to tell jokes, or Michael Jordan made $30 million a year to play basketball, plus another $50 million to sell hot dogs and sunglasses, it can seem like the only things of value are trivial and materialistic. Just as you did when you began to look for small gifts, review the mission and values of your organization when you begin to look for major donors. Fundraising is just the means to an end—the mission—and everybody, rich and poor, has something to offer.

Inside Research

First, and always best, are your own donors. Who loves the organization? Who has seen his or her children flourish because of this group? Who has volunteered? Who has donated consistently?

The best place to look is your own membership and your list of annual donors. If you do not have a membership that pays dues or a donor base that donates every year, build that base before you launch the major gift campaign.

Your Donor Base

Recruit two of your board members who have extensive connections in the community. They need to do the intensive, vital, and boring hands-on job of going through your current list of prospects name by name. Is the information current? Who is missing? Who should be giving more? Does every donor have a board member or volunteer assigned as a "worker"?

On your own lists, look for (obviously) the largest gifts and (not so obviously) the people who have given to you every year for more than three years. Even small gifts, given consistently, can indicate the possibility of giving a larger gift if asked.

Look for people who give an odd amount of money, like $27 or $358. An odd dollar amount can be a clue the donor is allocating his or her total annual charity budget among several nonprofits. This suggests the donor plans his or her charitable giving, and your group is already on the short list of good organizations. Look for the best addresses, multiple addresses (summers in Lake Wobegon, Minnesota, and winters in Lake Okeechobee, Florida), the names of the local aristocrats, celebrities, and entrepreneurs, and other indications of commitment or wealth.

For new organizations, you have to start with your own board and active volunteers, and then branch out. For older organizations, look for second- or third-generation members and multiple members from the same family.

Then ask the grapevine who won the lottery, inherited money, sold the ranch, or made a fortune by inventing a better mousetrap. For old money, look for people who went to elite schools, belong to private clubs, or summer and ski at exclusive resorts. For new money, look for the entrepreneurs, especially people of color, women, and immigrants, who want to leverage an entree into the established (white-male-Anglo) power structure.

You can also tailor your research to match the mission of the organization. Historic preservation groups can check the historical society and genealogical society to find the people with deep roots in the community. Environmental, hunting, and fishing clubs can find wealthy outdoorsy types by checking their state department of motor vehicles for owners of campers and recreational vehicles and their state department of conservation of game and wildlife for owners of boats and yachts.

In order to continue doing business in a small town, merchants have to be very discreet about their customers. Especially now that people can shop on the Internet, they can easily take their business elsewhere. But even if merchants may not be willing to name names, those who handle high-priced products may be able to verify prospects. For example, one of the best fundraisers in a small town in Iowa was the travel agent. The richest family in town would pay for their monthlong winter cruise in cash because they did not want the people at the bank (who would blab) to know where they went or how much they spent. Since the travel agent proved she could keep her mouth shut, she got their repeat business. She could guide her charity's fundraiser to the right people in very discreet ways that helped the organization and preserved her business relationships.

After you have worked the names already on your list, ask your board members to think of new names. Just as you asked your committee for ten names who could donate $20 each in the exercise in Chapter 5, now ask each board member to give you names of new people they could ask for larger amounts. Depending on your organization, try for three names at $200, one at $2,000, and one at $20,000. Review the kinds of people your committee members know. Then think about who has access to money through family connections or their professions. Even if you want to ask the bank for a donation, somebody signs the check. Asking for names of prospects for larger gifts may produce new people you have not asked before.

Outside Research

Charity begins at home. The first place to look for major gifts must be your own board of directors, active volunteers, and senior staff. Do not think that total strangers will support your group if the cause cannot compel your own leadership to give.

After you get support from your own leadership and your own donors, then you can research outsiders who share a commitment to your cause and can make a large gift. All these research sources, from corporate annual reports to divorce court records, are legal sources of information available to the public. Reading them is how gossip magazines, venture capitalists, opposing lawyers, political parties, and giant charities collect their ammunition. These resources can help your organization, too.

Many of your best prospects for major gifts can give not only from their own personal accounts, but also from a business account or a corporate foundation, plus a family foundation, a supporting organization, or a donor-advised fund at the local community fund. This chapter shows you how to research individual donors. We will discuss researching corporate donors in Chapter 11, foundations in Chapter 13, and other grant makers in Chapter 14.

There is a surprising amount of information you can find out about other citizens. Although people are often horrified when they discover what anyone on-line can learn about them, this is all public information. Major donor research is a great place to put your introverts, the people who do not want to ask for money, anybody who is housebound, and anyone who likes to play detective. Here are some of the sources you can use to learn more about your prospects. Ask your librarian, a prospect research professional, or an Internet researcher for other suggestions.

Magazines

Town and Country runs a feature called "The Most Generous Living Americans," naming donors of more than $10 million a year. *Worth* magazine also runs rankings of the all-time most generous American donors, currently topped by George Soros at $2 billion, Walter Annenberg at $1.2 billion, William R. and Flora Hewlett at $835 million, Charles F. Feeney at $700 million, and Laurance S. Rockefeller at $386 million.[3] *Worth* also features a section called "The American Benefactor" highlighting stories of individual philanthropists. *Fortune* runs an annual issue updating us on the latest billionaires and millionaires worldwide. The *Fortune* 500 issue tells which corporations are making money;

the *Inc.* 100 tells about the 100 fastest-growing small companies; the *Forbes* 400 tells about wealthy individuals. Most cities have a city magazine that does an occasional article on the fifty richest people in town and covers the social whirl of the elite. Trade magazines all include a gossip column on people in the business.

Newspapers

Follow the *Wall Street Journal,* local business papers, and the daily papers in every community where your best major donor prospects have homes. Assign someone to download, edit, and organize into your database current information from the business section, news, and gossip columns. Although there is no longer a "society page," most papers have replaced it with a "style" section that will report on clever, expensive, or star-studded gala events.

Assign someone to track the obituaries and key this data into your database daily. My dear sainted father used to say that the obits were the Irish sports page; if he got through the Fs and did not see his name, he knew he had to go to work. Obits can tell you about family relations, religious preferences, and memorials.

Reference Books and Websites

You can get started with *Who's Who,* including the regional versions like *Who's Who in the Southwest* and professional versions like *Who's Who in Banking.* These are fun to read and tell you about your prospect's jobs, schools, family, clubs, religion, political party, military service, awards, and other information. Also check *Standard and Poor's Register of Corporations, Directors, and Executives;* Moody's directories; and state as well as local professional directories for lawyers, accountants, and other professions. The *Social Register* lists people in twelve cities who come from old money.

Ask the librarian in the reference room or the researcher for a big charity to give you more ideas. All of these are available in book form at most public libraries or on-line at the public library through the computer-assisted reference center. If you do not have access to the more expensive services, recruit a researcher from a big financial institution, law firm, or business school to help you out.

International

Major donor research can be international. American and Canadian charities can research good prospects in other countries just as other countries are seizing the opportunity to look for good prospects here. My all-time favorite example of making the case bigger than your institution is the vintage poster from Canterbury Cathedral's successful campaign in 1975 that raised £7.5 million (see Figure 8.1). In addition to their promotions saying "You can adopt a gargoyle," they sold the intangibles, making the cathedral the symbol of all of Western civilization. I got this poster when I was visiting the cathedral in 1977.

In 1997 Canterbury Cathedral's fundraisers came to Chicago. Hosted in the home of one of their major donors and advisers, they had found more than one hundred people with the ability and interest to give to their campaign to raise $17 million to build a new educational center. Twenty years ago they were raising money from "every man, woman, and child in Britain." Now they have segmented their goal to raise $2 million from American donors, $2 million from Canadian donors, and $13 million from their English donors.

Nonprofit Sources

Many wealthy people give away money from their own checkbooks, through one or more foundations, and also through their jobs. Check out your prospects' foundation connections by name in the Foundation Center's *Guide to U.S. Foundations, Volume 2: Foundation Trustee, Officer, and Donor Index and Foundation Locator* and corporate connections through the name index of the *Corporate Foundation Profiles*. Ask all your volunteers to bring into the fundraising office copies of the donor lists from other charities' programs, newsletters, and annual reports. These donor lists can tell your volunteers who is giving how much to the competition and may remind them of good prospects they already know. It is futile to cannibalize these lists if the names are all strangers to your volunteers. If none of your leaders know any of your community's current major donors, work on recruiting people with wealth or power for your board before you launch your major gift campaign.

FIGURE 8.1 **Fundraising Poster**

ST AUGUSTINE FOUNDED IT.
BECKET DIED FOR IT.
CHAUCER WROTE ABOUT IT.
CROMWELL SHOT AT IT.
HITLER BOMBED IT.
TIME IS DESTROYING IT.

WILL YOU GIVE TO SAVE IT?

Canterbury Cathedral needs help from every man
woman and child in Britain. Please give generously

*Grateful acknowledgment is made to the dean and chapter of Canterbury Cathedral
for permission to reprint this fundraising poster.*

How Americans Build Wealth: Stocks and Real Estate

In the last twenty years the American stock market has enjoyed an un-
paralled increase in value. We hear about the scores of Microsoft millionaires who have made fortunes on their company's stock, but there are
millions of white-collar, blue-collar, and no-collar Americans who have
also built successful portfolios of stocks and bonds. In the same way,
most real estate in America has appreciated nonstop since the building
boom at the end of World War II. Your organization may have many
loyal donors who give you a small gift every year, but who have the po-

tential to make a substantial, major gift from the value of their real estate.

In most cases, the value of publicly held stock and the value of real estate can be estimated from print and on-line sources. You may be surprised to learn that your best major-gift prospects are not your highest annual givers, but people who live and give much more modestly.

Publicly Held Companies

If your prospect is a director, officer, or major stockholder of a publicly held corporation, you can find out more about his or her assets, income, and retirement package through the annual reports and 10-K forms required by the federal government.

The Securities and Exchange Commission (SEC) requires that publicly held companies publish annual reports. These reveal the largest stockholders, salaries of the officers, and retirement benefits. If you know that Mr. Smith retired from the Widget Corporation back in 1998, get the corporation's annual report for that year to learn his retirement package. If a private company is sold to a public company, the SEC data will tell you the selling price. All of this and more can be gleaned from the annual report of publicly held companies and on-line at www.sec.gov/edgarhp.htm.

Recruit a stockbroker or the researcher from a big investment company for your committee. Ask him or her to teach you how to retrieve information on publicly held companies from on-line services such as DIALOG and Dow Jones News Retrieval. By building a database that cross-references individuals' corporate and civic board memberships, you will see who knows who. This can help you find allies to persuade your prospect to give to your organization.

In the same way you can recruit a real estate agent to show you how to find the value of local real estate from the county assessor's office and to estimate the value of national or even international real estate through on-line research. Combining the value of your prospect's real estate holdings with the value of his or her securities will give you an excellent estimate of his or her assets.

There are also several vendors who will do on-line research for a fee. For computerized research services, see the advertisements in the trade magazines, shop the vendors at fundraising conferences, and ask local researchers whom they recommend. Always test the service with one or two names of people you know well, to see how accurate, complete, and current their information really is.

This kind of research is especially valuable for researching large, national organizations with many constituents, because you can identify the best prospects from a great mass of small donors. There are a dozen competent software companies that can help you identify your best donors based on a company's internal fundraising data, such as the recency, frequency, and lifetime total amount of their giving as well as the value of their stocks and real estate. This overlay of public financial information with your donors' giving history can reveal fabulous opportunities, especially for those charities that have a broad base of loyal donors. For example, when the California Division of the American Cancer Society used CDA/ Investment and Marts & Lundy software to filter out the capacity of their best prospects, they discovered hidden treasure. One donor had made a total of fifteen gifts to the American Cancer Society, the largest was $50 and the most recent was $25, but the enhanced database revealed he had securities with a net worth of $206,724 and property worth $508,000. With careful cultivation by Group Vice President Ted Meyers, the prospect eventually made a gift worth $206,000 to the American Cancer Society.

Obviously the well-established charities with the largest base of long-term donors have the most opportunity to benefit from the use of financial data overlays. But any charity can mix its own meticulous records with SEC and real estate data as well as advice from local experts so as to not underestimate a prospect's ability to give.

County Offices

After an estate is probated, probate court files are public information. If you suspect someone has inherited wealth, write the county where the estate was probated. Ask for the will and the inventory that tells you about real estate, stock, and other property. Today shrewd planners avoid probate by setting up trusts for one or two future generations, but probate court is a good source for the others.

If someone's divorce became final today, the information about it is available at the clerk of court's office in the county of residence. Court records can include financial statements and even IRS returns. However, remember that divorce lawyers specialize in hiding the assets of the party they are representing, so always assume this information is very conservative.

The county treasurer or county assessor will have data on property owned in that county, including its assessed value and taxes.

If your prospect contributes to political candidates, his or her donations may be public information, depending on the size of the gift and the integrity of the campaign office. (Bags of cash on Election Day are not yet a thing of the past in Chicago, Louisiana, and other bastions of participatory democracy.) Legal contributions to local city and county candidates are recorded by each campaign and available at the county board of elections; records of donations to candidates for state office are available through the state board of elections in your state capitol. Most states require disclosure of gifts of $100 or more.

At the federal level, records of donations larger than $200 per year to candidates for president, senator, or member of Congress are available from the Public Records Office of the Federal Elections Commission (FEC). Your researcher can retrieve data from 1978 to the present by donor's name, city, state, zip code, or amount. You can also retrieve data for Political Action Committees (PACs). For more information call the FEC at (800) 424-9530 or log on www.fec.gov.

Especially look for donors who gave to politicians who ran on issues defined by your organization. If the politician won, remind your prospect that the politician won because your group cut the issue for the public. (It doesn't hurt to have a letter from the elected official saying this.) If the politician lost, remind the prospect that politicians have a fifty-fifty chance of winning an election, whereas a terrific organization like yours is out there fighting for the citizens every day, regardless of who is in City Hall or the White House.

Cautions

Assume that any research using books or databases is incomplete and out-of-date. Especially families with old money pride themselves on avoiding publicity. They find ways—get married, change their names, move to Montana—to stay off these lists. Merry pranksters have been known to fill out the *Who's Who* questionnaires with the names of their pets and other nonsense.

Doing research is a way to expand your prospects beyond your own list. Just be sure you take anything in print or on-line with a grain of salt. Whenever possible, verify your research with another source; ideally, insiders who know the prospect.

Do not be misled by people who flash a lot of cash. With easy credit, almost anyone can look rich. I knew a salesman who dazzled his clients with a $130,000 sports car. He confessed to me that it was 102 percent financed; he even financed the license plates and insurance. On the other hand, there are people worth millions who drive the same compact car for fifteen years. Ken Wolfe at the Colonial Williamsburg Foundation found that one of his most generous donors, who left more than $2 million to the Foundation, was living very modestly in a $65,000 house and getting Meals on Wheels because she used to volunteer at Meals on Wheels and liked the people.

Actually, most of the millionaires in America are not flamboyant movie stars or sports idols; they are boring types who get up and go to work every day. Demographic research tells us that the average American millionaire is John Doe, age fifty-seven, who has been married for thirty-two years to the same woman, owns a highly productive small or medium-sized business, has two children, and works ten to fourteen hours a day, six days a week. The wealthiest 1 percent of the population hold 33 percent of the private wealth, 60 percent of the corporate stocks, and 9 percent of the real estate. Nearly twice as many are in sales or marketing than are doctors. They do not work for big corporations, but instead own their own businesses or shares of private companies. Less than 1 percent are movie stars, entertainers, athletes, or (har-de-har) writers.[4]

Your goal is to find the people who share your values and to give them a chance to help your organization. Always begin with a broad base of annual givers, and then add on the wealthier people who can and will give more if you ask them. According to a U.S. Trust study the wealthiest Americans—those with annual adjusted gross incomes of more than $225,000 or net worths of at least $3 million—gave an average of $29,400 in 1997, and they can give more in future years.[5] It will take time to find, educate, encourage, and involve these people, but on the other hand, how much time will it take to sell twelve hundred $25 memberships? You need and want both large and small donors.

Records

It is vital to keep up-to-date records on all of your donors and to collect more extensive information on your best prospects. Several excellent software packages are designed just to help you track and retrieve donor information. These range in price from $1,500 to $8,000. Attend two or three sales demonstrations to see what the biggest packages offer, and then interview local fundraisers to see what they recommend. Be sure to talk to both the director of development and the person who actually keys in and retrieves the data. Get your donor data on a computer from day one, because one of the best indicators of a major donor prospect is repeat gifts over several years. It is especially important to keep cumulative records. While a person who gives $2,000 this year will leap out as a major donor prospect, the loyal donor who has given you $100 every year for twenty years is *also* a $2,000 donor. Especially if James Madison paid his $25 dues, gave $25 to the Bill of Rights dinner in December, and sent $50 to the year-end appeal, it is easy to miss him in the multiple reports. If you are keeping only flat lists of each campaign, or publishing only annual reports, you will miss some of your very best prospects. Once you get on-line, hire someone or get a great volunteer to feed in the historic data on your best long-term givers.

Back up the information every day, and always keep two duplicate sets of the data outside the office. I like to use the "odd-even" backup system. On the odd-numbered days, you back up the data on your odd disks, and on the even-numbered days you back up the data on your even disks. Then if the worst happens, and the office burns down while you are at lunch, destroying the hard drive, the original disks, and one set of backups, you have another set of backup disks that are at most one day behind.

If your records are not on computer now, make this your priority for the next month. Start today. Hire temporaries or high school and college students to key in your data. Even with the most zealous volunteers, you cannot compete in today's fundraising market doing paper retrieval. A manual system is too fragile and too limited; learn to like computers.

For more advice, contact the data-processing people at the best charities in town and shop the vendors at national conventions. Twenty-four cities now have technical assistance providers who specialize in knowing the best computers, software, and websites for nonprofits. These members of the Technology Resource Consortium (TRC) are not pushing any particular brand of merchandise; they allow nonprofits to try out a variety of equipment and software and help you analyze which system is best for your current and future needs. For a list of TRC members, log on to www.npo.net/itrc managed by the IT Resource Center (ITRC). You can also get advice from local technical assistance providers, some United Ways, or software user clubs. The sophomores in the high school Tech Club may be more savvy on the latest software and websites and more enthusiastic about using the latest technology. Someone who enjoys working with the computer can infect the rest of the office with a good attitude, too.

Do not buy anything until you check with your national organization. Make sure the hardware and the software are compatible with the system your state and national offices are using or will be using next year. Many national organizations can purchase what you need at a deep volume discount, so ask your national office before you go crazy and pay retail.

Professionals and Volunteers

Prospect research has become such an important part of successful fundraising that it is now recognized as a profession, complete with a professional association to advocate for access to public information and to uphold ethical standards for confidentiality of private information. (See the listing in the Resource Guide for information on the Association of Professional Researchers for Advancement.) As the information age continues, the ability to access, retrieve, and analyze data on donors and prospects will become more and more critical.

Although the field is becoming more professional, the best prospects remain your own leaders and the people they know. Surveys and fundraising war stories all show that donors make big gifts because they care passionately about the cause. Of course, interests in tax benefits, status, and possible shortcuts to heaven are always at work, but most big givers give because they want to give. All the databases on the Internet cannot replace one local insider who has the trust of the people you want to reach, because he or she will know the stories that make a difference.

For example, volunteer Margaret Standish is working in Boston's Back Bay Area to preserve and protect the Commonwealth Avenue Mall. This landmark, built on the model of the great French esplanades, is not a shopping center but a landscaped area between two boulevards that contains the largest urban stand of elm trees in the United States.

One elderly woman gave the project $1,500 to buy a new maple tree in memory of her husband; it will shade the park bench where they courted sixty years ago. Many of the project's donors have such personal reasons to care about the area; their individual support helped leverage a six-figure gift from a major Boston business.

Romance and memories are not, and never will be, in the legal records. So, successful prospect research needs teamwork between your professionals who know what is in the documents and databases and your veteran volunteers who know what is in the hearts and souls of the donors.

The following sample shows some of the information that is useful to collect and retrieve. The better software will allow you to cross-index and update data in multiple files. So, on the John Adams file, it will say, "husband of Abigail Smith Adams, father of John Quincy Adams, and grandfather of Charles Francis Adams." When any of these files changes, so will all of the others.

Prospect Research Form

Devise your own form to record information you learn about your best prospects. Add anything else that your organization or your national office wants. There are many versions of ready-made software that are simply fill-in-the-blank. Some are much easier to use than others.

The most important field here is the last one—the "worker" field (it may be named something else on your software). It is the person from your organization who knows and asks this donor for money. When it is time to sell foursomes to the golf outing, or get sponsors for the gala, or sell advertisements for the newsletter, you can just print out a list for each volunteer and turn them loose.

"People give to people" is the mantra of every good fundraiser. Track every donor and every worker meticulously, and your major donor list will grow every year.

Prospect Research Form

Name: _____ Birth date: _____

Spouse: _____ Birth date: _____

Business/profession: _____

Address: _____

Website: _____

Title: _____

Phones: Office: _____ Car: _____ Pager: _____

E-mail: _____ Fax: _____

Assistant: _____

Assistant's phone: _____ Fax: _____

How long at this job: _____

Previous employer: _____

If retired, year retired: _____

Legal residence (dates): _____

Address: _____

Country: _____ Registered voter? Y/N Citizenship:_____

Phones: Home: _____ Car: _____

Second home (dates): _____

Address: _____

Phones: Home: _____ Car: _____

Directorates and other companies:

1. _____

2. _____

3. _____

Do we have matching gift forms on file? Y/N

Estimated annual salary: _____

Bonuses: _____

Estimated profit from business: $ _____

Other sources of income:

1. _____

2. _____

3. _____

Securities market value: _____

Estimated net worth: _____

Other evidence of wealth: _____

Real estate market value: _____

Education:

School/College/University:	Dates attended:	Degrees:

1. _____

2. _____

3. _____

Military service: _____

Religion: _____

Political party: _____

Organizations:	Offices held:

1. _____

2. _____

3. _____

Clubs: Offices held:

1. _____

2. _____

3. _____

Who in the organization knows this prospect? _____

Name: Relationship:

1. _____

2. _____

3. _____

Interest in our program: _____

Giving history:

Last gift: $ _____   When: _____   Why: _____

Largest gift: $ _____   When: _____   Why: _____

Cumulative total: $ _____

Years given: 19___ to 20___

Last contact: _____   When: _____   How: _____   Who: _____

Last meeting: _____   When: _____   Where: _____   Who: _____

Volunteer history:

Local/State: _____   National: _____   International: _____

Board: _____

Committees: _____

Special abilities: _____

Program interests: _____

Children's names: Birth dates: Remarks (schools, marital status,
                                                 role in family business):

1. _____

2. _____

3. _____

Attorney: _____   Name: _____   Phone: _____

Financial adviser: _____   Name: _____   Phone: _____

Banker: _____   Name: _____   Phone: _____

Researched by: _____   Name: _____   Create date: _____

Worker: _____   Daytime phone: _____

E-mail: _____
_____

Major Gifts: The Big Gift—Now   9

Do your giving
while you're living.
Then you're knowing
where it's going.

                           —Folk wisdom

SOME YEARS BEFORE SHE DIED, LILA WALLACE remarked that she knew her will by heart: "I, Lila Acheson Wallace, being of sound mind . . . spent it."[1] She spent it locally and globally. Her money renovated the Great Hall at the Metropolitan Museum of Art in New York City; restored the flower gardens at the home of artist Claude Monet in Giverny, France; and preserved the villa of art critic Bernard Berenson in Tuscany, Italy.

Of course, she had plenty of money to spend, since she and her husband founded *Reader's Digest*, the world's most popular magazine. As the daughter of a painter and a Presbyterian minister, she knew the importance of both beauty and giving to the things that matter. Before she had money, she spent her time for good causes, teaching high school, working for the YWCA, and serving as a traveling organizer in World War I, setting up recreational centers for women factory workers. She became what fundraisers call a "good prospect"—someone who has the experience, know-how, values, vision, and means to make a major gift to an important cause.

Asking person-to-person for big gifts is the fastest way to raise the most money with the least expense. When you ask openly and sincerely for a big gift, you are giving the donor an opportunity to make a big difference in your organization's work. Making a big gift makes the donor feel proud. You get the gift of his or her money; the donor gets the gift of self-esteem.

In Chapters 6 and 7 you learned how to build a broad base of donors using mass-marketing techniques like E-mail, direct mail, the Internet, phones, and going door-to-door. In Chapter 8 you learned how to identify the best prospects out of your current donors and how to find other good prospects outside your current donor list. This chapter will show you how to train your fundraisers to ask those prospects in person for a large gift. The next chapter will discuss how to ask for planned gifts like bequests. Here we will focus on how to get living individuals to make a big gift now (see Figure 9.1).

FIGURE 9.1 **Individual Donor Development**

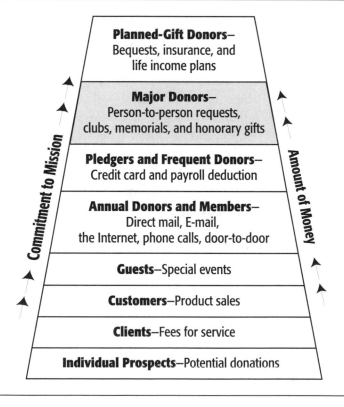

Getting Started

With the bull stock market of the 1990s and the transformation of the American economy away from manufacturing and into technology, entertainment, finance, and retail, there are now more millionaires than ever before. An amazing 142,556 people reported adjusted gross incomes of more than one million dollars on their IRS Form 1040 in 1997.[2]

Anyone in the stock market, including the 25 million Americans who have their pension funds in 401(k) retirement plans, made an amazing amount of money. Meanwhile more than $1 trillion is moving from the Depression and World War II generation to the baby boomers. There is plenty of money out there.

You are competing for the assets of each donor. Have the courage of your convictions. Your organization will make the world better; you deserve this money just as much as, or more than, manufacturers of luxury goods. Believe you're worth it, and ask for it!

There are now universities running capital campaigns for more than $2 billion, and the elite prep schools are running capital campaigns for more than $300,000. More than 60 percent of the funds for these campaigns come from really big gifts, from $1 million to $100 million. These institutions can get these gifts because they are appealing to their alumni who are in the upper 1 percent economically and control one-third of the country's assets. But they also have dozens of professional fundraisers and hundreds of trained volunteers who focus on nothing else but asking for big gifts. Your goals may be smaller, and your list of current donors may not all be aristocrats, but any nonprofit organization can ask for larger gifts, and get them.

Who Can Ask

The key to success in major gift fundraising is the person who asks. Since most major gifts take months or years to cultivate, you want to find and train the best volunteers and staff to build respectful relationships with your top two hundred prospects. Frankly, almost anyone can do a special event or manage the sales. Major donor development takes people who are personally involved with the mission, and committed to raising bigger money.

The best askers are people who have personally made major gifts to this cause. It is much easier if the fundraisers also have experience from other major fund drives and have either wealth or status themselves. However, almost anyone can learn to ask for major gifts if the person has the courage of his or her convictions.

It is ideal to combine one person who has personally benefited because of your work and one who has the confidence to ask for the gift. Do not feel you have to be limited to two people, nor should you always take the same two people. If your first team does not work out, be sensible: send another team. One time a donor did not click at all with my partner and me, two boring middle-class white people, but really liked the next pair, an African-American pregnant lawyer and a priest. They got $35,000. Another donor was put off by the professionals and their slick presentation; she loved the woman who had conceived the idea and gave her $3 million. Avoid using children of the prospect; kids cannot close on their own parents. However, they can open the doors for other people to ask.

Skills

Successful fundraising requires volunteers who can do three things: listen, think, and ask. Even when they do not get a gift, good listeners will collect invaluable advice to improve your programs. Although we can all name names of the exceptions, most people did not get rich being stupid. Be eager to get good advice from the experts at making money.

Second, you need volunteers who can think. Someone simply reciting the script will never raise big gifts. Volunteers who really care about their organization and really want to get a gift will find solutions that are profitable and ethical for both parties.

Third, you have to ask. The prospect cannot respond unless he or she knows what you want. If you know what you want and say what you want, the prospect will admire your sincerity and simplicity. You both know why you are there—ask.

Use the CEO

Although volunteers are the best at asking for major gifts, this also has to be a major part of the CEO's job. If you are the boss, at least half of your time should be spent cultivating current and future donors and asking for gifts. More is better, and full-time may be necessary if your group is in debt.

When Beverly Sills took over as CEO of the New York City Opera, the opera raised $5 million and spent $6.5 million the first year. Then its warehouse burned to the ground. The company lost $10 million worth of costumes and settings; the insurance company paid $1.5 million. Then the unions went on strike. (And you think you have problems?) Beverly Sills could have filed for bankruptcy; many people, including her own husband, encouraged her to do it. Instead, she determined to succeed.

She focused all her energies full-time on asking for big gifts from the city, corporations, and mostly major givers. As she jokes, "I got the reputation of being the most expensive breakfast in New York."[3] Results: she got the financial support she needed and in five years had the company in the black with a budget of $20 million a year. Of course, she did not do it alone. She also had excellent professional counsel and many high-powered friends to help. But it was her resolution that made it possible.

Every CEO must care heart and soul about fundraising, especially working with the people who can give you major gifts. Even if you are not a world-famous prima donna, you can make the effort to meet with a major-gift prospect every day. Put major-gift fundraising first on the CEO's work plan every day. Any committee can recruit members and put on special events. The leaders, and the people who want to be leaders next, need to focus on getting the big gifts.

If your CEO is famous enough, you can use access to him or her as one of the perks of giving higher amounts. Colleges and universities have used small dinners or golf foursomes with their high-profile football and basketball coaches to raise money for both sports and academics; college presidents and symphony conductors know that working with wealthy prospects is a major part of their job descriptions. Even religious charities use this technique. For example, if you give more than $10,000 to the Canterbury Cathedral's capital campaign for an educational center, you get invited to the completion service in England. For $25,000 you get dinner with the dean, and for $50,000 you get to meet the Archbishop of Canterbury himself.

Before You Ask

Unlike asking for smaller gifts, asking for large gifts will take several meetings as you develop trust with the prospects, learn what they want to do, and devise the best way to meet their goals. Because this is a long-term process, your fundraisers need to be prepared before they begin to ask for major gifts.

Make a Gift

Before the first meeting, the people who are going to be asking for major gifts must make a major gift themselves. Board members, volunteers, and senior staff can make a one-time gift or a multiyear pledge. Many charities make it easy for paid staff to make a major gift through payroll deductions.

The organization's president, the chairperson of the major-gift campaign committee, and the CEO must show leadership by making a major gift. As Rev. Willie Barrow, associate pastor of the Vernon Park Church of God in Chicago, reminds us, "You can't lead where you won't go, and you can't teach what you don't know."[4]

Even better, practice what you preach, and change your habits to improve your life. Then donate the money saved to the major-gift campaign. Quit smoking and give $1,000 to the Lung Association; wear a cloth coat rather than fur and donate $15,000 to the zoo; ride the bus rather than buy a new statusmobile and give $60,000 to the group organizing for better access for disabled people. You get the idea.

People believe what they see more than what they hear. It does not matter what you say—if volunteers and donors do not see the leadership making major gifts, they will never believe that the cause is important or urgent. Making your own big contribution is the most important step to guaranteeing your success in asking for big contributions.

Practice Asking

After you have made your gift, practice asking for a major gift. Act out saying, "We want you to give $1,000" (or $1 million, or the balance of your estate, or whatever your goal is). Practice smiling, making eye contact, and listening. Brainstorm in a small group to come up with possible tough questions you might be asked, and rehearse the most-effective honest answers you can give.

Have the team of people who will ask for large gifts act out a request; this will show you each person's strengths. Then you can match the best storytellers with the best closers.

Videotape each person doing the ask. Especially if you will be involved in a very long campaign, will be asking for very large gifts, or will have only one chance to solicit a key donor, videotaping is a great tool to use to improve your skills.

Attitude

If you perceive any negative attitudes about asking for money from rich people, this is the time to discuss them frankly. Some volunteers are terrific at organizing events and selling memberships but not good at asking for major gifts. For whatever reason, they cannot get over their anger toward rich people. This is not the time for amateur group therapy. It is the time to find any volunteers who manifest negative attitudes toward major donors and assign those people to different fundraising committees.

As with any minority group, major donor prospects can be sensitive to language that they perceive as offensive. Most rich people hate to be called "rich people." Patricians talk about "people with wealth" or simply "the right people." Rich ranchers say "Bubba has a bunch of money," and the top financial advisers call rich people "high-net-worth individuals." Some very wealthy, very conservative, and very old-money people cannot bear to discuss money at all and instead will use euphemisms like "Mary's trust fund" or "Bill's portfolio." Check your own language and attitudes to be sure you are speaking and acting in a way that respects your donors.

Overcoming Fear of Asking

Do not think it is a personal weakness to be afraid to ask for a large amount of money. For most people, this level of dealing is outside their normal experience at home or at work. Everyone has been taught a lot of taboos about money. Even the bravest people can have trouble with asking for money, and more trouble asking for big money.

For example, General H. Norman Schwartzkopf, nicknamed "Stormin' Norman" during his leadership of the Persian Gulf War, was recruited by filmmaker Steven Spielberg to chair the $60 million capital campaign for Starbright, an organization that uses technology to enable seriously ill children to play and learn to forget their pain. He has succeeded in getting big gifts from both individuals and corporations, but he confessed in an interview that asking for million-dollar gifts is still hard for him. "I'm still uncomfortable asking people for money," he said.

If it is awkward for a four-star general, it is going to be awkward for most of your volunteers, too.

Except for a few people who were born or made themselves into super salespeople, everyone is afraid to ask for money, and more afraid to ask for big money. So discuss this frankly with your team; work as a group to find ways to make it easier, such as practice and going in pairs; then go ahead. As Joan of Arc says in Jean Anouilh's play *The Lark*, "Say to yourself, yes, I am afraid. But it's nobody else's business, so go on, go on. And you do go on."

Assemble Training Materials

Prepare a kit of materials for the volunteers and staff who will be asking for money. This can include a brief history of your organization, highlights of its most outstanding achievements, the need for this particular request, and the way it fits into the big picture of the organization. Include a menu of funding needs and the opportunities for recognition; for example, for $5,000 you get your name on a chair, for $50,000 you get your name in the lobby, for $5 million you get your name on the theater. Remind volunteers about the tax advantages of giving to a tax-exempt nonprofit organization. Include the names and numbers for leadership, the fundraising staff, and the organization's legal, insurance, and tax advisers to help with complicated gifts.

Give a simple step-by-step list of exactly what you want volunteers to do, including the reporting, paperwork, and thank-you notes. Include all of the organization's stationery, envelopes, and brochures they will need.

Also, spell out what volunteers may not do, such as offer to rename the college for a donor. For larger institutions, specify the name of one executive who will approve and sign all agreements.

It goes without saying—but say it anyway—that all information about a prospect's personal or financial circumstances will be held in strictest confidence by the volunteer and the organization. Major donors will need to feel they can tell you about their wishes and fears about money, their own future, and the future of their loved ones. Fundraisers who earn a reputation for complete discretion will get the most repeat major gifts.

Rate Your Prospects

The last step before approaching the prospects is estimating how much money they can give and how much you can ask for at this time. Convene your committee, including people who know the prospects and a few people who have had experience rating prospects for other campaigns. Assign a specific dollar amount for each prospect so it is easier for both the asker and the askee.

Aim high. It is flattering to the prospect to be asked for a large amount, and people like a challenge. If it is too high, do not worry—the prospect will suggest a lower amount.

Setting dollar goals in a group assures that prospects who are committed to your cause and have the ability to give are not deprived of the joy of giving a large amount to your organization. This saves everyone from the fainthearted, who will want to murmur, "Any amount will be appreciated." Since the group has set specific goals for the campaign and for each prospect, the solicitor has to ask first for the amount set by the consensus.

Do not project your own financial limits onto other people. Your salary may be in the tens of thousands, but the bonus for a CEO now can be in the tens of millions. Maybe the most that you can give Spelman College is $220 or $22,000, but Bill and Camille Cosby can (and did) give $22 million. Maybe all you can buy is a box of UNICEF greeting cards, but media mogul Ted Turner has pledged $1 billion to the UN. No one can keep up with the world's most generous philanthropist, hedge fund CEO George Soros. Through an assortment of foundations, Soros has given a few foreign countries more money in grants than the U.S. government has supplied in foreign aid. Practice what you preach. If you believe that all people have something important to give to your organization, act as though you mean it. Ask the people who can give time to give their time, and ask the people who can give major money to make a major gift.

How to Ask

If you are asking a donor or volunteer from your own list, begin by finding people within the organization who have worked with the prospect. For instance, who served on the board or a committee with Ms. Money? Who knows her from conventions, parties, or office work? What are the prospect's major areas of interest? Why did she give money in the past? Did she support Duke Ellington or Donizetti? Affordable housing or African art? Senior citizens or the sophomore class? Who asked her? How?

Write a letter thanking the prospect for her support in the past. Say you want to meet with her to discuss the goals of the organization now, and ways she can support these goals. Call to confirm that she got the letter, and ask to meet with her in person. Let her set the date, time, and place, but be prepared with some specific choices: "I'll be in your neighborhood on Friday morning for the dedication of the computer resource center. May I see you at your office at 10:00 A.M.?"

Prepare a menu of choices of what the particular prospect might like to fund, based on his or her giving history and what your research tells you. Always include at least one choice that seems to be a real financial stretch, because you never know all about the prospect's commitment or ability to give. Take along someone the prospect knows, from the same neighborhood, congregation, workplace, or age group. Or take someone this person would like to know, such as the charismatic founder of your organization or the prize-winning doctor from your clinic.

Cultivation

Even if you know the prospect through work in the organization, find out more about the person. Why did he join? Why did he stay involved? What does he like best about the organization? What does he think should be improved? How? What victories is the prospect most proud of? What does he think will be the most serious areas of need for the next ten years?

For strangers, people who are not already in the organization's "family," you need to take even more time and care. Since these prospects are new to you (and you to them), you need to develop relationships and do more research on the spot at the same time.

Listen

The goal at every meeting is to learn all you can about this prospect's particular interests and needs. Listen, listen, listen. It is enormously helpful to have two people making the calls, so you can debrief later and make sure you both heard the same thing. With two people, one can listen while the other one talks. A partner is also invaluable for those of us prone to talk too much. Many times I have been saved by "Gee, Joan, that's very interesting, but I'd like to hear what Mr. Soros has to say."

Depending on the prospect's current interest in your work, personal timetable, and rapport with you, you may be able to make a match in one or two meetings, or you may need one or two years to build a relationship of trust—or more for very large gifts. Keep in touch between meetings with phone calls, letters, and clippings. Alert the prospect when your leaders will be on the radio or TV. Be sure the prospect gets a good seat at the benefit if he or she likes parties, and is introduced to your top leaders, staff, and other donors.

Ask

Don't forget to ask. You do not need to ask every time you meet, but you'd better be asking at least every other time. Think of your first request as your opening bid. It is a place to start. Then, as you both find out how serious the prospect is, you can refine the deal to meet the individual's needs. Does she want her name on the building? Or would she prefer this gift to be in honor of her father? Or does she want complete confidentiality as a requirement for making the gift? Would she rather make a lead gift to kick off a campaign and motivate other givers? Or is she a "wait and see" type who pledges to give the last million if you can raise the first three million? Does she want her husband, lawyer, and accountant to approve this donation? Or can she make the transaction on her own?

What does he want to get? A seat on the board? A press conference announcing this gift? Entrée to the inner circle of big givers? A private meeting with the founder? Can you deliver what he wants?

Are there any strings on the gift? If so, are they acceptable according to the organization's policies?

It may help to tell the prospect what others are giving. You can tell Jane Addams, "Well, Ms. Addams, eleven other members from your class of '82 have given $1,000 gifts." This makes it easy for her to match this gift or, if she is a competitive type, to show off and give a $5,000 gift. Even more persuasive is to remind your prospect that you personally believe in this cause so much that you have made your own major gift.

Yes!!!

The close of this gift, and the cultivation of the next gift, begins when the prospect says yes. Most people capable of making a large gift can make more than one gift, and many of our best donors know other good prospects. So the actual experience of donating a large gift should be made simple, clear, and reassuring. Then it will be easy to repeat and easy to recommend to other prospects. If you are using a printed pledge card, fill it out and ask the prospect to sign it immediately. If you are not using pledge cards, ask your prospect several questions to be sure that you understand what he or she wants to do with the money, stocks, property, or other gifts. Write down the answers, hand the page to the prospect, and ask, "Is this what you want?" Ask the donor to make any changes; if possible, in his or her own handwriting. If there are other people present, such as a spouse or lawyer, ask them to review your notes with the prospect's additions and to agree that it is what the prospect wants.

Thank the prospect in person immediately and ask what kind of formal recognition he or she would like. Repeat that all information will be kept strictly confidential except for the recognition approved by the donor, such as listing the gift in the annual report.

Put a handwritten thank-you note in the mail the same day. Then send an official letter confirming the agreement as you understand it from your notes and ask the prospect to confirm your understanding. Verify the spelling of all names. Also, send thank-you notes to the person who made the introduction and any advisers.

If the prospect has any questions after receiving your letter, work them out as soon as possible. Use your legal and financial experts to make it easy and pleasant (cost free) for the donor. Encourage the donor to include his or her advisers to finalize the agreement.

Many successful fundraisers benefit from a split personality. On the one hand, they love risks, aim high, and believe anything is possible. On the other hand, they know nothing is more important than attention to details. For major gifts, this means good fundraisers will ask for large amounts of money and motivate their volunteers to ask for large amounts. It also means no detail is too small for their personal attention.

Always verify that the financial department handles all financial arrangements promptly and courteously. When the financial department sends the checks for payments from annuities or pooled income trusts, the fundraiser or CEO can attach a personalized note for each donor. Be compulsive about listing all names and amounts correctly in your newsletter, campaign reports, and annual report. Push the public relations department to get news releases out to all the media serving the donor's communities and profession. In a small office, the fundraiser may also handle these financial and publicity chores. In a larger institution, the fundraiser must personally make sure the best staff handle follow-up in a way that will encourage future gifts.

No...

If you get a "No," call again in a year or two. If you get a "Not now," call again in six months. If you get a "Let me think about it," call again in three months. For any response that is more encouraging, ask before you leave when you may call again.

Follow-Up

After the meeting, send a thank-you note the same day, even if the prospect says no. Debrief with your partner, the staff, and the committee. Write down any suggestions for other prospects, such as ways to improve the material or program ideas, and send them to the office. Strategize on what worked best and what needs to be changed before the next meeting. Most major gifts will require several meetings with the donor. Keep careful records and keep trying until you succeed.

As discussed in Chapter 8, the most important record is the name that goes in the "worker" field on your software. This is the person, ideally a board member or campaign committee member, who will *personally* maintain a relationship with this donor. This means a personal, handwritten note on the year-end letter, a personal phone call to ask the donor to sit at his or her table at the spring gala, and a personal invitation to dinner in the board member's home with the president. Each board member or campaign worker should be able to maintain contact with five to ten major donors in a significant way, and probably twenty-five to one hundred via mail and E-mail.

Naming Names

Some major donors prefer to remain anonymous, but most people like to see their names in your written materials, such as the annual report. Ask the donor if you may publish his or her name, and ask how he or she would like to be listed. For your protection, be sure to specify that the name goes up when the pledge is *paid*, not when it is made.

Today there are many more choices for listing names, so be sure you find out what your donor wants. Never simply lift a name from another charity's list, because some donors will choose a different style for different organizations. For example, Martha Washington may be listed as Ms. Martha Washington in the annual report from the Mount Vernon Women's Center, but her contribution to the veterans' group could be from General and Mrs. George Washington, her contribution to the neighborhood group from George and Martha Washington, and her contribution to her elementary school from Patsy Dandridge (Mrs. George Washington).

Names are news, and a photo is worth a thousand words. Put the names and photos of your donors in the newsletter, the annual report, and anywhere else they will fit. Theaters, hospitals, art museums, and colleges put the names of donors in their lobbies. Religious congregations have allowed donors' names on specific buildings, windows, organs, and artwork. In the Renaissance, church donors actually got their own likenesses included in stained glass windows next to the saints and the Holy Family. Today, most people settle for a brass plaque and recognition at the annual meeting.

Some donors love to get their names (or those of loved ones) put up in light. In fundraising jargon, displaying names of donors is marketed as "Designated Gift and Memorial Opportunities." If your group chooses to use designated gifts, set a policy on prices, recognition, and what is or is not for sale. For example, every building owned by the American Red Cross is just called a Red Cross building, but specific rooms or equipment may be named for donors, such as the Clara Barton Bloodmobile.

More and more charities are finding ways to let a donor put his or her name on a specific piece of their programs. Obviously this is easiest if you have a new building, but almost anything will work. For example, at the National Cathedral in Washington, D.C., you could sponsor a Gothic pinnacle for $400,000 or pay for a single carved angel for a bargain $5,000. At the world-famous Topeka Zoo you could underwrite the Lion Night Quarters for $75,000 or get the lions a scratching post for $5,000. My personal favorite is the University of Southern California's program to peddle each position on its football team. The quarterback and the center are already gone, but if you act fast, you can still get a defensive back position named for you for only $250,000.[5]

The organization wants donors' names placed where they will be seen. So if you sponsor the Gothic pinnacle, your name goes up in the lobby of the cathedral where most people will see it, not on the pinnacle where only the pigeons would see it. High schools and colleges can create the "Hall of Fame" for alumni who have been successful and supported the school. (The Topeka Public High School complements this with the "Teachers Hall of Fame" for the faculty who helped the achievers on their way.)

In addition, many organizations use premiums for their donors, from tote bags and T-shirts for small donors to valuable jewelry and artwork for their big donors. Private time with a charismatic leader can be a great incentive for major donors if it fits the style of your leader. Some noted nonprofit CEOs are like successful politicians and love to glad-hand their best donors.

The ideal form of donor recognition costs the organization little or nothing but is highly coveted by major donor prospects. Universities with popular football teams designate parking spaces near the football stadium as rewards to their biggest donors. For example, membership in the Texas A&M booster club known as the "Twelfth Man" costs from $12 per semester for students and up to $25,000 for the most zealous "Aggies." The best donors are given the best parking spaces for their tailgate parties before the home games.

Choose a recognition system that is consistent with local practices. Big-city art museums in the United States literally put their donors' names in lights in an electronic display in the lobby. One art museum in Canada puts the names of its donors in small gray type on a small gray display in the back of the lobby under the stairs, because anything flashier would not be considered to be in good taste.

The ultimate recognition for your best volunteer fundraisers and donors is to ask them to serve on your board of directors. Then you get talent that has been in the trenches and knows the organization well. Most major donors will not want to serve on your board unless they have a deep personal interest in the cause, but some will lend their endorsement by allowing you to use their names on an honorary board.

Anonymous Donors

Not everyone wants his or her name in lights. One of the largest gifts ever made by an American was from Paul Mellon to the U.S. government to create the National Gallery of Art. He donated art worth $31 million, plus $15 million for the building and $10 million for an endowment. Mellon stipulated that the museum must not bear his name, so that it would be easier to get more gifts from other benefactors.[6] If a donor asks to remain anonymous, you must rigorously protect the name of that donor.

Memorials

Some donors may prefer to give a gift as a memorial for a loved one. This strategy is used effectively by religious congregations, hospitals, hospices, and disease associations, whose donors appreciate any system that makes their lives easier at a very stressful time.

For example, the B.C. & Yukon Heart Foundation acknowledges memorial gifts by sending the next of kin a card bearing a picture of the foxglove plant (*digitalis purpurea*, which is used to make a drug for heart patients) and the words "To Honour the Memory of _____ a contribution has been received by the B.C. & Yukon Heart Foundation from_____." The names are added in calligraphy. The dollar amount of the gift is never disclosed.

The next of kin also gets a smaller version of the card that he or she can send to the donor. It says, "Thank you for being so thoughtful. Your In Memoriam gift to the B.C. & Yukon Heart Foundation is truly appreciated." The foundation itself sends a thank-you card to the donor that thanks him or her for the gift and encloses another donation envelope for the donor's convenience.

The Role of the Staff

The staff's role is to manage the overall campaign. This means collecting names of possible prospects, supervising research to determine the best people to ask, convincing your fundraising leaders to give major gifts themselves, and then training the leaders to ask for big gifts. Some volunteers are naturals at all this and love going eyeball-to-eyeball with a prospect.

Other solicitors have a more deliberate style and work best in steps. Instead of going right for a gift, they will ask, "Would this be a good time to discuss your gift?" If they get a "No" or a "Not now," the door is still open to ask another time. However, some leaders who can give a gift themselves and care heart and soul about the cause still have great difficulty asking for a major gift. This is where staff can help the most.

Staff can pair a person who has a great story to tell with someone who has great closing skills. Or a member of the staff can go along with the leader and ask the right question at the right time: "Joan, wasn't there something you wanted to ask Mr. Soros?"

Fundraising staff can also use what organizers call the "fixed fight." If a staff person already knows that Jane Addams is going to make a big gift to the organization, the staff person will take someone who needs to get a confidence boost to "ask" for that gift. Of course, the request succeeds, and the next one will be easier.

If all else fails, staff can ask for a gift. This is the least desirable scenario, because then the relationship is being forged between the donor and a staff member, rather than between the donor and a leader. If the staff person gets hired away by another organization, who has the relationship with this donor? Your leader or your ex-employee?

In theory, paid fundraising staff should never ask for big gifts, certainly never alone. However, in practice, sometimes the very best leaders will simply strangle with panic, and it is in everybody's interest for the paid fundraiser to ask for the gift so the donor can make the gift he or she wants to make and the leader can be saved from cardiac arrest. Of course, the leaders will get credit for getting the gift, and they will see that it is possible to ask and survive. Your hope is that praise and practice will give them more determination next time.

Professional fundraisers must have a working knowledge of the current tax laws and help you hire or recruit the best lawyers, accountants, and insurance people who are experts in their fields. Always involve your own legal counsel and the donor's tax advisers in structuring a gift, but remember that most big donors' major motivation is not getting a tax break. Donors give because they believe in your mission and want to see you make the world better.

As you can see, unlike selling memberships or gala tickets, asking for a major gift requires great diplomacy. You need to build a relationship of trust so the prospect can feel free to tell you what he or she wants. Have the courage of your convictions to articulate what the organization needs and not sell yourself short.

Where to Ask

Ask where the prospect wants to be asked. Most often this will be in the prospect's office or home. Some prospects prefer to meet at their club or at a restaurant. Meals are fine for getting to know people better and sharing your stories, but they are less-effective settings for closing the deal.

People with new money and who are using gobs of it to buy their way into the status charities may want to be seen being courted in public. Other people, especially old money or closet rich people, may want to keep everything sub rosa. I know one fundraiser who wanted a gift from a wealthy workaholic from Tiburon in Marin County north of San Francisco. Since the prospect did not want his neighbors or his colleagues to know the deal was being negotiated, the fundraiser would drive from San Francisco, across the Golden Gate Bridge, and around the bay to Tiburon. Then he and the prospect would ride the first ferry for an hour to downtown San Francisco. At night the pair would ride the last ferry back to Marin County, and then the fundraiser would drive back to San Francisco. He spent three hours driving in the dark to spend two hours in private with the donor. After eight months of these meetings, the organization received a seven-figure gift.

Where Not to Ask

Never ask for money at a party. It is awkward for your prospect, embarrassing for your host, and guaranteed to make you look gauche and greedy. *Time* magazine reported that Joan Kroc, owner of the San Diego

Padres baseball team, widow of the founder of McDonald's Corporation, and legendary philanthropist, was invited to a party at the home of Dr. Jonas Salk. What happened? "So many other guests accosted her with solicitations for money that she excused herself and left."[7]

If the host or hostess knows both of you, it is appropriate to ask for an introduction to a wealthy person and a glowing reference to your great work: "Mr. Tipton, I'd like you to meet Mary Smith. She's the one who has done the terrific job expanding the children's museum." Then make polite party conversation, trying to listen and learn as much as possible about the prospect.

The next day send your prospect a brief letter—one paragraph on how much you enjoyed meeting him or her and one paragraph on how you would like to have an opportunity to tell more about your project. Include one recent clipping and one brochure. Send a copy of your letter to the host or hostess with your thanks for making the introduction.

When you meet a wealthy person in a social setting, it is tempting to seize the moment and ask for a contribution right away. However, this makes you look desperate and makes the prospect feel as though you want only his or her money.

If you want to build a long-term relationship with the wealthy person, look at every contact as a step toward building a lasting partnership. This relationship needs respect on both sides. The prospect respects the seriousness of your work, and you respect the seriousness of the prospect's philanthropy. In this way, you do not annoy a prospect at a party, and he or she does not trivialize your work. You both gain.

When to Ask

As long as the donor is not in stress, there is no bad time to ask for money. Do not ask someone if there has recently been a death in the family, or a divorce, or if there is a serious illness in the family. Otherwise, any time you can get to the prospect is a good time. Door-to-door canvassers have proved that heat waves, downpours, and blizzards all increase the evening's take. The biggest annual increase the United Ways have ever seen was 50 percent in 1942—the first year of World War II.

One fundraiser had been pursuing a certain donor for months and was always getting a polite postponement. Finally, on a winter day when it was twenty below zero, of course, the prospect thought this was the day to meet with the fundraiser. The fundraiser had to wade two blocks through thigh-high snowdrifts to get to the house; she got a gift worth $3 million.

National and international organizations have a great advantage because they can double-team the best prospects. For example, Miles and Priscilla cultivate the prospect on Martha's Vineyard in the summer, while Bill and Amy work on him in Palm Springs in the winter.

For bigger organizations and bigger goals, major-gift solicitation goes on all year long. Since many wealthy people have more than one home and travel often, you operate on their timetable. Be ready for any opportunity for a personal meeting, and keep sending positive reports to keep your organization in the prospect's mind.

More than 50 percent of gifts of stock are made in the last quarter of the year, and 35 percent are made in December. Although you want to cultivate your best prospects all year long, if you are asking for a gift of stock, be sure you have asked for the stock by October.

For small organizations and smaller goals, it is easier to choose two months in the spring or the fall and focus your work in one very well-organized campaign. The easiest way to help volunteers overcome the natural inclination to procrastinate is to compress all of your asking into one tight campaign.

Like Aristotle, most volunteers prefer working with a beginning, a middle, and an end. Before the campaign starts, the staff and leaders will have recruited the top campaign leadership, made their own gifts, researched and ranked the prospects, set a dollar goal, and recruited the troops. The first week, you train the askers; the second week, they set up their appointments; weeks three to six, they ask for gifts; week seven is for follow-up with tough cases; and week eight is wrap-up and celebration. If you end on time, it will be easier to get good recruits next year.

What to Ask For

The easiest gift to get is just good old cash. This can be one lump sum or a multiyear pledge. Today giant charities are asking for ten- and twenty-year pledges in order to leverage bigger gifts. Most charities ask for three- to five-year gifts. You can make it easy for the donor through electronic funds transfer or credit card payments arranged through your banks. Or the donor may prefer to get monthly or quarterly reminders (nonprofit jargon for a bill).

Noncash Contributions

Of course, you are glad to get gifts that are worth money as well as plain money itself. It may be in the self-interest of your donor to give you the ranch, the Renoir, or the Rolls Royce. Get a professional appraisal of the property, and be sure it is also in the interest of the organization to take this kind of a gift. Ask other charities how they handle noncash gifts, and involve the donor's tax advisers in planning for the gift.

Donors may want to give property to a nonprofit to avoid paying capital gains taxes themselves or to avoid estate taxes if the property passes to their children or grandchildren. The money they save by avoiding these taxes can be invested in a "replacement policy" of life insurance, so the children or grandchildren will still see an equal or greater dollar value at the time of the donor's death. This is a win-win-win scenario: the donor, the donor's beneficiaries, and the charity all gain. The charity may want to use the property for its own programs, rent it out for earned income, or sell it for cash.

If the donor wants to give you a work of art, be sure to get an appraisal for the value of the work and an estimate of what it will cost to insure. Ever since Van Gogh paintings have been auctioned for tens of millions of dollars, some private collectors and small institutions have found they cannot afford to insure their works of art for what is considered fair market value. Work with the donor's tax advisers to negotiate the most advantageous deal for both of you.

If the donor wants to give you something like a boat or a car, consider whether it is best to use the vehicle for your program, sell it off for cash, offer it as a raffle prize, or make it a production prize for your workers.

For any noncash donation of more than $500, the donor is now required to file Form 8283, "Noncash Charitable Contributions," with the IRS. If your agency sells or trades the contribution in the first two years, it is required to file Form 8282, "Donee Information Return," with the IRS. Both of these are intended to reduce tax fraud by the rich and devious.

Loans

Once you have a good relationship with a wealthy donor, he or she can also make you no-interest or low-interest loans. This can be a good source of venture capital in low-income communities denied credit from financial institutions. Be sure everyone knows that a loan is a loan, not a gift or a grant. Make all payments on time, or even better, pay off the loan early.

Appreciated Stock

In the 1959 movie *The Young Philadelphians*, Paul Newman plays a lawyer specializing in the "new" field of tax law. On Christmas Eve, Mrs. J. Arthur Allen comes into his office looking for someone to write a codicil for her will to guarantee care for her pet Chihuahua. The lawyer finds out Mrs. Allen is worth $100 million, kisses the dog, and says he will be glad to fix her will.

Mrs. Allen laments that some people do not care about animals and that is why she gives $5,000 every year to the Society for the Prevention of Cruelty to Animals (SPCA). The lawyer sees his opening and asks, "In cash?"

Once he learns Mrs. Allen always gives her contribution in cash, the lawyer suggests she donate appreciated stock instead. For example, if Mrs. Allen purchased stock for $1,000, and it is worth $5,000 at the time she sells it, she will owe capital gains tax on the $4,000 profit. On the other hand, if she gives the stock to the SPCA, she can deduct $5,000 from her taxable income, and she avoids paying taxes on $4,000.

As you can imagine, the multimillionaire loves this idea and decides to throw all her business to Paul Newman's character's law firm. This movie is more than forty years old, but the same idea still works today. If you have a donor with appreciated property, giving it to your non-profit organization will reduce the donor's taxes and give you the value of the appreciated stock.

Clubs

Clubs are a strategy to urge annual donors to give more money. You buy your way into the club by giving a certain dollar amount. People who regularly give $25, $50, or $100 easily can be asked to give $500 to be a Silver Spartan or $1,000 to be a Golden Gopher. This strategy is now commonplace in the fundraising community—as evidenced by the illustration below.

Colleges and universities have used these clubs for many years, usually at the $500 or $1,000 level to get annual donors to think bigger. As prosperity has driven incomes up and inflation has driven the value of the dollar down, the oldest clubs are now too large to be exclusive. So organizations add on new categories at the $10,000, $100,000, or $1 million level.

The United Ways have had great success using their $10,000 club called the Alexis de Tocqueville Society. So far they have started the clubs in more than ninety cities; in 1998 their 13,000 members gave $317 million to the United Way. These clubs enable the United Way to reach major donors who are not part of the traditional corporate executive leadership already active in the United Way. Gifts range from $10,000 to $900,000 and are given and solicited by major donors with staff support.

One of the most successful American nonprofits to use major gift clubs to achieve their goals is Ducks Unlimited, the world's largest private-sector waterfowl and wetlands conservation organization. A general membership starts at $20 for one year and has to be renewed every year. If you want to make a bigger gift and never have to renew again, they offer big-money clubs starting at $10,000.

Major sponsors range from a Life Sponsor, who donates $10,000 within four years, to a Legacy Sponsor, who gives $250,000 over a lifetime. Life Sponsors get a gold Life Sponsor pin, lifelong listing in the annual report, and an engraved plaque. Legacy Sponsors get their names listed on a Legacy Sponsor Plaque at the Ducks Unlimited National Headquarters and a replica of the plaque, a white gold pin inlaid with diamonds, and perpetual listing in the annual report.

One terrific innovation of Ducks Unlimited is their Grand Slam Life Sponsor, which combines three national programs into one recognition category. To qualify, a donor becomes a Life Sponsor in the United States, Canada, and Mexico. The cost is $10,000 within four years to Ducks Unlimited in the United States, $10,000 Canadian within five years to Ducks Unlimited Canada, and $2,000 within one year to Ducks Unlimited de Mexico. Each country has its own symbol of recognition and lists the donor in its annual report. This way the organization can market three big-money clubs at once in three countries and at the same time raise awareness of the importance of preserving wildlife habitats across national borders.

There is probably no limit to what status organizations can charge for a club. In fact, some colleges and universities have begun a club called "The First Fifteen" for the fifteen largest donors to the school. Then all they need are a few million-dollar gifts, and everyone on the list needs to jump up his or her giving to qualify for retention.

Make up some categories to fit your cause. The American Cancer Society calls its big donor club "Excalibur," based on its symbol, the Sword of Hope, and playing off the Arthurian legends of the elite knights of the Round Table. The Statue of Liberty/Ellis Island Foundation created the Torch Club for gifts of $1 million or more. One member is the Disabled American Veterans, which earmarked its gift for making the entire area accessible to physically impaired people.

Putting It All Together

Most organizations can use a combination of gift clubs, credit card and electronic funds transfer, and naming opportunities to make it easier to get large gifts from major donors. But the professional and volunteer fundraisers still have to make the personal calls to build the relationships that will motivate the donor to give. Most big gifts are made because the donor cares deeply about the mission of the organization. The more you can share your victories and your dreams with your prospects, the more they will want to be a part by making a large gift.

The Need for Big Gifts

Today there is more competition for more money for more expensive needs. Although some self-help groups intentionally choose to remain small, most nonprofit groups need to grow, raise more money, and get more political power. To meet those goals, they need to be able to raise dependable big money.

Money is power, and more money gives you more power. The ability to raise and spend big money enables good organizations to solve problems as well as treat the victims. In his autobiography, *Is That It?*, Irish rock star Bob Geldof tells how he organized the Band Aid concerts and telethon that raised $117 million in 1985. Then he tells how the Band Aid organization went about spending the money to relieve the famine in Africa. In one effort, Band Aid did a one-to-one match with the U.S.

government to build a multimillion-dollar bridge over the River Chari in Chad. Before the bridge was built, supplies had been brought across the river by canoe.[8]

Major Gifts: What to Ask For

Possible Gifts   *Amount Requested*

1. *Money:*

   Annual gift   _____

   Membership   _____

   Pledge   _____

   Club   _____

   Special gift   _____

   Major gift   _____

   Challenge/matching gift   _____

   Interest-free loan   _____

   Other   _____

2. *Noncash Assets:*

   Art   _____

   Real estate   _____

   Vehicle   _____

   Other   _____

3. *Stocks:*   _____

4. *Bonds:*   _____

5. *Life Insurance Policy,*
   IRA, 401(k) Plan: _____

6. *Others:*   _____

This is the metaphor for fundraising today. If you can raise more money, you can forge partnerships with other major players, both public and private. You can build the bridges that enable everyone to work better. Is your group burning out because you can afford only canoes? How many more problems can you solve if you focus first on raising big money, then on applying it to big solutions?

Major Gifts: What to Ask For

Ask your major-gift staff and volunteers to rate your best prospects on the size and type of gift. Start with a gift to the annual campaign or a membership on the first visit, and then move on to other possibilities.

Wealthy people may have other resources to help your group. They may be able to host a party at their mansion, lend you art for your offices, or sign over stock proxies to enable your members to attend the annual meeting of a corporation.

Cultivation Records

Your cultivation of each prospect needs to be intentional and recorded. Some computer software has a sort of tickler file that can remind you of birthdays, anniversaries, and religious holidays. Or you can buy a tickler file at any office supply store, and file paper reminders by days and months.

Keep a record of every time a volunteer or staff fundraiser contacts your major donor prospects. This is especially helpful when you are working with a large number of people or when your staff and volunteers turn over quickly. Most fundraising software has a field called "worker," for the person who is the primary contact for each donor or prospect. Keep this information up-to-date, and your major donor campaigns will go like silk.

In her autobiography *Twenty Years at Hull House*, Jane Addams wrote, "The first gift I made when I came into possession of my small estate was a thousand dollars to the library of Rockford College, with the stipulation that it be spent for scientific books." Today that thousand dollars would be worth $20,000. Let's get into the Wayback Machine and see what a fundraiser's cultivation record for Jane Addams would look like:

Name: Jane Addams, Rockford College Class of 1882

Dates	Contact and Comments
2/1	Mail annual report—flag page 8 with her name.
3/5	Visit. Ask for library books.
5/3	Mail Mother's Day appeal.
5/17	Received $10 gift from mailing.
5/18	Mail thank-you letter with invitation to graduation. Receipt sent from office.
6/11	Graduation; Addams's speech to science club.
6/12	Mail thank-you for speech.
6/19	Mail photo of speech to science club with article from the school paper.
8/7	Visit. Asked for science books; left list of suggested titles.
9/6	Mail birthday card.
9/13	Mail invitation to homecoming.
10/2	Homecoming: toured library. Dinner with librarian and science students. Revised list of book titles.
11/9	Mail Thanksgiving card—"We're thankful for your support."
12/2	Received check for $1,000 for library, for science books (see list from 10/2). Thank-you note sent from me.
12/3	Receipt sent from office, with thank-you note.
12/4	Thank-you letter from the college president.
12/12	Mail Christmas card with photo of students holding new books.

Planned Gifts:
The Big Gift–Later   10

It is the job of the organizer to make the obvious explicit.
—Heather Booth, founder
Midwest Academy

THERE ARE MANY REASONS WHY YOUR organization should be asking for bequests and other forms of planned gifts. You already know it is a lot of money. Americans gave more than $13 billion dollars to charities in 1998 through bequests. This is more than the $9 billion donated by corporations. In other words, dead people give more money than corporations. How much time do you devote to getting gifts from corporations? Are you also spending that much time with your best donors to help them plan a bequest for you?

Bequests are the fastest-growing form of philanthropic gifts. Experts predict that the amount of money going to charities from bequests will triple in the next decade. As the World War II generation passes away, their assets having have benefited from an unparalleled bull stock market and real estate market, they will leave at least a trillion dollars to the baby boomer generation. These transactions will present a great opportunity to serve families and your organization at the same time.

However, there is one reason it is very difficult to get started in planned giving. People do not want to talk about dying. Combine death and money and you get the last two great taboo subjects in America. Now how are you going to feel right about going out and discussing dying and giving? Even worse, how are you going to motivate your volunteers to do this?

My mentor Heather Booth always says, "The job of the organizer is to make the obvious explicit." Usually this has to do with a campaign such as, "No, we do not want the toxic waste dump next to our school." But the same advice will work with planned gifts. It is obvious that we are all going to die. It is also obvious that your wonderful organization will still be going and have even greater needs in twenty or thirty years. Planned gifts are the bridge between these two facts. If you have the courage of your convictions, you can create the way for people to leave a legacy to the organizations that have given them joy and strength. By looking at planned giving as a way to create a permanent, powerful organization and as a way to give donors financial peace of mind, you can make it easier for your staff and volunteers to begin asking for planned gifts.

FIGURE 10.1 **Individual Donor Development**

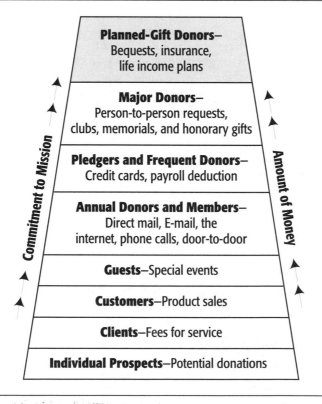

This chapter will discuss the variety of planned gifts, how to ask for them, and how to get legal and financial expertise to help. These gifts usually take the most time to develop and involve by far the most money. Therefore they are at the pinnacle of the fundraising pyramid (see Figure 10.1).

After you have built a broad base of annual donors, you can consider asking for planned gifts. These used to be called "deferred gifts," but fundraisers found that prospects wanted to defer forever, so the name was changed to "planned gifts." A donor plans now to give your non-profit organization money later, most often through a bequest in his or her will.

Bequests are the most volatile source of philanthropic dollars. In the big picture, bequests can account for from 3 to 13 percent of the total given in the United States. The high end (13 percent) came in 1982, with the $1.3 billion bequest from oil tycoon J. Paul Getty to his own foundation in Malibu, California. This gift has multiplied into $7.5 billion in assets, enabling the J. Paul Getty Trust to build and fill a flamboyant $1 billion art museum on a hilltop in Los Angeles and to expand their grant-making beyond their own properties. In 1997 the largest bequest was $4 billion from David Packard, founder of the Hewlett Packard computer company. We will continue to see mega-bequests as the first generation of computer moguls pass away. Most years, bequests account for about 7 percent of the philanthropic dollars, more than corporation gifts and equal to foundation grants when the stock market is doing well.

How do you get in on this gold mine? You have to ask. As noted in Chapter 1, surveys show that over 77 percent of Americans give to charity every year, and they give to between eleven and fourteen charities every year. Americans with a will remember two to five charities in their will. So of the charities they fund every year, two to five get in the will, and nine are left out. The ones that are left out are usually left out because nobody asked.

Bequests are the easiest way to get started in planned giving for any nonprofit organization. After you have begun asking for bequests, also explore using life insurance, retirement plans, annuities, trusts, and other instruments to allow your donors to get the satisfaction of giving.

Advantages to the Donors

Planned gifts are a service to your donors. They get to give a big gift in a way that gives them credit now. They can strengthen their financial situation through reduced taxes or dependable income. And they can be motivated to do something they ought to do anyway. In some cases they will get the peace of mind that their property will be preserved for a purpose they want—for example, to serve as a historical site or a wildlife refuge. Donors can provide for their heirs or honor their spouse, parents, or grandparents.

Advantages to the Organization

Asking for planned gifts forces a nonprofit organization to do real long-range planning, looking ahead not two or three years but three or four decades. The staff will need to hire or recruit lawyers, accountants, stock brokers, and insurance experts to guide the organization and advise your prospects. With this process in place, you have the security of knowing that more money will be coming in the future. Although the money takes longer to get, planned giving can add up to much, much larger dollar amounts.

You should be eager to explore any fundraising strategy that requires you to think big, think long range, and get serious about your financial management.

Asking for Bequests

Giving through a will is a time-honored fundraising strategy. William Shakespeare had a will. In 1616 he left his land to one daughter, £300 to another, his clothes to his sister, and his second-best bed to his wife.[1] (The Globe Theatre should have been in the will, but nobody asked.) Often a will makes a great difference by providing a major gift at the right time. One generous bequest resulted in one of the first restoration projects in the United States at the Touro Synagogue in Newport, Rhode Island, in 1827. Completed in 1763, the synagogue was in deteriorating condition when it received a $10,000 bequest for its repair from the will of Abraham Touro, son of Isaac Touro, one of the synagogue's founders.[2] Obviously the Touro Synagogue's planned-giving committee had done its job.

Statistically, half of the people in your organization already have wills, and the rest know they should have wills. Your volunteers may already know about bequests for charities from their religious congregations, universities, or hospitals. They can also give and ask for bequests for your group. However, probably the scariest "ask" for a fundraiser is the first time you ask someone to remember your charity in his or her will. Despite the pioneering work of the hospice movement to improve the way people think about end-of-life care, most of us do not like to think about death and dying, let alone talk about it.

The depth of this denial is exposed by the fact that more than half of all Americans do not have a will. Even worse, a third of all the U.S. lawyers do not have a will—and they can do their own for free! So how can we bring up this touchy subject? Somehow we need to say:

1. Yes, you are going to die.

2. No, you can't take it with you.

3. So, please leave some of it to this wonderful organization.

The answer is to practice what you preach. Tell your members that they can take control of their own lives and they can control their own money. They do not have to lie down and let life run over them. So there are only two choices. They can choose to write a will and choose which of their family, friends, and favorite organizations will get their estate. Or they can choose to procrastinate and risk having the state or province make all of the choices for them. Almost nobody believes that Montana, Mississippi, or Manitoba will make the same choices the deceased person would have made.

Never underestimate people's ability to procrastinate on financial matters, even when they know they should do it, when they and their loved ones will gain from it, or even when they legally have to do it. Thousands of American taxpayers ask for an extension past April 15 every year to file their taxes. Eighty percent of these people will *get* a refund. They have nothing to gain, and money to lose, by procrastinating, but they do it anyway.

In the same way, some people may procrastinate when it comes to writing their wills. They know they should do it, but they prefer to do it tomorrow. One of the greatest services that a fundraiser can give to a donor is urging that person to make the choice to write a will today. Donors will be grateful and relieved when they finish the planning.

Practice What You Preach

The best way to get started on a program for bequests is to write your own will and include bequests to the organizations that matter most to you. You will never be sympathetic with your bequest prospects unless you know how hard it can be to make these choices. If you already have a will that is more than five years old, update your own will and include a bequest to the charities that matter to you.

Since every state and province has different laws, it is wise to hire a lawyer to help you prepare or update your will. Some handwritten "do-it-yourself" wills can stand up in court, but you are much smarter to ask a professional to make sure that your wishes are carried out. Books, software, and fill-in-the-blank forms can help you make a first draft, but good legal advice will guarantee that your wishes will be carried out.

Also review the current materials on planned giving available at your library. Ask a veteran fundraiser, especially a planned giving specialist, to be your mentor. Interview leaders who have chaired an endowment campaign in your community. Say "yes" whenever another charity asks if you might be interested in making a planned gift, so you can see how they operate.

A Little Knowledge Is Dangerous

With regard to bequests and other planned-giving strategies, a little knowledge can be a dangerous thing. Your own fundraising staff must have a working knowledge of current tax laws, insurance options, and investment opportunities. In addition, you can recruit legal, insurance, and investment experts from your community to help on this committee. Their self-interest is that they meet more potential customers at the same time they help the cause.

As your organization's base of renewed members and repeat donors grows, you may choose to hire a professional to work full-time to encourage those people to give your organization planned gifts. For a smaller agency, one person may be able to handle research, training, and cultivation. For larger organizations, you may want to create a separate department with several professionals to handle research, publications, planning, training, and follow-up. The ability to respond quickly with current accurate information to donors' inquiries is often the determining factor in which charity gets the planned gift.

Planned-giving specialists have created councils for mutual support and education in about 110 large cities in the United States and Canada. Planned-giving officers from some of the largest national programs also meet in groups sponsored by similar causes, such as health care, the Jewish Federations, or United Ways. For more information on the local professional association for planned-giving officers, contact the National Committee on Planned Giving, 233 McCrea Street, Suite 400, Indianapolis, IN 46225-1030; (317) 269-6274, www.ncpg.org. Also ask for their order form for their excellent publications such as *A Guide to Starting a Planned Giving Program* (see Resource Guide) and attend their annual conference to meet the leaders in the field.

Outside Counsel and Advice

In addition to your own staff and volunteers, you can hire fundraising counsel with expertise in planning and managing a planned-gifts program. Several firms specialize in planned-giving literature, newsletters, training, and management of campaigns. You can get recommendations for the best firms through their satisfied customers in your community, or shop the advertisements in the fundraising periodicals and the exhibitors at national conventions. Professional counsel will make the planned-giving process much easier for you and your volunteers.

You can also buy special software designed to calculate the tax deductions and annual payouts of different planned-gifts options. This is one of the greatest tools to make planned-giving an option for every professional. Attend demonstrations by dealers and ask planned-giving specialists which software they recommend.

Always work with the professionals retained by your donors. Be glad to have their CPA, attorney, banker, or stockbroker involved in this transaction, because such professionals know more about the prospects and their current and future financial goals than you do. Also remember that these people are not court retainers; all good professionals have other customers. If you work well with them, they may recommend your charity the next time someone says, "I'd like to give/leave part of this to a good charity. What do you think?"

When to Ask for Bequests

Most people write (or update) their will when certain events occur:

- They inherit money or property.

- They marry or divorce.

- They have a baby.

- They leave for a war zone.

- They buy a home.

- They start a business.

- They are diagnosed with a life-threatening illness.

- They acquire a great deal more money—win the lottery or make a killing in the stock market.

- They plan to take a trip out of the country.

- Someone in their family becomes a lawyer.

With the exception of weddings and babies, which generally are publicly announced and eagerly awaited events, your organization has no way of anticipating these occurrences. You can't know when someone's grandfather will die or when someone plans to fly to Tahiti. An active, diverse board and many volunteers can give you early warnings about these trigger events. For most of your prospects most of the time, you simply have to ask often and give them several opportunities to respond.

Your website, newsletter, annual report, and reply envelope should always include a box to check for information about your bequest program. At least once a year send a letter about wills. Include a "success story" about a donor who remembered your agency in his or her will and what you can now do with that money.

Add an advertisement for your program to your publications. Figure 10.1 is an example developed by Ken Wolfe, director of principal gifts for the Colonial Williamsburg Foundation. He says his first ads were much longer, much wordier, and much less effective. Over the years he has learned to simplify his planned-giving ads and maximize their impact. Colonial Williamsburg is an entire community that replicates life as it was when it was the capital of the colony of Virginia in the 1700s.

FIGURE 10.1 Advertisement for a Life Income Plan

Restrained at Colonial Williamsburg's pillory and stocks, John Hamant laments his misfortune.   *Dave Doody*

Locked Into Your Stocks?

Are you locked into appreciated securities you can't afford to sell? Then join the many friends of Colonial Williamsburg who are discovering the special benefits of life income gifts. By contributing your appreciated stock to one of our life income plans you too can enjoy

- income during your lifetime
- a current income tax deduction
- avoidance of capital gains tax
- reduction of your taxable estate

What better way to provide for Colonial Williamsburg's future and your own? To learn more, complete and return the enclosed reply card, or contact Ken Wolfe or Ingrid Blanton in the Planned Giving Office at (757) 220-7203; fax (757) 565-8062; e-mail: kwolfe@cwf.org.

Through the architecture and live actors, they teach millions of visitors about the politics and personal lives of the European visitors, American colonists, and African slaves. Ken was able to use an old device for punishing criminals, the stocks from 1798, to persuade people holding high-value, low-dividend stock in 1998 to help themselves and Williamsburg by donating the stock to the foundation (see Figure 10.1). You can be just as creative to connect your work to the interests of your readers and prospects.

Humor does not work all the time, or for every kind of organization. But this and other well-conceived ads, letters, meetings, clubs, and personal contacts have produced great results for Williamsburg. As of 1997 they had received 165 life-income gifts with a total value of $13.6 million, plus 115 bequests worth a total of $11.2 million.

Also add bequests and other deferred gifts to the menu you offer your prospects whenever you discuss ways they can support your organization. You never know when it will pay off. For example, Christ Church in Alexandria, Virginia, has more than two thousand communicants and also draws many tourists, since it was the home church for George Washington and Robert E. Lee. The congregation's regular Sunday program includes this section titled "Stewardship":

> Christ Church is almost entirely dependent upon the discipline
> of annual pledging to support its ministries. The Biblical tithe
> is the standard of giving encouraged by the Vestry.
>   Please remember the mission of the Church in all of
> your giving and the Christ Church, Alexandria, Virginia
> Foundation, Inc. in the structuring of your will and when
> memorials are appropriate.

This is a terrific example. First, notice they begin by asking for the annual gift. Also, the church's board knows what it wants and says what it wants (10 percent of your income). Finally, they ask you to remember the church in your will.

The church's own members will see this at least fifty-two times a year—every Sunday. The tourists will see it at least once, maybe more. As long as it is in writing, this message is easy to throw into a desk or file as a reminder or to delegate to your accountant or lawyer. If you ask often and put it in writing, your prospects can more easily respond when the time is right for them.

You Never Know

Let me tell you a story to illustrate the importance of asking. Democratic congressman Richard Durbin of Illinois was trying to get onto a flight on which he had no reservation. He started with, "Any seat will be fine—just get me on this plane." The reservations clerk informed him that the only seat left was a center seat between two smokers. Rep. Durbin did not want the middle seat between two smokers.

The clerk noticed his disappointment, then saw from his ticket that he was a member of Congress. So the clerk apologized for the bad seat, acknowledged that smoking hurts both customers and employees of the airlines, and asked Rep. Durbin, since he was a congressman, could he do something about it? Rep. Durbin cosponsored the legislation that outlawed smoking on all U.S. flights of less than six hours.

I learned three lessons from this story. First, it never hurts to ask. You may get results far beyond your wildest expectations. The reservations clerk probably heard travelers and airline workers complain every day about tobacco smoke. Because she took the initiative and asked, all airline travelers are safer today. Asking gets results.

The second thing I learned is that anyone can make a big difference. It is a tendency to think you cannot talk about wills unless you are a lawyer or a member of the clergy. But do not let your volunteers think planned giving is only for the lawyers or the clergy. Of course, involving the experts is important, but anyone can open the doors and begin the discussion.

Third, I learned that it pays to respond to good ideas. Richard Durbin now serves as U.S. senator from Illinois, partly because he acted on a good idea when he heard it.

I told this story to sales expert Barbara Pierce Braugham. The lesson she pulled from it was, "You see—you never know who you're talking to!" Retail stores teach the sales force that (except for repeat customers) you do not know until you ring up the order how much someone will spend. Every day, they get a big sale from someone who does not look like a big spender. In the same way, fundraisers never know whom they are talking to. You can do good research on your prospects, especially people in the public eye, but you never really know their level of commitment or their ability to give. One way to find this out is to ask and keep asking.

Whom to Ask

The best prospects for planned gifts are the same as the best prospects for major gifts:

- Yourself.

- The board, planned-gift committee members, and senior staff.

- Your own donors who have given for three to five years.

- New people with a commitment to your cause and the ability to make a planned gift.

With your own donors, look for continuity of giving. There are many stories of some regular but modest lifetime donors who leave a very large bequest. Thelma Howard was Walt Disney's housekeeper for thirty years. In the 1950s Disney gave her some shares of stock, which she never sold and may not have even known the value of. When she died in 1994, she left half of her estate, worth $9 million, to the California Community Foundation, enabling it to award $250,000 a year in grants to organizations for poor and disabled children.[3]

For your own list and researching new prospects, look for people over sixty years old, single people or married couples with no children, and people who like to plan. Some planned-giving experts have focused on specific markets that have a need, such as older people who have a farm but do not have any children who want to be farmers. One expert counsels you to walk to the farthest corner of the parking lot around the newest shopping mall you can find. Look around. If you see cows, that farmer is a prospect.

Demographic research is a popular tool of some fundraisers looking for good prospects, and many charities are experimenting with market segmentation. This will help the largest charities that have a popular cause and the money to invest in market research. However, most organizations still find their major donors and their bequest prospects one by one. Start with the people who have demonstrated that they care about your cause, and then ask them to give, to give a larger gift, and to put the group in their will.

If you choose to include asking for bequests in your fundraising strategy, it must be a priority for the CEO and volunteer leaders. You need to discipline yourselves to include one or two visits every week to talk to a prospect about a bequest. Because you may not see a return for five to fifty years, it can be hard to keep yourself motivated. But the key to success is patience, persistence, and asking.

To urge their board members, senior staff, and best donors to give bequests, some charities give them more recognition. For example, the American Red Cross has the "Codicil Club" for donors who have remembered the Red Cross in their will or with another planned gift. Members of the Codicil Club get a lapel pin to wear as recognition of their generosity and to enable them to advocate for the program when curious people ask, "What is that pin for?"

Anyone can include your group in his or her bequest. Some people will say that they do not know anyone rich enough to have a will, but more likely they know people who do not plan but should. Of course, asking for bequests is much easier when you are working with middle- and upper-income people. More of them know about working with lawyers and making long-range plans. As Gloria Steinem said, "Rich people do plan for two generations hence, and poor people will plan for Saturday night."[4] However, do not assume that simply because someone is wealthy, the person's will is made and his or her estate is in order. Every community has a story about one of the richest families who lost everything because the patriarch never wrote his will.

Other Ways to Give

Actually there are only two kinds of giving: planned giving and unplanned giving. All fundraising strategies are designed to make your organization more intentional about asking for money and to make your donors more intentional about giving their money.

Here are some of your other options available for planned giving. They are just a sample of what is available.

Life Insurance

To raise money from people in their thirties, forties, and fifties with higher incomes but fewer assets, the perfect tool is life insurance. For a relatively modest contribution, the donor will get credit now for a very large gift that will benefit the charity later.

For example, in the plan used by the American Red Cross, a forty-year-old woman can pay $1,199 a year for five years for a $100,000 life insurance policy. She can deduct the payments from her taxable income as a charitable gift. So for a total contribution of $5,995, less than $100 a month, she leverages a $100,000 gift and is recognized as a major donor *now*. Although her real annual expenditure is less than $1,200, she is perceived as, and treated as, a $100,000 donor. The payment to the charity is a certainty, there is little paperwork, and the gift does not have to go through probate. The charity can borrow against the policy now, will receive annual policy dividends, and, at the time of the donor's death, will receive a substantial gift.

There are many ways that donors can use life insurance policies to benefit their favorite organizations. Check with your own insurance agent and contact the firms that specialize in selling insurance for non-profits. These advertise in the fundraising periodicals and will have a booth at the national conventions. Also ask a local charity that uses insurance for planned gifts to give you advice and leads on good firms.

Retirement Plans

Much like insurance, many people acquire a large part of their estate through annual contributions to a 401(k) retirement plan at their job (about 25 percent of working Americans), through deposits to an Individual Retirement Account (IRA), or through other retirement plans. All of these ask you to name a beneficiary. Anyone can name a charity as the first or second beneficiary. Because of the booming stock market, the totals for these plans have often soared beyond the investor's needs. Investors can allocate part of this windfall to the organizations that have made a difference for their lives.

Life Income Gifts

Life income gifts are a way for donors to give your organization cash or appreciated stock and, at the same time, get a dependable annual income, often at a higher rate then they were receiving before. There are several different kinds of annuities and trusts that can provide this advantage to your donors. Ask your lawyer and financial planner to give you an introduction to the choices.

Charitable annuities are not new ideas. Clara Barton had a charitable gift annuity in 1877. She had gone to Europe in 1870 to help the victims of the Franco-Prussian War, with funding from the Boston Relief Committee. Seven years later Barton was straightening out her finances and discovered she still had $3,241 of the organization's money. (That $3,241 was worth about $50,000 in 1999.) She returned the money to the committee, which in turn gave it to the Massachusetts General Hospital to invest, with the provision that the annual interest should go to Clara Barton in her lifetime. After her death, the hospital got to keep the money. Barton said this was "perfect."[5]

What is new is the number and complexity of instruments fundraisers can use to help their donors: pooled income fund agreements, charitable remainder unitrusts, charitable remainder annuity trusts, revocable charitable trusts, and charitable lead trusts. Through all of these methods donors give cash, securities, or real estate to your organization and in return receive a tax deduction and income for themselves or another person.

This is definitely an area where a little knowledge is a dangerous thing. You should have a basic understanding of the vocabulary and the legal, tax, and personal benefits of each kind of product. For example, some people like trusts more than wills because they keep the family's finances private by never going through probate. But keeping up with the tax laws is a full-time job, and any fundraiser already has a full-time job. Recognize what your responsibilities are as the professional fundraiser and recruit other professionals to handle the other responsibilities.

Planned Giving in the Big Picture

Make it a goal to learn more about all of the planned-giving strategies available to your organization. Attend the planned-giving track at national conventions, and if you like the trainers, sign up for other training offered by the same firm. Recruit the best local lawyers, CPAs, stockbrokers, trust officers, and insurance agents to organize your planned-giving efforts. Retain a good planned-giving consultant, and if your first efforts do well, consider hiring a full-time director of planned giving.

However, do not segregate the planned-giving staff and volunteers from the rest of your fundraising efforts. In smaller organizations, you have only a limited pool of prospects, so you need to offer them all the choices that are best for them. In larger charities, the work to develop a bequest may also lead to a current gift, and vice versa.

Planned gifts will take longer than other donations to pay off, and the entire agency needs to budget and plan for this. If you want to hire a planned-giving firm, do multiple mailings, and offer a few seminars every year, then the program is going to be a money drain for the first five to ten years. In that case, the other fundraising staff and volunteers will need to commit to using other strategies for raising the money to cover the expenses of starting up your planned-giving program.

Conclusion

Experts predict that bequests to nonprofits will triple in the next decade. Life insurance, real estate, trusts, pooled income funds, and other forms of planned gifts will also become more popular ways to give a large gift to the nonprofits that donors like the best.

With the graying of America, the number of prospects for planned gifts will expand, too. In the year 2000, one in five Americans will be at least fifty-five years old. Successful fundraisers can establish or expand their planned-giving programs to serve these donors and their agencies better.

Work Sheet for Planned Giving

Do I have a will?

Have I remembered my favorite charities in my will?

Whom could I ask to include my organization in his or her will?

1. _____

2. _____

3.

Whom do I know who could use small, deductible premium payments to purchase a large life insurance policy to benefit my organization?

1. _____

2. _____

3. _____

Whom do I know who may want to help us, and whom we can help, through a planned gift?

1. _____

2. _____

3. _____

Whom do I know with expertise in estate planning and tax management who would also be a good addition to our board of directors or planned-giving committee?

1. _____

2. _____

3. _____

Corporate Grants   11

—Donna Alexander, president of the
Edmond, Oklahoma, Public School
Foundation to the president of the
Edmond Realtors Association

LOCAL BUSINESSES AND MULTINATIONAL corporations can be great partners for your nonprofit organization. You will find you have a lot in common. Your members are their customers, employees, and stockholders.
Both of you have an investment in the community and a commitment to
its future. No matter how much money you are making now, you both
would like to make more.

Although corporate giving as a whole accounts for only about 5 percent of the total philanthropic dollar in the United States, in most communities the impact of corporate giving seems much greater. Because of
their stature in the community, receiving funding from the major bank,
business, or employer gives you not only renewable funds but also a very
positive endorsement. Most businesses can give you relatively large
amounts of money (larger than most individual gifts) and many other
noncash donations—most important, their products.

This chapter will show you how to research corporate charitable giving: donations of money, goods, services, and people. For these kinds of
gifts, you ask the boss or the vice president designated to handle corpo-

rate contributions. Some corporations also give grants through foundations. Foundation research will be covered in Chapter 13.

Chapter 12 will look at corporate sponsorships. These can be as simple as the local bank buying an advertisement in your benefit program
for $100 or as significant as Texaco sponsoring more than fifty years of
broadcasts from the Metropolitan Opera for more than $100 million.
All of the marketing dollars that go from corporations to nonprofit organizations are now called strategic philanthropy. Last, but certainly not
least, will be a consideration of the ethics of asking for money from for-
profits.

In both Chapters 11 and 12, I will use the term *corporation* to mean
any for-profit business. Because they make the highest profits and spend
the most money, we typically think of corporate donors in terms of the
giants such as IBM, Merck and Company, Johnson & Johnson, Pfizer,
Hewlett-Packard, General Motors, Eli Lilly & Company, Bristol-Myers
Squibb, Microsoft, and Intel (the top ten corporate donors in 1996).[1]
However, remember that 99 percent of the businesses in the United
States employ fewer than five hundred workers; 80 percent of businesses employ fewer than twenty workers.[2] Even if your community has
no big corporations, you can still ask for money from the local businesses, such as your grocery store, hardware store, car dealer, gas station, and restaurant.

Corporate Charity

Conservative economist Milton Friedman thinks no for-profit company
should make donations to nonprofits. Instead he says for-profits should
work exclusively to make profits for their shareholders; then those people can choose to support good charities from their dividends. Fortunately, most corporations ignore Friedman's opinions. They consider
corporate charity to be a smart strategy to win goodwill in their communities, and they know that most people think most corporations
should be giving more money.

Advantages to Charities

Asking for money from corporations offers many advantages. First of
all, corporations are a huge source of money. In 1998 corporations as a
category gave $9 billion to charities. For the biggest givers, much of their

donations were their own products and services. Forty-one percent of corporate giving from computer companies and 33 percent of giving from pharmaceutical companies was in-kind products and services, both because software and drugs have a very short shelf life and because the companies can tax-deduct the market value rather than their cost to produce. Much of corporate cash gifts are matching gifts to their employees' donations. In 1998, almost 55 percent of Microsoft's cash giving went to match its employees' gifts of $9.5 million. Other generous companies that gave more than 20 percent of their cash gifts to match employees' gifts were Nationwide Insurance, Bankers Trust, J. P. Morgan, Enron, Textron, and Prudential Insurance.[3]

The reported dollar values of corporate gifts understate the total value of what corporations actually donate. Many of their noncash gifts, especially products, facilities, and loaned executives, are never reported as charitable contributions but are just considered "what we want to do." Also, it is not unknown for employees to do photocopying, on-line research, and other work for their favorite causes on company time without this contribution being reflected in the company's total gifts. The real value of corporate contributions is probably three to five times higher than the reported figures.

Unlike foundation support, which often runs out after one to three years, corporations can support a good cause for decades. If you give them what they want in terms of recognition, they can support you with cash and noncash contributions year after year.

Challenges

Corporations are usually more conservative givers than are individual donors. Since they are accountable to their lenders, stockholders, customers, unions, and bosses, they prefer to back a sure thing. Like banks, they more willingly give money when there is little or no risk. So most corporate gifts go to safe causes like health and human services (35 percent), education (30 percent of corporate giving), social services (12 percent), and noncontroversial arts (10 percent).[4] Less than 1 percent of corporate gifts go to religious congregations.

Education is a big winner because it is in the organization's own interest (the business needs smart workers) and is nonthreatening. The biggest change in recent years has been the growth of giving to elementary and secondary schools.

Corporations' conservatism works against gifts to reform movements, avant-garde art, new causes without a track record, or causes with many aggressive supporters on opposing sides of an issue, such as abortion. Also, it is common sense that most businesses will not fund any nonprofit that is, or is perceived to be, antibusiness.

In recent years winning corporate grants has been harder because of the numerous mergers and downsizing of American corporations. There are fewer doors to knock on and fewer smart grant makers at the companies to advocate for the good charities. Especially in smaller communities, what used to be the local bank is now a branch of the bank holding company headquartered in another county, or even another state. Instead of seeing the bank president you know at the Chatterbox Café, you see only a photo of some stranger in the annual report. Instead of seeing the executive in charge of funding at the jazz festival and sounding her out on your new idea, you are told to submit your proposal on-line if you want to be able to compete.

The good news is there are more new small businesses, twice as many started by women as by men, with more family-friendly styles of operation. You may not have as many big corporations to ask, but there may be more for-profit businesses all together. Do not overlook the newer, smaller, more unorthodox businesses and services, and you may be able to build a very big and profitable base of for-profit donors.

Advantages to the Corporations

Corporations choose to spend money with nonprofits for many reasons, but in every case, they give to get something they want. Some individuals at the company may share your values and vision, but do not be misled by their expressions of solidarity, no matter how genuine. For a corporation, charity is considered a "cost center," which has to compete with every other corporate department for what management considers to be scarce resources. You have to prove that, dollar for dollar, your organization is the best place for the company to put its money.

What can a for-profit company get from allocating dollars to a good cause?

- One benefit is goodness by association. Advertisements claiming "Our company is terrific" do not work. Advertisements saying "Our company is proud to bring you affordable housing, or computers in the schools, or a free night at the art museum" make the company look good to the general public.

- The corporation can get a deduction on its income taxes for cash and noncash gifts. However, for most companies, tax savings are not the primary motivation for giving. (The same is true of individual donors.)

- The rank-and-file employees will be proud to work for a company that supports their causes. In some companies, employees can be nominated for "volunteer of the month." If Arlette is selected, she gets her picture in the company newsletter, and her charity gets $500, which then confers major-donor status on Arlette. You can bet the people in her organization know where she works and will want to know about any job openings, too.

- Supporting charities with snob appeal enables the company to show off for its best customers. It can use private showings at the sold-out museum show, champagne with the prima donna, or lectures by the Nobel Prize scientist to dazzle favored clients. World-class culture makes it easier to recruit world-class executives.

- Conversely, supporting projects for low-income people not only puts money where it is needed the most, but can also alleviate charges of elitism or lack of social conscience.

- Corporate philanthropy provides opportunities for leadership. In a survey of one thousand young professionals, more than 80 percent believed that companies should apply their employees' entrepreneurial talents to public service.[5]

- Company people can work with politicians and bureaucrats as peers involved in the same causes. Then when they need to contact the government for a business-related need, they can call a friend.

- It can give businesspeople a chance to sample the best nonprofits, then select their favorites for a pro bono job when they retire.

Some retired workers are thriving in second careers, serving non-profits they met through their company's involvement.

I saved the best two for last:

- Love. It can be lonely at the top. Working with a nonprofit enables even the top CEOs to meet their needs for genuine friendship and respect. The CEO of a worldwide bank on the West Coast told me he liked to volunteer as the treasurer at a seminary because it was "collegial rather than hierarchical." At his job he was always The Boss; he was obeyed, and he was feared. At the charity he was part of a team; he was needed, and he was liked.

  Romances can develop. There are many sound reasons why it is foolish to date people at your own company, but volunteering to work on the company's favorite charity gives you a chance to meet other nice people who do not work for your company.

- Money. Spending money in a targeted way with charities can increase sales and customers. In 1984 the American Express Company raised $1.7 million for the Statue of Liberty by offering a donation for each time customers used their credit cards. Of course, patriotic shoppers wanted to link up with a cause that was American, urgent, and easy to do. American Express increased usage of its card by 28 percent and signed up 17 percent more card customers.[6]

The corporations' needs are your opportunities: more profits, more customers, and happier workers. Develop a strategy for how your non-profit organization can help local corporations achieve their goals.

Research

Do your homework to find a company that is interested in funding your kind of work. Then find a person who can say yes, and make the case for funding. Like any source of funds, corporate givers need cultivation, education, encouragement, and thanks.

The giant charities employ staffs of people who do nothing but research companies, foundations, and wealthy individuals. In big cities, ask for advice from a fundraising researcher at a university, hospital, or national charity. In smaller towns you can also get good advice from the librarian in the business section at the public library, a business professor, or a business reporter. The following paragraphs offer some other ideas to get you started.

The Grapevine

First and always best is the grapevine, one reason you want businesspeople on your board of directors. If your board is restricted to low- and middle-income people, create a "corporate advisory board" made up of business leaders to get you into the gossip loop of commerce and industry. You want to know which executives have a personal interest in your cause. Who has dyslexia? Whose daughter is a dropout? Whose son is in prison? Whose aunt has cancer? Whose uncle is an artist? Whose mother feeds the hungry? Whose father had a triple heart bypass? The insiders can give you the tips you need to make the best match.

Begin with the business and professional people on your own board. Ask them for leads in their own companies, at their vendors, at their competition. Every business has a professional or trade association; assign your leaders to look for prospects when they go to conventions or trade shows.

Ask anyone in the company to share the employee newsletter. How do the employees feel about the company? If they have a union, what does the union leadership recommend?

Other Organizations

Who else in the community already has data on local corporations? Ask for information from the United Way, the chamber of commerce, banks, brokers, industry associations, city or state departments of tourism, economic or community development organizations, and business reporters. Best of all, ask other local charities that receive gifts from corporations whom to ask, what to say, and what not to say.

However, be very cautious about pulling prospects off lists in programs of other charities. This can result in what Joe Breiteneicher of the Philanthropic Initiative calls the "Claude Rains syndrome." Rains played the inspector in *Casablanca* who let the real target get away while he went out to "round up the usual suspects." A few highly visible companies get inundated with requests, while other good prospects may be overlooked.

Who makes money from your organization? Ask all of your organization's vendors at least once a year. Most towns have more than one bank, travel agent, printer, computer store, and office supply company. If your vendors are not supporting the organization's mission with a generous contribution as well as excellent service, shop the competition.

Publications and Websites

Corporate foundations are going on-line slowly but surely, led by the telecommunications and technology companies. About six hundred companies now offer information about what they fund and how to apply for grants as part of their website. You can find information on companies such as Abbott Laboratories, Deere & Company, General Electric, Microsoft, Sara Lee, Texaco, and Weyerhauser.

A few will also accept your application on-line. Sylvia Clark of the NEC Foundation in America reports that the number of applications tripled when they went on-line. Go to the company's home page, then look for a link to grants or guidelines.

Some corporations include information on their grant making in the company's annual report, and a few publish an annual report just on their philanthropy. Most do not publish anything, so you will need to find the most prosperous companies, then look for an interest in your cause.

Recruit a volunteer with access to the business databases to read, download, organize, and file the business information. Ask two volunteers to read and clip the business sections of your local newspapers, the *Wall Street Journal*, and national magazines such as *Forbes*, *Fortune*, and *Advertising Age*. Be sure to get the annual issues on the *Fortune 500* (most profitable corporations), the *Inc. 100* (fastest-growing public companies), and the *Forbes 400* (highest-paid executives).

If one industry is dominant in your town, read its trade magazines. For example, if you want to ask oil companies in Houston or Calgary, read *Oil Daily*, *Petroleum Intelligence Weekly*, *Automotive News*, *Nucleonics Week*, and *Sludge*. (Never again will you think your newsletter is dull!)

Go to the business section of the public library, and get to know the librarian. He or she can show you how to use local reference materials, especially the directories for your city, state, or province, and the directories for specific industries, such as agribusiness, computers, or franchises. Ask about the major reference books such as the *Standard and Poor's Register of Corporations, Directors, and Executives*; the *Directory of Corporate Affiliations*; the Dun & Bradstreet directories, and the Moody's manuals.

Also ask your librarian about computer-assisted research opportunities. Many libraries can access hundreds of databases, including journal and magazine articles, technical reports, and government documents. You can use directory files to search for companies by your geographic area, company size, or product. If you choose to start your own business, other files can facilitate searches for patents, standards and specifications, and export information. For publicly held companies, read the company annual report from cover to cover. If the financial section is new to you, ask an investor, your accountant, or a broker to interpret it.

Directories of Corporate-Giving Data

The Foundation Center, Taft, and Public Management Institute produce directories of data on corporate giving in America. You can use these for free at the Foundation Center Cooperating Collections website (www.fdncenter.org), some public libraries, or the research departments of friendly large charities. Or you can purchase your own books or CD-ROMS.

The directories make your job easier by indexing each corporation's cash and noncash giving by the location of the company's headquarters and operating locations, which will get preference over communities where the company has no employees. You can also research grants by type, such as money for a conference or an endowment, or by recipient, such as education or health care, or find allies who can give you advice. Collect data on the officers and directors and present it to your leadership to see if any of your people know any of the corporation's decision makers.

International Corporations

As for-profit businesses become increasingly global, so does their philanthropy. Corporations headquartered in the United States are giving more overseas in response to new opportunities in Central Europe, Africa, and Asia.

In the same way, more and more Japanese, English, Dutch, German, and Canadian companies are becoming effective grant makers in the United States. Grants to American nonprofits help foreign companies to recruit good workers, improve relationships with state and local governments, get a federal tax deduction, meet the business and social leaders in the community, and support worthwhile causes.

For more information on foreign-based or foreign-owned corporate grant makers, ask their local employees and check the current directories of international corporate giving.

Corporate Foundations

If the company has a company foundation, it will, like other foundations, have information at the Cooperating Collection of the Foundation Center (www.fdncenter.org). At the Collection, you can also check out the Foundation Center's *National Directory of Corporate Giving*. This is the most current and complete data on 1,800 of America's leading corporations. Learn where they give cash as well as noncash contributions such as supplies, equipment, and products. All this information is cross-indexed six ways, so you can research by name of a person, name of the company, location, type of business, type of support, or subject area of funding. The directory also includes explicit lists of what each firm does not fund, so you will not waste your time on a sure rejection.

To research the giants, see the *Corporate Foundation Profiles*, which gives you detailed information on the grant making of the 250 top American corporations with assets of more than $1 million or annual giving of more than $100,000. This reference contains the data you want to know: where money has actually been given, background on the companies' officers and board members, and detailed financial data, all cross-indexed by location, subject field, and types of support (grants, scholarships, loans). The Cooperating Collection also offers more directories and how-to books on corporate fundraising.

Questions to Ask

As you are doing your research, use the following Corporate Research Work Sheet. Ask committee members to add other questions they want to get answered.

Corporate Research Work Sheet

Name of the company: _____

Address: _____

Phone: _____ Fax: _____ Website: _____

Our contacts: _____

Executive we want to reach: _____

Connections to our cause—personal or professional: _____

Projected profit for this year: _____ Next year: _____

What are the company's greatest achievements? _____

What are its goals? _____

What are its greatest needs? _____

Who makes up its workforce? _____

Who are its customers? _____

Who is the competition? _____

Does it have a foundation? _____

What other charities has the company funded? _____

Charity: _____ Amount: _____

Why did the company give there? _____

What did it get? _____

Finding the Right Person

Who has the power to say yes to your request? If you can get to the president or CEO, that's great: of course the boss can say yes. Or your point person may be a vice president for corporate affairs, community affairs, or public affairs. Some companies have a pool of money available for good causes and any employee can ask for some.

What matters is whom you know. Even if you don't personally know the "right" person, you may know somebody who does. If you want to get an appointment with a manager, ask his or her best customer to set up the appointment. Or ask the manager's predecessor, spouse, doctor, lawyer, best friend, or mentor. It does not matter whom you use, if he or she gets you an introduction.

If all else fails, try the cold call. Make cold calls first thing in the morning on Tuesday, Wednesday, or Thursday when you are both fresh. Practice saying in one minute who you are, what you want, and what you can offer the company. Call a friend and practice over the phone, recording it. Redo it until your pitch is irresistible. Then prepare to be resisted. Make a goal to call ten companies a week, and assume you are doing well if three let you through to the right person and one of them wants to hear more.

Does this work? Yes, if you are persistent. In 1970 Stan Calderwood, the president of the Boston public television station (WGBH-TV) called fifty corporations to give them the opportunity to get thirty-nine hours of BBC television at the bargain price of $390,000. All fifty companies turned him down. On call number fifty-one, he reached Herb Schmertz at Mobil Corporation (who answered his own phone) and got him interested. A few weeks later, Calderwood got the money to launch *Masterpiece Theatre*. The partnership between Mobil and WGBH-TV is still strong after three decades.[7] *You* have a lot to gain and nothing to lose from making cold calls, so try a few each week.

The Package

Companies are different, so be sure you get current advice from employees and other local charities they fund. Generally speaking, the companies want a short (six-page) package from you. This will include one page on each of the following topics:

1. What, exactly, do you want to do and how will that advance your mission?

2. How much money do you want? Outline the budget for this project and state how this fits in the organization's total budget. Name names and amounts from other funders.

3. Why can your group accomplish this goal? Give your credentials. Specify results, using numbers.

4. Who is on your board? How much money have they given to this project? Who is the boss? Who will be working on this project?

5. What specific benefits can you offer the company? How will its support be acknowledged and publicized?

6. Include a copy of your 501(c)(3) tax-exemption Declaration Letter from the IRS. Offer to send a copy of your audited financial statement and other pertinent documents such as blueprints or research, as desired.

Some companies make it even simpler. McDonald's Corporation has a four-page application that merely requires you to fill in the blanks. Others may want more, but they will tell you. Do not overwhelm the company contact with your newsletters, annual reports, and videotapes if all the person wants is your plan, budget, and leadership. You want your organization to look cost-effective, right? Therefore, do not send twenty bucks' worth of propaganda the recipient does not want and will not read or return.

Send your package with a cover letter from your organization's president or the CEO. Then follow up with a phone call and ask for an appointment. Use the name of the customer, board member, or employee who can open doors for you. If possible, ask that person to send a short note alerting the company to watch out for this exciting package.

The corporation contact may be able to make a decision just from the package. Or this person may want you to come in to provide more information. Very rarely will someone from the company come out to see your project. In any case, you present your organization as a terrific opportunity for the corporation to work with a partner to meet its goals and yours.

What Can You Ask For?

American corporations may take tax deductions for up to 5 percent of their pretax net income. Of course, the most extreme is Newman's Own food company which indicates on every bottle of salad dressing, "100% of aftertax profits to charity." Started by movie star Paul Newman with a great recipe, a gorgeous face, and $40,000, the company had funneled more than $90 million to charities by 1998. A few more-conventional companies give more than 5 percent such as Cummins Engine, Safeway Stores, Paramount Communications, Pillsbury, and Soft Sheen Products. Most for-profits give away about 1 percent of their pretax net income in cash and noncash contributions.[8]

Unlike most foundations, which have only money to give, corporations can give you money, goods, people, and services. Within each of these categories are many choices for you to consider. What can the corporation give that will meet your needs?

Money

The easiest thing to get is money. Giving money requires the least work for the company. Someone simply writes a check.

Ask for a specific amount for a specific project. Depending on your relationship with the company and what you want, you can ask for a gift of money, plain and simple, or a large challenge grant to motivate other gifts.

Many corporations will match contributions from their employees, retirees, and directors (and their spouses), and some companies match more than one-to-one. For example, IBM does a two-to-one match. So if you want to find a $1,000 donor, ask an IBM employee to give you $334 (less than a dollar a day) and let IBM match it to $668 to raise $1,002. Even better, if you can get individual gifts from corporate bigwigs, they can apply for multiple matches as the employee at one company and the director of another.

Besides gifts and grants, corporations can also make loans at or below current market rates. These may be called "program-related investments," or PRIs in fundraising jargon. In this way, oil companies, insurance companies, and others have invested in affordable housing and new businesses in credit-starved communities.

Things

Companies can give you anything, from their products to their recyclable trash. In particular, any product with their name on it becomes an effective advertisement to the entire community. Ben and Jerry's ice-cream factory in Vermont gives a free ice-cream cone to each citizen who registers to vote; any merchant could copy this idea.

What does the company do that no one else can do? DuPont makes the special paint used on railroad cars. At $150 a gallon, the paint is priced out of the budget of the National Railroad Museum in Green Bay, Wisconsin, which owns the train used by General Dwight D. Eisenhower in England during World War II. But the Railroad Museum persuaded DuPont to donate enough British Railways green paint to make the train shine as part of Ike's birthday centennial celebration in Abilene, Kansas.

What does the company do best? If one company is recognized as the best in its field, ask it for products and advice. IBM in Europe, the Middle East, and Africa donated IBM hardware and software, as well as skilled employees and cash grants, to the United Nations' Global Resource Information Database (GRID). The total gift was worth $6.5 million and will enable the UN to literally operate on a global scale. IBM now markets computers in 132 countries and builds goodwill through its Corporate Social Responsibility (CSR) programs in all of them. For example, IBM has donated computers to help compile data for support of legal action in child-abuse cases in Great Britain, to improve teaching in rural Denmark, and to evaluate new farming methods in Zimbabwe.

Think big. The Funding Information Center in San Antonio, Texas, got Valero Energy Corporation to give it an entire building, got the carpeting from La Quinta motel chain, and got skilled workers from nearby Kelly Air Force Base.

You can also use donated products as part of another fundraiser. A local store donated seventy-five teddy bears to the Lubbock General Hospital. Executive Director for Development Jacque Hastings sent out a simple mailing that depicted a child's drawing of a bear in a Santa hat and offered, "For each $25 donation a teddy bear will be donated in your name to a child." In three weeks the hospital netted $3,000 and several new donors, including a number of physicians.

People

Do you need help getting the computers up to spccd? Designing a market strategy? Setting up competitive pay and benefit packages? Doing an energy audit? Starting a business? Ask a local company to lend you its best brain in that field. Assign two of your own people to learn all they can from the borrowed businessperson.

Services

What services do you need that a local company could supply? In their slow times, firms can give you assistance with printing, trucking, global teleconferencing, translations, art design, data searches, or scientific analysis.

Most nonprofits lack the discretionary money for the frills like an art collection or a nice meeting space. For-profit companies may be able to offer you art on loan to improve patient or employee morale. They can give you great spaces for meetings or retreats with state-of-the-art audiovisual and computer networks. For much more advice on noncash gifts, get *Resource Raising: The Role of Non-Cash Assistance in Corporate Philanthropy*, by Alex J. Plinio of the Prudential Insurance Company of America and Joanne B. Scanlan of Independent Sector. For ordering information, see the Resource Guide.

How to Ask

Once you have researched the local corporations, decide where your interests and values match, and then choose what you will ask for and prepare your package. Call to double-check the exact spelling of all names and titles. Then send off your package with a cover letter saying you will call in two weeks. This gives the recipients a week to open the mail and route it to the right person. Do not wait for them to call, or you will wait forever. Call the person to whom you sent the letter and ask if you can meet. The company staffer may say your package is plenty, may ask for a specific addition, such as your audit, or may want to meet with you. Ask to bring another person and try to get a time in the morning.

Once you set the meeting, call at least three charities that get funding from the corporation and ask for their advice. Try to talk to two or three people in the prospect company for their suggestions, too, on the corporate culture and needs. Talk to your partner and set goals for the meeting.

It is much easier if you have a partner; one of you can listen while the other one talks. The ideal pair is one person who has personal experience with the project and another person who can ask for the desired donation.

Image

I thrill to the marrow of my bones every January 15 when TV airs the 1963 speech by Dr. Martin Luther King, Jr., in which he said, "I have a dream that my four little children will one day live in a nation where they will not be judged by the color of their skin, but by the content of their character." In a perfect world, we and our projects would be judged only on our merits, not on our appearances.

Unfortunately, we do not live in a perfect world. As organizer Saul Alinsky often said, "You have to begin with the world as it really is, to get to the world as you would like it to be."

For corporate fundraising, this means conforming to the corporate dress code. You do not want someone who can write a big check to balk because he or she is threatened by your appearance. Unless unorthodox clothing is part of your job, as it is for zoo directors who wear safari clothes year-round, look like the people whom you want to listen to you.

When Nancy Abbate began the Youth Service Project (YSP), she was a college student herself and had a pretty flamboyant style. For example, not only were her proposals on purple paper, her hair was dyed purple. Once she began asking corporations for money, she discovered that no one at American Airlines, AT&T, or Amoco had purple hair. Since her image was standing between her and her goal—getting funding for her program—she quit dying her hair. Results: She built YSP from two volunteers with no money to fifty staff running award-winning programs for three thousand youths at a cost of $1.5 million. In 1997 she won corporate support from seventy businesses, including the three just mentioned.

People Who Get Places, Get Places Early

Get there at least half an hour early to get cleaned up and get the feeling for the company. In large, controversial, and phobic corporations, you will need to pass through several layers of security. The worst that can happen is you will arrive early enough to read the company brochures and the *Wall Street Journal*. The best that can happen is you will get more time with the executive and make a good impression.

When you meet the executive, take a few minutes to get acquainted, but resist the temptation to just visit. After five to fifteen minutes, get to the reason you are there: you are representing a terrific program, and you are able to offer the Widget Corporation a great opportunity to support your newest (biggest, best, most-effective) project. Say why you are unique, special, superior; say why you are cost-effective. Dollar for dollar, why is this the best program in town?

Engage the executive in discussion. Ask for advice, and write down any suggestions. Most of them will be good and can help you improve your funding package and the program.

Be prepared to answer questions, and be specific. Quote facts and figures, briefly, whenever you can. If you are asked a question you cannot answer, promise to get the answer and send it the next day.

As graciously and firmly as possible, say exactly what you want from the company and what you will give: "We would like you to advertise in the program for our new play to raise awareness about AIDS. Because you are the biggest chain of pharmacies in town, we would like you to have the first chance to reach this audience. The back cover is $1,000 and will give your ad the most visibility. We will also list your gift in our annual report."

Or you might say, "We would like you to underwrite the production of our new play to raise awareness about AIDS. We project our total cost will be $100,000. We will put your company's name on the marquee on 42nd Street, on all the posters and other advertising, on the playbills and the ushers' T-shirts, and on all mailings to subscribers. We have set aside one hundred seats on opening night for you to use for your own employees or customers. As the largest chain of pharmacies in town, you understand what a serious problem this is; your support will give us credibility and will position your firm as the one that is really concerned about preventive medicine."

What Not to Do

Never criticize another nonprofit agency. Even if it is a terrible group run by your worst enemy, do not be lured into a discussion about another nonprofit organization. Just say, "They do A, and we do B. If you want to know more about them, call their office. Now let me tell you about our program and why we are so excited about it."

If you admire a group, say that, and then say how yours differs from it and is distinctive: "You're right; that group is doing a terrific job saving the bluebird habitats. We're lucky to have such a fine organization here. Now let me tell you about the work we are doing to restore the courthouse . . ."

Do not discuss partisan politics. Remind the executive that it is illegal for a tax-exempt charity to endorse a candidate and of course your organization always follows the law. Then say, "Our research shows that a majority of citizens agree with our stand on the need for more good jobs. So we are eager to work with all the citizens who share our goals."

Ask and Follow Up

Keep your eye on the ball. Your job is to ask for a specific dollar amount and get it. Ask at least three times for the gift you want. Leave a reply card or a pledge card with a stamped envelope.

You may also ask for the names of other companies that may be interested in this sort of project. In most communities there are a handful of companies that contribute to and participate in several fundraising projects. If you get one leader, he or she can introduce you to other savvy funders.

Before you leave, confirm a date when you will know the decision. Some gifts will be decided while you are in the office; others will go to the committee to decide if it can go on the agenda of the meeting six months from now. Either way, ask what you should do until you hear from them.

Immediately after your meeting send a thank-you note to the company's contact person. This means that the day before the meeting you have written a short note saying, "Thank you for meeting with us." This can be printed off the computer, or handwritten if your handwriting is legible. Add a postscript if you want.

Some people are now using their fax machines for thank-you notes, saying something like, "I just couldn't wait to tell you how much I appreciate your taking the time to meet with us today." But this is much more impersonal and can be read by anyone near the fax. Also, remember the wisdom of *Thoroughly Modern Millie*: rich people can nickel and dime you to death. An executive at a multibillion-dollar company once told me, with a straight face, that he resented other people faxing their thank-you notes to him, because they were using his paper instead of their paper. Better to spend your own forty cents and look distinctive than to spend his penny and get a penny-pincher riled up.

When your organization gets the company's check, send another personal thank-you note the same day. The office must send an official receipt with all the information needed for the company's tax records, including the organization's federal tax identification number, and the signature of an officer. Since the amount the company may deduct on its federal taxes is determined in part by what the money is spent on, keep meticulous records of every expenditure made with corporate funds, and send the totals with the final report to the company. If this is your first contribution from the company, ask for the name of someone in its accounting department who can brief your bookkeeper on exactly what the company wants.

Deliver everything you promised and more. Send multiple copies or photocopies every time the company's name appears in print in your literature. Put the company on the newsletter mailing list and invite representatives to your special events, too. Go to the company's annual meeting and tell all the stockholders what a terrific company it is.

Best of all, measure and report the results you got from the company's gift. Try to meet again in person at least once to ask for advice. Then go back and ask for a larger gift next year.

Conclusion

Good nonprofit organizations make it easier for corporations to compete for top executive talent, retain the best employees, and market their products to the public they want to reach. Successful fundraisers know they have a lot to offer, and a lot to gain, by raising money from the business community.

Corporate Marketing Partnerships   12

The chief executives are all asking, What kind of value are we getting for our investment?

—Curt Weeden
        Vice president of corporate contributions
        Johnson & Johnson
        New York Times

THE FIRST TIME I HEARD A CORPORATE EXECUTIVE tell a room full of fundraisers that she looked at her company's philanthropy as a "cost center," I could feel the winds of change blow through the room. Half the people were thinking, "Uh, oh. My sentimental stories are not going to work here anymore." The other half were thinking, "Yes! At last there is something my board can understand."

Realistically, philanthropy has always been a cost center for most businesses. It is just that it had a very soft way to measure. The benchmark was the CEO's degree of satisfaction. If the corporate philanthropy guys were giving to the boss's alma mater, his wife's favorite museum, his brother's hospital, his son's Little League team, his mother's library, and his father's disease, they thought they were doing their job. Then American Express shook up the competition in the 1980s by showing you could connect your giving to your marketing and produce irrefutable proof of greater profits because your brand was linked to a good cause. Suddenly, every savvy marketer knew there was money to be made by finding the right partnership between a good nonprofit charity and a good for-profit business.

Experienced proposal writers already knew how to get grants and products from corporations. Marketing your charity's brand can be something, no pun intended, brand-new for most fundraisers. It requires a new way of thinking about the value of who you are, what you do, and how you do it. Mastering the art of making good deals at appropriate corporations offers you an immense amount of money, even more visibility, and the opportunity to learn a lot of skills that can improve your organization.

Marketing Partners

This chapter will discuss how to win marketing and advertising dollars from business partners. For advice on winning grants from corporations see Chapter 11.

In 1998 American corporations gave $9 billion in philanthropy. In 1998 corporations spent about $1.5 billion on marketing deals with nonprofits. The real difference is in the future projections. Corporate charitable giving has been almost flat for a decade, actually going down slightly in terms of dollar grants as the percentage of product gifts goes up. In contrast, marketing dollars for nonprofits have quintupled in the last decade, and will probably grow even faster in the next ten years as more charities get as good at doing deals as they are at writing proposals.

The deals are getting bigger and better. For example, the Boys & Girls Clubs of America negotiated a $60 million contract with Coca-Cola in 1997. It is a multifaceted agreement that benefits the Boys & Girls Clubs in several ways. First, they get a large amount of cash, more than $22 million the first year and a half. They get vending machines in their 2,073 clubhouses that produce revenue for the local clubs. They will get sponsorship for local special events such as golf outings, in both cash and Cokes, and sponsorship for a national event. They get royalties for the use of the Boys & Girls Clubs' logo. They get an introduction to scores of local bottlers who have joined local boards and volunteered with hands-on projects like repainting the local clubhouse. To top it off, their work for children is highlighted in 44,000 special packages of twelve-packs of Coke products during the holiday season, just when most individuals are making their year-end gifts.

This partnership took more than a year to negotiate and will last for a decade. It benefited by having the CEO of Coca-Cola on the National Board of the Boys & Girls Clubs, which are both based in Atlanta. Most of all, it benefited from the astute development skills of the Boys & Girls Clubs Senior Vice President for Marketing and Communications Kurt Aschermann, who spent eight years learning how to negotiate a deal. Aschermann insists that the visibility of this kind of campaign is worth even more than the money. The Boys & Girls Clubs anticipate a total of 44 million positive impressions, which could not be purchased for any amount of money.[1]

This chapter will discuss how your organization can use corporate partnerships to raise money and awareness for your mission. You will learn how to do it in a way that is right for the values of your group. If you are looking for a simple donation, go back to Chapter 11. If you are interested in starting your own businesses or selling your products and services in a businesslike way, review Chapter 3.

Strategic Philanthropy, Formerly Known as Cause-Related Marketing

Strategic philanthropy is combining marketing and philanthropy to make more money for both the nonprofit and the for-profit. In the simplest form of this strategy, the for-profit advertises that it will contribute a specific amount or a percentage of each sale of its products in a certain time period to the nonprofit. The corporation gets to connect itself to a good cause, persuade its customers (the stores) to buy more of its merchandise, and promote the cause better, because the consumers have an incentive to spend money.

The Alpha Case: American Express

The American Express Company was the outstanding pioneer in developing the concept of cause-related marketing. When President Ronald Reagan cut funds for social programs, urging Americans to "return to self-reliance," he unleashed thousands of fundraisers, all knocking on the same corporate doors. Although many for-profit companies wanted to support good nonprofits, there were serious limits to what "checkbook philanthropy" could do to replace the lost government funding.

American Express assigned its marketing department to devise a way to raise more money for the nonprofits and at the same time make more money for the company. As Warner Canto, Jr., senior vice president for worldwide marketing, development, and communications, said, "Why not admit without embarrassment that there is nothing wrong—and everything right—with doing well for American Express by doing good in the communities where we do business?"

Since the program was launched in 1981, American Express's cause-related marketing has generated more than $35 million in donations and advertising support for eighty-eight causes in the United States and seventeen other countries. They are most famous for raising $1.7 million for the Statue of Liberty restoration, the campaign that increased usage of American Express cards by 28 percent and increased customers by 17 percent.

Because of the effectiveness of the advertising that is aimed at consumers, charities selected for a cause-related marketing promotion get more than money from the corporation. Heightened public awareness of a good cause produces more individual and corporate gifts. Performing arts groups see ticket sales skyrocket during a promotion. Employee and volunteer morale goes up because the print and broadcast ads highlight the value of the cause. For example, the Lincoln Park Zoo in Chicago featured its blue rhino in ads to urge American Express cardholders to "Charge Wildly for the Zoo." As one of the few free zoos in America, it benefited not only from the $152,000 raised through the promotion but also from all the new members and customers produced by the advertising.

Outreach to Consumers

For nonprofits, cause-related marketing is an ideal way to reach millions of consumers who may not be givers to charities. Forty percent of Americans never respond to mail; less than half have access to the Internet or live in a neighborhood suitable for canvassing; and although the dollar results prove me wrong, my dinner-party surveys show 98 percent of people loathe the intrusion of phone calls. But almost everybody buys food and household supplies. Corporate tie-ins enable millions of people to learn about your cause and give in an easy way. A lot of small donations can add up to a large dollar gift for the charity.

One good example is the partnership among Nabisco Foods and the American Red Cross (see Figure 12.1). In 1991 during the month of March, which is Red Cross Month, Nabisco ran special advertisements to urge shoppers to buy its products and support the work of the Red Cross. The 2,700 local Red Cross chapters encouraged their millions of members, donors, and friends to purchase Nabisco products, and urged local retailers to feature Nabisco products, during the promotion. Nabisco paid a $500,000 sponsorship fee as part of the national Red Cross Disaster Relief Fund and established an additional incentive fund to reward local chapters. Using a formula based on increased sales, Nabisco also donated money from the incentive fund to local retailers, who in turn donated it to their local Red Cross.

As John Linderman, the director of trade marketing for Nabisco Foods, explained, "Cause-related marketing improves Nabisco's impact in the local markets. We get into more stores, and our products are bought by more customers. It also gives the local stores a way to stand out, to stand for more than just a place to shop for food. Internally, this kind of promotion also makes the Nabisco sales force feel proud of the support they can give to the Red Cross that teaches kids to swim, helps in local emergencies such as house fires, and helps around the world in times of war."

Nabisco products are popular with millions of consumers anyway, so the advertisement provides an easy way for shoppers to support a good cause. What a great opportunity to reach millions of possible donors who may never respond to your letters, E-mail, phone calls, or door-to-door canvassers.

Steve Delfin, officer for corporate development of the Red Cross, explained, "Cause-related marketing provides a new source of money and visibility for our work today. Plus it positions us with senior marketing personnel, a talent pool for many of tomorrow's CEOs."

The Red Cross is the kind of nonprofit organization that corporations like because:

- It has a long history of productive partnerships with corporations. A Red Cross magazine from 1918 shows a Wrigley Gum advertisement promoting the Red Cross War Relief Fund.

- It has a very high visibility. The Red Cross logo is—surprise, surprise—a red cross on a white background. What is surprising is its

FIGURE 12.1 **Cause-Related Marketing Advertisement**

Grateful acknowledgment is made to Nabisco Foods Company for permission to print this portion of the March 3, 1991, FSI for the American Red Cross.

logo is the number-one most easily recognized logo in the world, scoring even higher than Coca-Cola, McDonald's, or Playboy. Awareness of the importance of Red Cross work skyrockets in times of disasters such as Hurricane Mitch.

- It has a universal appeal.

- It has an immense, extremely committed corps of volunteers, including many of the local retailers whom national marketers want to reach.

If your organization is also recognized and respected by corporate decision makers, then cause-related marketing can also be a good fundraising strategy for you.

Making a Deal

Ask your fundraisers to collect samples of cause-related marketing from stores, television, magazines, and newspapers. Discuss these samples and brainstorm on possible partners for your organization.

What does your group have to offer? Think about the size of your base, especially members, donors, and volunteers. Can you measure and show the purchasing power of your donors, the visual appeal of your constituents, or the urgency and popularity of your cause? What does the corporation want in terms of markets, credibility, selling more products, or improving its image? Where is the match?

You do not need a Harvard MBA, but you do need to know how to speak the corporate language and, more importantly, do the math. Recruit a few aggressive marketers to be your mentors, and learn what they do, how they measure success, how they get reviewed. Read what they read, log on to the websites they use every day. Your job is to honestly and ethically describe the advantages of connecting to your "brand," the value of the tangibles and intangibles of your organization. What can you tell a brand manager that he can easily understand, appreciate the value added to his company, and then sell to his boss? If his job is to sell more spaghetti sauce, then your job is to use your imagination to help him achieve that goal.

Note this is totally different from traditional foundation fundraising. The most serious problem with the classic format for a foundation proposal is that it begins with a "needs assessment." Once you begin working with for-profit marketers, you need to change your introduction from "we need" to "you get."

Steve Delfin of the Red Cross cautions, "Charities must ask, 'What do we bring to the table that will help this company sell more product?' We may love our organization because of the wonderful work it does, but our business partners love our organization because we make their sales figures look wonderful."

Review the last chapter's ideas for finding a corporation to ask for money. Focus on meeting with the manager of marketing or advertising.

Once you have found a corporation that likes your presentation, you need to be politely persistent. It can take months for all the right people to approve the deal, from the marketing manager to the brand manager, plus approval from both the subsidiary and the parent companies, plus approval from the lawyers at every level. So allow plenty of time and assign your most determined and diplomatic fundraiser to negotiate the deal.

To close the deal, create a deadline by connecting your promotion to a date linked to your cause, such as February for Heart Month or Black History Month. Or connect it to your special event that is important to the community. If you have a celebrity on your board, you can connect to an event where he or she stars such as the Oscars or the Indianapolis 500. Or simply give the company a finite "window of opportunity." If the company has not signed an agreement by your deadline, cancel the negotiations and pitch the competition.[2]

How to Find Corporate Partners

Cause-related marketing works best for organizations that are highly visible and appealing. Very narrow causes, partisan causes, or causes without visual appeal are much harder to sell. Realistically, strategic philanthropy will not be an option for every organization. However, for most organizations it is a growing source of renewable money that is well worth investigating.

You know your members, donors, and allies. Which companies want to reach that particular market? Consider this: L'Eggs pantyhose did a five-city promotion that raised $10,000 for WAGES, the national alliance of programs that helps women who have been out of the workforce prepare for job interviews, including providing them with head-to-toe business attire. John Deere & Co, the world leader in farm equipment, and Pioneer Hi-Bred International, a seed company, supported Farm Safety Just 4 Kids, based in Earlham, Iowa, to develop a safety demonstration for kids who are exposed to moving farm machines.

What for-profit companies need and want your particular expertise and exposure? The National Center for Accessible Media (NCAM) grew out of the pioneering work done at public TV station WGBH in Boston of providing closed-captioning on popular TV shows for people who are deaf or hearing impaired. With start-up funding from the Dole Foundation, NEC Foundation of America, and Mitsubishi, NCAM quickly established a track record of technical competence and policy expertise. They developed the Web access symbol that looks like a keyhole in the corner of Web pages that makes website information accessible to people who are blind or visually impaired.

In 1995, NCAM created the Business Partner Program to develop strong relationships with leaders in the media industry. The Business Partner Program gets four levels of annual financial gifts—$5,000, $10,000, $15,000, and $25,000 and above—plus in-kind support such as on-line resources and government-affairs expertise. The Business Partners get personal contact with people, with and without disabilities, who are experts in universal access to the Internet and other media.

Through the Business Partner Program, NCAM has built partnerships with digital-broadcast equipment manufacturers, such as Lucent and Panasonic, which must fulfill federal requirements by providing closed-captioning capabilities using standards from a subcommittee chaired by NCAM. NCAM's experience with VBI encoding (adding data to TV shows as a postproduction process) attracted interest from Intel and Microsoft. NCAM's role in changing Web standards is the basis for consultations with the Web-masters at Chicago Tribune on-line services, New York Times Electronic Media Company, Disney on-line services, and many others. NCAM has combined technical expertise, standard setting, policy involvement, and advocacy to promote its mission of access to public media, and these victories are crucial to attracting support from media business leaders.

Your staff and leaders can also market your organization's expertise to the businesses that need your know-how or share your advocacy goals. NCAM's Jennifer Gormley recommends making contacts through trade shows, demonstrations, industry conferences, and individual meetings. Ask your board members with business contacts to give you introductions and ask your media friends for leads, too.

Advertising Sponsorships

Another way for-profit companies can support nonprofits is through intentionally advertising in or on certain media, or supporting certain projects, in order to connect with their constituents. In advertising jargon, the goal is to target a certain market, which means the company is going to spend money to reach a specific group of consumers.

This has worked best for companies that support artistic projects aimed at upscale audiences. For example, Mobil Corporation paid for *Masterpiece Theatre* on American public television. This classy British TV show attracts well-educated, affluent people. In Mobil's survey of upscale viewers, 31 percent of the respondents said they bought Mobil gasoline most often, compared with 16 percent for Exxon, 15 percent for Gulf, and 10 percent for Texaco. When Mobil surveyed new stockholders, most gave investment goals as the reasons they bought the stock; however, 7 percent said they bought the stock because Mobil sponsored quality television programs.

Advertisers for Grassroots Organizations

Advertising expenditures are not limited to million-dollar highbrow projects. Creative fundraisers can ask for advertising dollars for almost any project. For grassroots groups, simply look at which local merchants do the most advertising. Who takes the largest display ads in the local newspaper, the yellow pages, the high school yearbook, the theater programs, the backs of church programs, and politicians' ad books? Use all of these for leads, as well as the suggestions in the last chapter.

For example, a high school in Abilene, Texas, wanted to send its band to march in the Rose Bowl parade in Pasadena, California. Fundraisers knew they could never sell enough candy bars to send the band out of state. So they decided to ask for money from local retailers, targeting the merchants with a musical advertisement. For a contribution, the band would play the merchant's jingle during time-outs and halftime. While the band played "Did somebody say McDonald's?" the local franchise flashed an advertisement up on the scoreboard.

It was a good partnership. The retailers got music to go with their visual advertising, they reached an audience they wanted to attract, and they supported a good cause. The band made more money outside its regular donors (families, friends, and candy customers) and learned to play songs the students actually recognized.

Ethics

The last step of your fundraising strategy is to plan where you will not ask for money. You can be intentional about what sources of money you want and which sources you do not want. Your organization must have a written policy on fundraising ethics that has been approved by the board of directors and distributed to every fundraiser, volunteer, and consultant. A written policy on fundraising makes it easier to review the performance of your fundraising employees and train your volunteers.

The most important safeguard is an assertive group of board members with experience in marketing and negotiations to review every deal. If you are a national organization, recruit two or three savvy people from local chapters from this group, too. If your board has corporate CEOs, ask them to assign their best marketing people to you. If your board is all low-income people without this kind of expertise, start a "Corporate Advisory Board" and recruit the best marketing, advertising, and sales people in your community. Be sure to have a way to vet every agreement with your advisory committee well before the deal is done.

This will help you avoid the fiasco that became a front-page embarrassment for the American Medical Association in 1997. A staff vice president had approved an exclusive deal for Sunbeam to use the AMA's name on its health-care products. Unfortunately, the deal outraged both the AMA national board and many state and local leaders who felt it was wrong for the association to sell an exclusive endorsement of any products, let alone products that were not noticeably better than the competition's. Although the staff person resigned, the AMA suffered from the bad press outside and ongoing mistrust inside the organization. As Queen Victoria's prime minister Benjamin Disraeli said, "There is no education like adversity." Now the AMA has a very thorough system for clearing corporate partners and a very active oversight committee.

There are strings attached to all sources of money, and it's advantageous when for-profits are explicit about the strings they attach to the money. In the same way, it's helpful if your nonprofit organization is explicit about the rules it has for accepting corporate contributions or choosing to participate in a marketing partnership.

You need to be careful about both real strings and perceived strings. For example, in 1989 the board of directors at APRN, the public radio network in Alaska, rejected a $32,000 contribution from Exxon. The board of the radio network believed it would appear to some people that their news reports on the Exxon Valdez oil spill that threatened the animals and economy of Alaska could be compromised. APRN's written policy on underwriting specifies that it may not accept money that even "creates the appearance of a conflict of interest." Although Exxon attached no strings to the money, the suspicions raised from accepting the contribution could have cost the network's news department some of its credibility.

Get It in Writing: Your Policy

A written policy connected to your mission makes it easier to resist temptations. If your organization is well respected, for-profit corporations will want to connect to your positive image. Or your members may be the market they want. For example, in Chicago, Bethel New Life sponsored Umoja Fair to raise money to reduce infant mortality in its community, which is 99 percent African American. (*Umoja* is Swahili for "unity.") Bethel had brought the infant mortality rate in the West Garfield neighborhood down from thirty-three per thousand to seventeen per thousand in four years by promoting better health habits for pregnant women, including abstaining from alcohol and drugs.

A beer company that wanted to get a bigger share of the African-American market offered to underwrite expenses of the fair. Of course, this was a tempting offer, since it was a lot of money for no work; all the brewery wanted was the company name on the printed materials and its giant inflatable beer can at the fair. But Bethel New Life's board of directors turned down the beer money, since alcohol consumption is one cause of infant mortality. The board members knew their organization ethically could not tell pregnant women that drinking was wrong and, at the same time, accept money from a beer company.

Bethel now has a written policy that connects the organization's goals and values to their corporate fundraising strategies. Thus every staff member and fundraising volunteer knows ahead of time who is— and who is not—an appropriate corporate sponsor. Far from putting a chill on corporate fundraising, a clear understanding of who makes a good corporate partner can energize your corporate fundraising program. For example, the year that Bethel New Life voted to reject the money from the beer company, its budget grew 35 percent to $4.9 million, including contributions from for-profit businesses such as

Allstate Insurance, Amoco, Tribune Co., Illinois Bell, Sears, and Walgreen's.

The Boys & Girls Clubs of America uses a one-page set of "Guiding Principles for Strategic Alliances." These include points such as:

- We do not endorse products, promote the sale of products, or mandate our Clubs to endorse, purchase, or sell any product. We do not give "official," "preferred," or "exclusive" status to any company, product, or brand. The national organization does not sell to or through Club members.

- We seek relationships with corporations to support our cause without a quid pro quo. The business benefit we offer is that consumers are more likely to buy a product if it is associated with our cause. Also, by supporting Boys & Girls Clubs of America, corporations fulfill their social responsibility.[3]

- Above all else, all relationships must enhance—and never damage—our brand.

You can create a similar policy to guide your fundraisers, tailored to fit the way your organization works.

Get It in Writing: Their Policy

Written policies are a two-way street. Whenever you are negotiating with any funders, ask the company to put in writing exactly what it wants from your agency. Then you can be sure that its terms are acceptable to your leadership, and you can ethically conform to what the donor wants.

A written agreement can also eliminate last-minute surprises and embarrassment for either party. For example, IBM canceled its advertising for a Professional Golfer's Association (PGA) tournament three weeks before the event, when the company learned the tournament would be played at an Alabama golf club that excluded African Americans. "Supporting even indirectly activities that are exclusionary is against IBM's practices and policies," said Gina Chew-Holman, IBM spokeswoman.[4]

Self Interest—Your's and Their's

The growth of strategic philanthropy in the past ten years has provoked a great debate on the ethics of using this method of fundraising. Some fundraisers believe that charities should not get involved in promotions with the advertising or marketing people but should just stick with asking for donations from the corporate-giving people. The thinking is that nonprofits should accept money that is given only from purely charitable motives.

I think it is hopelessly naive to expect corporate gifts to come from pure motives. Do our friends and family donate only from pure motives? Individual donors give because they want status, power, and their name on the auditorium as well as beauty, truth, and justice. Why should corporations be expected to be less self-interested than the individuals who give nonprofits 85 percent of their budgets?

The corporation has a self-interest, and so does your organization. Put them both in writing, and if the deal and your values agree, then get a written contract and proceed with enthusiasm. If you cannot negotiate a contract that is right for both parties, use different strategies to raise your money.

Research

An organization can write into the contract specific limitations to protect its reputation if circumstances change before the campaign. Jamie McCreary, the March of Dimes director of national promotions, says they check a possible corporate partner with:

- The AFL–CIO

- The Federal Trade Commission

- The Environmental Protection Agency

- The *Directory of Corporate Affiliations*
  —Who owns them?
  —Whom do they own?

- Dun & Bradstreet

- The Better Business Bureau

- The corporation's annual report

Internally, the promotions department also checks any possible corporate partners with the legal, community services, science, and communications departments, regional offices, and the field staff.

This may be more research than your organization wants to do, especially if you are working with a local company you already know and trust. However, every group can do simple research in its own community. First, check out the corporation with all of the players, not just the marketing department. Talk to the unions, the business reporters who cover the company, and the competition.

Second, be sure the marketing dollars are a small part of your organization's budget. The core budget should come from dependable, renewable individual donors. Then you have the freedom to walk away from any relationship that is not right for your group.

Third, choose partners that are logically connected to your mission. For example, Gaines dog food company raised money for the American Humane Association. Johnson & Johnson, "The First Name in First Aid," raised money for the American Red Cross. Since 1969 Sears has donated paint to preserve and protect the Great American homes of the "Who's Who" of history; thousands of tourists see Buffalo Bill Cody's ranch in Nebraska, John Paul Jones's house in New Hampshire, and Helen Keller's home in Alabama spruced up with the same Sears paint they can buy for their own homes. Since 1989 Sears also has been the sole sponsor of the National Trust for Historic Preservation's contest to recognize the best restoration efforts by ordinary Americans. The closer the connection is, the better for both partners.

You need clear, explicit principles about money, as you do about the rest of your mission. Do not let your leadership demean your corporate partners or miss the opportunity to work with local businesses who care about your mission. As members of a worthwhile organization doing important work, your fundraisers want to find all the allies who share your goals and your values—including the best for-profit companies.

Conclusion

There are many advantages to working with a business partner. Your organization can reach beyond its current membership to everybody who shops. The talents that make a business profitable—good management, taking risks, and thinking big—are the same talents you need to be a successful fundraiser. Best of all, you get the chance to meet the people who think that profit is good. Working with the top marketing and advertising people in your community will help your fundraisers learn to "sell" your own cause with integrity, creativity, and profitability.

Foundation Grants   13

What are you willing to pay in order to live in the kind of society that you want to live in?

                 —Andrea Kydd, director
                 Health program
                 Nathan Cummings Foundation

FOUNDATIONS ARE NONPROFIT ORGANIZATIONS that exist to make grants to other nonprofit organizations. Because of the booming stock market and aggressive investing, foundation assets soared in the 1990s, resulting in increased grant making at all levels. Big, new foundations from information and technology fortunes such as Turner Broadcasting and Microsoft joined older giants such as the Lilly Endowment and the Ford Foundation. Small towns and rural counties learned to start community foundations. In Michigan, even high school students learned how to start foundations and make grants.

All of this means that today there are a lot more opportunities for fundraisers to ask for grants. A grant is simply a donation, usually relatively large, from an institution rather than an individual person. Grants range in size from hundreds of dollars to millions. Unlike a loan, a grant does not need to be paid back.

This chapter will look at how to research foundations and ask for grants. In every case, get more current detailed advice from a local group that the targeted foundation funds now. In the next chapter we will look at the other kinds of institutions that also make grants to nonprofit organizations, such as United Ways and alternative workplace funds, religious congregations, civic clubs and associations, and government agencies.

Getting to Know Foundations

A foundation is simply an institution that gives away money. Because foundations receive a tax break from the federal government, they are required to disburse at least 5 percent of the value of their assets, on average, every year. Unfortunately, nothing says they have to give it to your organization. Your job as a fundraiser is to convince a foundation that your organization is the best place to spend its money.

Foundations are the easiest grant makers to research. All foundations get a tax break from the U.S. government and in exchange have to file a detailed report on their activities with the IRS every year. They file a 990-PF just as your nonprofit organization files an IRS Form 990 and you as a good citizen file your IRS 1040 every April. The foundations' financial data from the IRS, including specific names and amounts, are made available to fundraisers in the Foundation Center's publications, CD-ROM, and databases.

Foundations represent an immense amount of money. In the United States, more than forty-six thousand foundations gave away more than $17 billion to charities in 1998.[1] In Canada in 1997, 1,072 foundations made grants worth more than $450 million (Canadian).[2]

Advantages

Asking for foundation money provides many advantages to your organization. The best thing that foundations offer is the requirement that you write a proposal. This is a written request for money that helps you to think through a new project from beginning to end. Even if you do not receive a grant, the process of planning the project, making the budget, and devising a way to measure the results is worth the effort.

Foundations are the venture capitalists of the nonprofit world. Some will fund the sizzle before there is a steak. Although the money usually runs out after one, two, or three years, it can buy your organization the time it needs to establish a funding base in its own constituency and create a track record.

The number of foundations is growing in both numbers and scale. From 1980 to 1998, the number of foundations more than doubled from 22,000 to 46,000.[3] Scores of new community foundations were created across the United States, with technical assistance and funding from the Kellogg Foundation and the Lilly Endowment. New public foundations are raising money for special populations, such as the one hundred American foundations that fund programs for women and girls.

With a red-hot stock market, plus investments in even more profitable hedge funds and other nontraditional investments such as leveraged-buyout funds, oil partnerships, and real estate, the rich got richer faster than ever before. The big foundations became huge and the wealthiest individuals created bold new foundations. Billionaire George Soros created a global network of foundations that make more than $350 million worth of grants in more than thirty countries from South Africa to his homeland, Hungary. Microsoft founder Bill Gates and his wife, Melinda, gave their foundations, the Bill and Melinda Gates Foundation, more than $17 billion in cash and Microsoft stock. The Gateses' foundations have designated grants such as $100 million to immunize poor children in developing countries and $20 million to the capital campaign for the Seattle Public Library. In addition, several huge foundations were created when nonprofit health-care institutions became for-profit companies. The largest was the California Endowment, which was created when Blue Cross of California became a for-profit business. It held almost $1.3 billion in assets at the end of its first year. Also, the David and Lucille Packard foundation received a bequest of $4.7 billion from Hewlett-Packard cofounder David Packard.

Foundations can give big money. The largest reported grants in 1997 were the pledge of CNN founder and Time Warner vice chairman Ted Turner to give $1 billion to the United Nations over a decade. In 1996 the Robert W. Woodruff Foundation gave $203 million to support health research at Emory University, and the Moody Foundation gave $140 million to the Moody Gardens in Galveston, Texas. Of course, the vast majority give much smaller grants, but there are enough of these jumbo grants to keep fundraisers smiling.

Some foundations can also give you loans or venture capital known as "program-related investments"—PRIs in fundraising jargon. This funding can be very helpful for groups working in low-income communities that are denied credit by conventional lenders.

The largest foundations have savvy staff who can serve as a helpful sounding board for new ideas. Foundation staff can put you in touch with people you should know; national foundation staff are especially good at getting the leaders of a certain field together.

Challenges

Foundation grant making is notoriously "trendy," going from cause to cause. You can get no money if your cause is considered passé. Even worse, you can get too much money if you ask the year your cause is hot, then get cut off the following year when it is not.

Unlike government, corporate, and United Way funding, which can be renewed year after year for decades, foundation funding usually runs out after one, two, or three years. On the one hand, foundations are always looking for new programs to fund. On the other hand, you can invest a lot of time and effort (and sometimes money) cultivating a relationship and mastering applications and reporting requirements, only to see the grant run out, leaving you to start all over on another source of funds.

Grant makers like to fund a specific piece of your overall work, since it is easier to understand and easier to take credit for a single program. There is also less risk of funding a failure. Never expect a foundation to pay for your organization's everyday operating expenses; that money needs to come from renewable sources like dues and donations.

Forty percent of the foundation money is controlled from New York City, which of course favors organizations that New Yorkers think are important. If your organization is in New York state, you could find more than six thousand foundations that made $3 billion in grants. If your organization is in Alaska, you could find thirty-six foundations that made $3 million in grants. Rural organizations are at a serious disadvantage in raising money from foundations, with the exception of a handful of foundations that are based in rural communities themselves.

Most foundation money goes to education (26 percent), health care (17 percent), human services (14 percent), and culture (14 percent). There has been great growth in giving to organizations for children and youth, science, international support for protection of global ecosystems, and use of computer technology.

Despite some growth, most organizations for minorities and women still get a tiny sliver of the foundation pie. For example, foundation funding for African-American organizations tripled in the 1980s but is still less than 5 percent of the total. Hispanic, Asian-American, and Native American groups got even less. Programs for women and girls received 5 percent of foundation grants. Religious congregations got 2 percent of foundation grants.[4]

Who May Ask

In the United States, foundations legally may give grants only to non-profits that are tax-exempt under section 501(c)(3) of the Internal Revenue Service tax codes. Every nonprofit is incorporated in its state, then applies to the IRS to be exempt from paying federal corporate income taxes. The federal government first imposed a tax on "all corporations organized for profit" in 1894; at the same time, it specifically exempted charitable institutions.

Twenty-eight tax categories including more than 1,200,000 not-for-profit organizations are exempt from paying corporate income taxes. These include 501(c)(4) for civic leagues, 501(c)(5) for labor unions, 501(c)(6) for chambers of commerce, and 501(c)(7) for social clubs. Only organizations in the 501(c)(3) tax code are both exempt from paying corporate income taxes and able to give their donors the right to deduct the value of contributions from their taxable income. The 501(c)(3) is often shortened in fundraising jargon to simply "C3." In 1997, 693,000 charities and private foundations had 501(c)(3) status.

American lawmakers want taxpayers to support good causes, so the IRS gives tax-exempt status to groups they want to promote. These include "religious, educational, charitable, scientific, literary, testing for public safety, to foster national or international amateur sports competition, or prevention of cruelty to children or animals organizations."[5] These all fall into the 501(c)(3) tax code, and gifts made to them are deductible from individuals' taxable income.

Most foundations will give grants only to 501(c)(3) organizations, but there are a couple of loopholes. For example, a volunteer fire department is legally a 501(c)(4) organization, but foundations and individuals may still give deductible funds to the volunteer fire department's work for "exclusively public purposes." Some nonprofits that are not C3s, such as chambers of commerce, may legally create a special charitable fund exclusively to do 501(c)(3) types of activities. In that case a foundation may make a grant to the chamber's charitable fund and deduct the grant. For more information on tax codes, get Publication 557 free from the IRS at (800) TAX-FORM or www.irs.gov.

Foundations may also give grants to governmental bodies, such as a park district for a new swimming pool, a library to computerize the collection, or a school district for a better building. More and more towns and counties have a foundation fundraiser in the office of economic development.

The IRS Tells All

It is easy to research foundations because every American foundation has to file a Form 990-PF every year with the Internal Revenue Service, just as an individual taxpayer has to file a Form 1040 or a charity has to file a Form 990. The 990-PFs are a gold mine of information, because they actually name names of the trustees, the staff, and the charities that received grants.

All of the data from the 990-PFs and other foundation materials are collected as a public service (and a very successful example of earned income) by the Foundation Center in New York City. This organization compiles the data in directories and a CD-ROM for easy access. Soon it will also be available on-line for a fee.

Resources from the Foundation Center

At your own public library you can probably find *The Foundation Directory*, which will introduce you to more than ten thousand of the largest American foundations. Ask the reference librarian for other information on local foundations, corporations, philanthropists, and scholarships.

If foundations are brand-new to you, get the Foundation Center's *User-Friendly Guide*, or log on to www.fdncenter.org. for on-line training on foundation research and proposal writing. They give the easiest and clearest explanation of how to find prospects and ask for foundation funding.

Cooperating Collections

The Foundation Center operates five free libraries in New York, Atlanta, Washington, D.C., Cleveland, and San Francisco and supports Cooperating Collections in every state and Puerto Rico. Find the nearest collection from www.fdncenter.org. Phone first to ask when the collection will offer an orientation. Take a partner and learn about foundation and corporate fundraising. Most of the cooperating collections sell the Foundation Center publications as well as state and city foundation directories. At the cooperating collections you can also look at copies of the 990-PFS for the foundations in your state and often neighboring states; at the five national collections you can see the 990-PFS for national foundations.

Most of the cooperating collections are staffed by professional librarians; others have expert volunteers to help you. They will not do the work for you, but they will teach you how to work most efficiently. The cooperating collections are by far the best sources of information on foundation and corporate giving. Your own local library may have more information on local philanthropists and scholarships.

For more knowledgeable computer users, foundation and grant data can be retrieved through a commercial on-line service called DIALOG. Your organization can subscribe to DIALOG, or you may access the files through the computer-assisted reference center at your public library or through a friendly nonprofit or for-profit that uses DIALOG. To use DIALOG, you need to learn special codes and commands, but you can retrieve more current information more quickly.

The big advantage of using the computerized services is that the computer does all the searching for you, and it will organize and print the data in whatever format is most useful for you. If your organization does a lot of foundation research, the computer searches will pay for themselves in saved time and labor costs. Since the one thousand largest foundations reported close to 250,000 grants in 1997, the field has outgrown the ability of even the most zealous volunteer to retrieve on paper. For more advice, check with the on-line support staff at the Foundation Center in New York at (212) 620-4230 or DIALOG at (800) 334-2564.

Foundation Center Publications and CD-ROM

These authoritative reference books and CD-ROM are published by the Foundation Center:

- *The Foundation Directory* includes information on more than ten thousand of the largest foundations that give out more than $8 billion. This is the place to start, and will be available at most public libraries. The same information is also retrievable on a computer through DIALOG File 26.

- *The Foundation 1000* gives you much more detail on the top one thousand foundations.

- *National Directory of Corporate Giving* has data on more than 2,800 corporate foundations and 990 direct-giving programs that gave away both cash and in-kind gifts. All the corporations are cross-indexed in seven ways, including by location (for example, California), type of charity (elementary school), type of support (endowment), type of business (banks), and name of officers, donors, and trustees (Michael Eisner).

- *Guide to U.S. Foundations* gives information on more than forty-six thousand U.S. foundations. This is the best guide to local funding, since many of these are quite small family foundations and all are listed by state. Brief information on twenty thousand of these foundations is also retrievable by computer via DIALOG File 26. The twenty-five thousand smallest foundations will be found only in Volume 1: *The Foundations*, so be sure to use it for smaller local family foundations. To research local, major donor prospects use Volume 2: *Foundation Trustee, Officer, and Donor Index and Foundation Locator*.

You may also use the Foundation Center's thirty-five *Grant Guides* which report grants of more than $10,000 to a specific issue, such as aging, alcohol and drug abuse, arts, health care, higher education, or information technology.

All of these books and databases give you the guidelines on where the foundations say they will or will not make grants. The reality check is another book and database that tells where the foundations really made their grants. This is *The Foundation Grants Index*, which lists eighty-six thousand grants of $10,000 or more made by more than one thousand of the largest independent, corporate, and community foundations. This information is also retrievable via computer on DIALOG File 27.

Although these data come from less than 3 percent of U.S. foundations, they represent about 60 percent of all grants from private and community foundations. *The Foundation Grants Index* or DIALOG File 27 names the grants given in your state, sorted by twenty-eight subjects, from "animals" to "youth."

If you see that a good local nonprofit has received a grant from a foundation you want to ask, get more information from the fundraiser who got the grant. Always add current advice from real people to the data in the books. Ask whom to approach at the foundation and whom to avoid. What does the foundation like and what does it dislike? What are recent changes?

The Foundation Center also publishes excellent how-to books and offers on-line training writing proposals and researching foundations. See the Resource Guide, log on www.fdncenter.org or call (800) 424-9836 to order the Center's publications catalog.

CD-ROM

Most cooperating collections will have the Foundation Center's CD-ROM *FC Search*. If your organization does a lot of foundation research, it is worth investing $1,195 to buy your own *FC Search* CD-ROM; for newer and smaller organizations, use it at the nearest cooperating collection. This is a great tool that enables you to search almost fifty thousand foundations and corporate givers by choosing from more than twenty-one search fields. Best of all, you can type a key word to find information on your particular need in the text-search field and retrieve information that would not be revealed through the current indexes, such as information on sudden infant death syndrome or Frank Lloyd Wright. *FC Search* offers you all the information from ten Foundation Center directories including close to two hundred thousand grants and almost two hundred thousand trustees, officers, and donors. You also get hyperlinks to the six hundred foundations that have their own Internet websites. Included in the cost is hot-line assistance, a newsletter, and a semiannual updated disk.

Caution

The Foundation Center has presented fundraisers with an embarrassment of riches. So much data is available on foundations that you can easily get overwhelmed or, even worse, distracted from your original mission by the lure of easy money. Always begin with your own organization's goals and values. With your leadership, decide what you want to do and how you want to do it. Be sure that your core operating expenses are already covered by a dependable fundraising base of dues and donations.

Then if you want to explore foundations, choose a specific program, and research foundation funding for that. Remember, independence comes from diversity in fundraising. Never depend on foundation grants, and never budget the money until the check is in your hand.

Types of Foundations

You can get more information at the cooperating collection, but basically there are five kinds of foundations: private, community, corporate, public, and operating foundations. There is also something called a supporting organization that is not a foundation but makes grants.

Independent Foundations

The Foundation Center defines an independent foundation as a nongovernmental, nonprofit organization that has a principal fund of its own, is managed by its own trustees and directors, and has been established to maintain or aid charitable, educational, religious, or other activities serving the public good, primarily by making grants to other nonprofit organizations. Most of the biggest foundations are independent foundations, such as the Bill and Melinda Gates Foundation (which has assets of $17 billion worth of Microsoft stock). This is the biggest and also the fastest-growing foundation as the Gateses' continue to make huge donations of Microsoft stock. Another computer fortune, the David and Lucille Packard Foundation, is the second largest foundation with $13 billion in assets. Both the Gates and Packard foundations were formed in 1994, showing the extraordinary growth made possible by the information age. The Ford Foundation, which had been number one for thirty years, is now in third place.

The rest of the top ten foundations are the Lilly Endowment, funded with stock from the Eli Lilly pharmaceutical company (those wonderful folks who brought you Prozac); the Robert Wood Johnson Foundation, which focuses on health care and public health policy; the W. K. Kellogg Foundation; the Pew Charitable Trusts; the John D. and Catherine T. MacArthur Foundation; the Andrew W. Mellon Foundation; and the venerable Rockefeller Foundation, founded in 1913.[6]

Family Foundations

If you are asking individuals for major gifts, some of them may choose to give to you from a family foundation. Foundations were invented in 1917, the same year the federal government began levying an income tax. Wealthy families found that one way to avoid paying taxes was to create a foundation. Then the money could be squirreled away tax-free in a foundation at a 2% tax rate, but the family could still control how it was spent.

Community Foundations

You can think of community foundations as sort of foundation co-ops. Many donors pool their trust funds in a community foundation and gain economies from a shared staff. Funds may be earmarked for a specific interest in the community. In 1997 there were more than five hundred community foundations which gave more than $1 billion in grants.

Community foundations are now the fastest-growing form of foundation in the United States, because they give a donor all the advantages and prestige of being a foundation without the headaches of running one's own foundation full-time. Also, their donors can get the blessings of anonymity if they want. The most generous community foundations in terms of grants paid in 1997 were the New York Community Trust, the Greater Kansas City Community Foundation, the San Francisco Foundation, the California Community Foundation, the Columbus (Ohio) Foundation, the Cleveland Foundation, and the Foundation for the Carolinas. Even smaller communities such as Elk River, Minnesota (population 6,785), and low-income communities like East Chicago, Indiana, are creating community foundations.[7]

For fundraisers, community foundations are a good source of money because they are, by definition, committed to the well-being of the particular community. They can be the first source of money for new issues. For example, when nine volunteers started Horizon Hospice in Chicago in 1978, there was no rubric in the directories for "hospice" because only a handful were in operation in North America. The Chicago Community Trust gave Horizon Hospice its first grant of $35,000 to hire staff and open an office.

Corporate Foundations

In addition to their direct-giving programs, 1,900 American companies have foundations to make grants to the causes they want to support. The largest company-sponsored foundations in 1997 were Wal-Mart, which gave $39 million in grants; AT&T, which gave $37 million; Ford, which gave $33 million; Chase Manhattan, which gave $31 million; Bank of America, which gave $31 million; and General Electric, which gave $30 million.[8]

Public Foundations

A public foundation raises money, then gives it away, so this type of foundation is both a donor and donee. This role gives public foundations the advantages of being included in the inner circles of foundations, such as opportunity for membership in the Council on Foundations. Most of these target their grants for specific constituencies; an example is the Black United Funds (BUFS).

Another example of public foundations is the fifteen local "alternative foundations" that raise money and make grants to fund progressive grassroots organizing. These include the Haymarket People's Fund in Boston, the Chinook Fund in Denver, and the Vanguard Public Foundation in Los Angeles. Unlike traditional community foundations, the alternative funds include low- and middle-income community leaders in the grant-making process and raise money from all economic classes.

Operating Foundations

Although operating foundations are called "foundations," you cannot ask most of them for money, because they do not make grants to other nonprofit groups. The most common examples are foundations run by hospitals as a way to raise money and maintain an endowment for the hospital foundation. These spend money only on expenses incurred by their own hospitals, usually for indigent care not covered by government funds or private insurance.

Supporting Organizations

In the 1969 legislation that revised the IRS rules for foundations, there was language defining something called a supporting organization. A supporting organization is a legal vehicle to transfer assets to nonprofit organizations. It is a good deal for grant makers because there is no excise tax and no required payout. It is a worse deal for most charities because there is no way to research or ask for grants from supporting organizations.

Unlike a donor-advised fund that may specify that grants should go to, say, health charities in Houston, a supporting organization has the donors actually name the specific charities. Then those named nonprofits get grants each year. Although the supporting organizations are de facto grant makers, they are not open to the public. Now some of the largest charities, such as the Jewish Federation, are asking their major donors who make gifts each year to name the charity to receive money through the supporting organization. Thus the charity knows it will get a major gift each year, and the donors save money on their taxes.

How to Ask for Foundation Grants

To ask for a grant from a foundation, begin with someone you know. If any of your board members or volunteers already know the staff or trustees of a foundation, begin with those donors. Research the foundation through the Foundation Center publications or databases and the groups it has funded. Send a one- or two-page letter outlining the program you want the foundation to fund, then call to discuss it further.

If you do not have any prospects from your own leadership, ask the fundraisers from similar organizations to recommend foundations that might fund your organization. Then research those and begin a dialogue.

If you have no leads at all, attend an orientation at a cooperating collection to learn how to use Foundation Center data to make a short list of foundations that might be interested in funding your kind of organization in your community. Begin with a list of ten or fewer. Never assume that more is better and send off your proposal to every foundation in Michigan or every foundation that ever gave to substance abuse. You will spend a lot of time and money for little or no return.

Instead, begin with an intentional plan to get grants for a good new program from one to five foundations the first year. After you have received some grants and developed good relationships with local foundations, ask them to recommend other local foundations and the best people at the larger national foundations.

What to Ask For

The best grant to ask for is a matching grant, where the foundation gives you money to match what you raise. You get a grant and a deadline, so your fundraisers will have another incentive to ask their prospects. The grant does not need to be a one-to-one match; for low-income communities, you may need a five-to-one or ten-to-one match. For the foundation itself, a matching grant reduces the risk of making a bad grant.

Otherwise, match your needs and the foundations' giving guidelines. Most foundations will prefer to fund a specific piece of your program. A few will offer a range of funding from endowments to capital campaigns to scholarship funds. Some foundations will also make loans and program-related investments (PRIs). Especially in low-income communities that are denied capital from conventional lenders, foundation loans and investments can provide the venture capital needed for bigger projects.

If your group is brand-new, controversial, or both, a foundation may be the only lender you can find (besides your own donors). For example, when the Roslyn Group for Arts and Letters wanted to present the very controversial Judy Chicago sculpture called "The Dinner Party" in Chicago in 1980, we were just a small literary salon with no treasury. So we asked the Playboy Foundation for a loan of $850 to buy a movie about the making of the sculpture, and then showed the movie at meetings and parties to raise money and recruit volunteers. After six months the loan was repaid. Film parties alone raised $7,800 (a nine-to-one return on the loan) and helped recruit thirteen hundred volunteers, both men and women. Overall, more than seventy thousand people paid to see the exhibit and shopped at the exhibit's gift shop. After all the bills were paid, the Roslyn Group contributed the surplus of $27,000 to the Chicago Foundation for Women (to fund grants to women artists); the Playboy Foundation's original loan was multiplied thirty-two times.

Proposals

Most foundations want you to ask for money in a written document called a proposal. This is similar to a business plan for a for-profit business: it must persuade the foundation that your organization is a good investment. Tell the foundation what you want to do, why this program is needed, how you will do it, how much it will cost, and how much money you want from the foundation.

Set measurable goals and specify how you will measure the results. Include a detailed budget that makes clear exactly how much you want from the foundation, how much your organization will donate, and how this fits into the total budget of the organization. If there are other funders, name them, and include projections for how the programs will be funded after the grant runs out.

Attach a copy of your IRS Determination Letter to prove your organization has 501(c)(3) tax status and a copy of your audited financial statement to show your organization is well managed. Also attach a list of your board of directors, with credentials, such as "president of the school board," "CEO of Widgets, Inc.," or "person living with cancer." Use one or two copies of positive news stories and letters of praise for your work. If part of the grant will go to pay for professionals already on your staff, include their current resumes.

For more details on how to write a proposal, use the Foundation Center books at the cooperating collection or the on-line training at www.fdncenter.org, or order the books listed in the Resource Guide.

If you can write a term paper, you can write a proposal. Keep it as simple as possible. Spell out every single acronym and explain or eliminate all jargon. You may know that DRG means "Diagnostic Related Group" and that it is a way for the federal government to restrict health-care payments, but there is no reason to expect that the average Joe working for a foundation should know that. Test your proposal on your mother or a teenager; substitute simple English for any word or concept that person does not know. Then double-check the proposal, especially the arithmetic, and triple-check the name of the person at the foundation.

Send your proposal off with a very short and very positive cover letter. Since most proposals begin with a statement of the need for the program seeking funds, your proposal begins by describing the problem. Marketing whiz Richard Steckel calls proposals a "competition of woes." When you lead off with your "needs statement," of course you have to say the South Side has more drugs, more crimes, more empty houses, more dropouts, and more problems than the east, west, or north side. Fundraising this way can demoralize the most determined optimist.

So in your cover letter and any meetings with the foundation staff, you need to be very positive and paint a picture of determination to succeed. Emphasize how your organization can get results and how, dollar for dollar, you are the best investment in your field. Give the foundation hope that its grant will stop the drugs, fill the houses, and keep the kids in school.

Person-to-Person

The largest foundations employ staff to screen the grants and interview the applicants. Foundation staff may be able to recommend a decision just from your proposal and reputation, or they may want to meet with your people. In that case, use the strategy you used to ask for corporate money. Take a team, get there early, listen hard, never argue, never lie, know what you want, say what you want, and send a thank-you note the same day.

In rare cases, foundations have staff who can make a site visit to see your organization and the work it does. Put your best foot forward, but do not make any major changes simply because the foundation folks are coming to visit. If they do not like the program the way you run it, there are plenty of other places to ask for money. Especially for low-income organizations, usually a trip to the neighborhood is the most persuasive part of asking for a grant, since the grant maker will gain much more appreciation of your work.

Smaller family foundations may not have paid staff, so you may need to follow up your proposal with a phone call to a trustee. Ideally this will come from someone the trustee knows, either a community leader or someone from your board. Simply verify that the foundation received your proposal, ask if the trustee wants anything else, and offer to answer any questions. If the foundation is not staffed, it is not likely that someone will meet with you in person or make a site visit.

After the Grant

The same day you are notified your organization will receive a grant, send a thank-you note. Be sure your bookkeeper or treasurer knows what kind of financial records are needed on the grant; be sure the fundraiser knows what kind of reports are needed when. Always send the foundation more than it requested about its grant. Mail before-and-after photos, letters from people helped, any kind of measurable data from an objective third party (police statistics showing crime is down, school statistics showing attendance is up, hospital statistics showing less use of the emergency room by victims of domestic violence). Invite foundation staff to your special events; notify them when your leaders will be on radio or television; try to meet in person at least once to report on progress.

If the foundation turns you down, ask for advice to improve your planning and proposal next time. Also ask if the foundation can recommend other grant makers.

As with any other major donor, you want to be building a good long-term relationship with the grant maker. Although most grants run out in one, two, or three years, the foundation world is small. Foundation staff know each other and can recommend you to other good funders when the first grant runs out.

Conclusion

As you build a respectful relationship, foundation staff and trustees can give your organization much more than money. They can gather people together who are (or should be) allies to consider collaboration; they can give larger amounts of money for a longer time to riskier projects; and they can give you an objective sounding-board for new ideas. Though your foundation partners can help you launch a new program, it is your responsibility to create a dependable income stream (ideally with dues and donations from the people who benefit) to replace the grant when it runs out. As Vartan Gregorian, president of the $1.5 billion Carnegie Corporation of New York, said, "We're not an oxygen tank" that tries to keep nonprofit institutions alive. "We're an incubator for ideas."[9]

Other Grant Makers

Religious Denominations, United Ways and Alternative Funds, Civic Organizations, and Government Grants and Contracts

14

We ought to be telling the world there are more than just oases of goodness.

> —Archbishop Desmond Tutu
> To Peace Jam students
> *Horizon*

FOUNDATIONS ARE THE MOST OBVIOUS SOURCE of grants because all that they do is give away money. But there are many other institutions that give grants to good nonprofit organizations. This chapter looks at all the places, besides foundations, where you can ask for a grant. These include the United Ways and alternative workplace funds that make grants, local congregations and religious denominations, local civic organizations like the Rotary Club or Kiwanis Club, and all levels of governmental agencies.

Charities received most of the $3.4 billion raised by the 1,900 United Ways in their 1997–98 campaign. United Ways fund primarily noncontroversial health and human services agencies. It is difficult for a new group to get into the United Way allocations, but it is worth the effort because this organization is a dependable, renewable source of money once your group is in.

Religious denominations are the hardest to research because they are accountable to their own governing bodies and not to the U.S. government. But it is well worth the work because religious grant makers as a group gave more than $20 billion in 1998, more than foundations. Unlike foundations and the United Ways, they are not limited as to the kinds of nonprofits they can fund.

Every community has an array of civic and social clubs that raise money and give some of it away in grants to other good charities. These can range from very small grants ($50) from student groups; to medium-sized grants from the Veterans of Foreign Wars, the Junior League, the Lions Club, and fraternities and sororities; to the giants like Rotary International, which has made grants totaling more than $250 million to eradicate polio around the world.

Government agencies also give grants and award contracts to nonprofits. For nonreligious organizations this is often a very significant part of their budgets.

Religious Grant Makers

Although religious grant makers give more money than either foundations or corporations, they are more difficult to research. Unlike foundations, they are not required to file a 990-PF with the IRS, and unlike corporations, they are not accountable to stockholders. So you need to ask each member of your board to do the work to research his or her own denomination through internal documents and current grantees.

In 1998 religious congregations gave an estimated 38 percent of their money, or $20 billion, to support other charities. This was in addition to $35 billion for their own local, national, and international work. The largest single religious grant maker is the United States Catholic Conference's Campaign for Human Development (CHD), which gave away $7 million in 1998.[1]

Asking for money from religious grant makers is complicated, because every denomination operates differently. The common factor is that each one operates at the local level through the church, synagogue, mosque, or temple. This level is the easiest for a member of that congregation to approach.

Local congregations can also give you a lot more than money. Most have a building with a kitchen and nursery. Many host musical and theatrical performances. Best of all, they are the best source for volunteers with fundraising skills, since religious congregations get less than 2 percent of foundation or corporate funding. For experienced volunteers who know how to raise big money from individuals, look to your local congregations.

After the local congregation, the next level up is known generically as a judicatory and may be called a diocese, synod, conference, or other term. At the top level are the national programs, which fund both in the United States and internationally. For the regional and national grant makers, ask your local congregation for advice, and ask other groups that receive funding from the denomination. Like foundation grants, most grants from the national level of denominations run out after one to three years. Support from a local congregation is more likely to be renewable year after year.

Religious grant makers give their grants to achieve their goals for peace and justice. They do not need to limit their money to only 501(c)(3) organizations but can give to any group that can do work they want, such as feeding the hungry, housing the homeless, or visiting prisoners. However, each denomination is explicit in stating that, in the words of the CHD application, "the project activity for which funding is requested must conform to the moral teachings" of the denomination.[2]

To find out more about religious grant makers, ask your own leaders to ask in their own denominations for the rules and applications for each funding level. Then ask your leaders to recruit an important layperson and a member of the clergy to work with them to investigate whether religious funding would be a good part of your strategy. For more information, get the current edition of the *Religious Funding Resource Guide*, listed in the Resource Guide.

United Ways

As mentioned earlier, there are more than 1,900 United Ways in the United States, each of which allocates money to local health and human services agencies. Some also make grants for special projects. In 1997–98 the United Ways raised a record $3.4 billion to allocate to more than forty-five thousand health and human services agencies. This makes the United Way by far the largest grant maker in the United States. In total, the United Ways give more money than the largest foundation, the Lilly Endowment, which gave $424 million, or the largest corporate donor, Merck and Company, which gave $190 million in 1998. Most United Way funds go to traditional agencies such as the American Red Cross, Catholic Charities, the Salvation Army, Girl Scouts and Boy Scouts, the Urban League, the YMCA, and the YWCA.[3]

United Ways collect money through workplace solicitation (64 percent), corporate gifts (22 percent), and a growing campaign for major gifts from individuals. They also get grants from private foundations, such as a grant from the W. K. Kellogg Foundation to increase minority participation, and they broker big grants, such as a $500,000 seed grant from the Ford Foundation, which leveraged $17 million in five cities for affordable housing.

Of the 61 percent of United Way money that comes from workers through payroll deductions, 50 percent is from employees of corporations and small businesses, and 11 percent from nonprofit and government workers.

United Ways are also getting more aggressive about asking for major gifts from wealthy individuals. They have created a major gift club called the Alexis de Tocqueville Society; membership costs $10,000 or more. For 1997–98, contributions of $1,000 or more comprised the fastest-growing category of gifts to United Ways.

For the really big gifts, the United Ways have copied insurance salespeople and created the Million Dollar Roundtable. Million-dollar donors include Leslie Wexner, chairman of The Limited Inc. in Columbus; Jenny and Sid Craig, founders of the Jenny Craig Weight Loss Centers in San Diego; and Bill Gates, chairman of Microsoft Corporation in Seattle. United Ways are also joining other big charities in working harder at asking for planned gifts and building up their own endowments.

History

The system of running one campaign to raise money for several charities at the same time was first tried in Denver in 1887. In the depth of the Depression, Community Chests raised more than $100 million to help the hungry and homeless.

The United Way name was invented in Detroit in 1949 and is now used across the United States. However, "Community Chest" still lives on in a few communities and in Monopoly games.

The United Way concept of one fundraising campaign to raise money for multiple charities has spread to twenty-eight countries overseas, including innovative United Ways working with the American and European business leaders developing joint ventures in the emerging free market economies in Central Europe and the former Soviet Union.

Advantages

United Ways can raise money with very low overhead, because most of the work is done by volunteers and most of the money is collected through corporate payroll deduction. Larger United Ways spend only 14 percent and smaller United Ways spend only 16 percent of their budgets to raise their funds.[4]

The United Ways demand high standards for the charities they fund. United Ways require that each group be run by volunteers and submit to an annual independent financial audit; provide services at reasonable costs; and maintain a policy of nondiscrimination.

The United Ways are probably the most widespread training ground for giving and asking for money. Since payroll deduction makes it easy to give larger gifts, they also help every charity by setting the standard of asking for larger gifts.

The United Way is usually the broadest based and most tightly organized structure working with nonprofits in any community. In some communities, it is the only forum where corporate executives come in contact with minority leaders from low-income neighborhoods.

Challenges

For corporate donors, it is hard to get recognition or "credit" for making a donation to the United Way, since it just disappears into a giant pot of money. Some corporations have chosen to use their corporate giving more intentionally to achieve specific marketing goals, so those companies prefer to do their own charitable giving outside the United Way. Other corporations earmark their gift to guarantee that it is spent on what they want. For example, the Mellon Bank in Pittsburgh designated that $100,000 of its total gift of $500,000 be spent to create affordable housing.

For charities, the United Way is a very exclusive club. In the 1980s local United Ways admitted an average of only half a new charity per year. Despite efforts by new organizations, the fundraising press, and a few enlightened United Way leaders to open up allocations to more worthwhile nonprofits, in the 1990s the average number of new charities admitted came up to only one new group per local United Way per year.

United Way has a written policy against coercion. Nevertheless, employees, especially at the lower levels, often feel coerced to give. Since workplace solicitation uses the structure that is already in place, and since it always works from the top of the pyramid down, it is inevitable that each boss, supervisor, or foreman asks his or her subordinates. The employees rarely feel this is a totally voluntary choice. Hopefully, as more United Ways allow more donor options, all employees will feel as enthusiastic about their gifts to the United Way as they do about their gifts to other worthwhile causes.

How to Ask for United Way Funds

United Way boards are dominated by business leaders, so you pursue United Way funding the same way you pursue corporate funding—what matters is whom you know. Contact your local United Way and ask for information on its application procedures. Each of the locals will be a little different, but most are limited to funding only noncontroversial health and human services agencies.

Find out who serves on the board and on the committee that admits new agencies. Then get your heavy hitters to lobby to get your group in.

Usually, only one or two new agencies will be accepted, so continue your other fundraising while you apply. If your agency is accepted, you must conform to the rules of the United Way. Most United Ways forbid you to do your own fundraising during their campaign in the fall. Most also put other restrictions on when and how you can ask for money, and they ask that your own employees give to the United Way.

The advantage of being a United Way agency is that it gives you credibility and legitimacy in the community, it gives you the opportunity (use it) to serve on United Way committees with the movers and shakers in your town, and it is a dependable source of money once you have been accepted. The amount the United Ways allocate will reflect the growth or decline of each local economy, but most United Ways see a small but steady growth of income every year.

If your agency is not accepted by the local United Way, consider organizing a donor option campaign or joining a local alternative fund, as described in Chapter 6.

Civic Organizations

Many civic and social organizations raise money for worthwhile causes in the United States and around the world. The biggest and boldest is the Rotary International, which raised almost $250 million in 160 countries to immunize more than 500 million children against polio. In Zambia alone, the number of reported cases of polio has dropped from 700 to 70 because of Rotary's fundraising.

The Junior Leagues of America raised more than $18 million in 1998 through special events, major gifts, cookbooks, thrift shops, and grants. They not only give most of this money back to their communities but also train volunteers, who go on to leadership roles in other organizations. Their most notable alumnae are former First Lady Nancy Reagan and Supreme Court justice Sandra Day O'Connor.

In smaller towns and rural communities, organizations like the Veterans of Foreign Wars (VFW), the Knights of Columbus, and ethnic clubs may be able to give you small grants for your cause. In minority communities, fraternities and sororities are often the place to look for small grants and leadership talent.

In any case, the easiest way to get a grant from a civic organization is to ask a member of the organization to advocate for your group. He or she will know the official and the unofficial application procedures. A woman in Brainerd, Minnesota, told me she was saved when an organization insider told her to ask again after her request was rejected the first time. The insider said the committee always turned down everyone the first time as a test to see who was serious; everyone who came back the second month got a grant. If the fundraiser had not had the tip and the encouragement from the insider, she might have lost the chance for an easy grant.

Civic organization grants are usually smaller amounts, but they give your group legitimacy in the community. With careful cultivation, you may be able to get the grants year after year and hopefully involve some of the organizations' volunteers in your group, too.

Government Grants and Contracts

Although Americans pride themselves on the pioneer tradition of self-reliance and neighbor helping neighbor, in fact more than one-fourth of all funding for nonprofit organizations comes from federal, state, and local funds. Of course, this percentage is much higher in some fields, such as health care, and much lower in others, such as community organizing.

The two big advantages of government funding are: (1) it is huge—after all, they *make* the money, and (2) it is ours. Like Abraham Lincoln, we believe in government of the people, for the people, and by the people. We *are* the government, and our revenue should go to support the worthwhile organizations that create a decent civil society.

There are three big disadvantages of taking government funds: (1) it will increase your total fundraising goal, (2) it is very restricted money, and (3) it makes it easy for undecided prospects to say no, since they can rationalize that they already paid their taxes.

Government money is not a free ride; it will always cost your organization in terms of bookkeeping hardware, software, personnel, and aggravation. It can also cost more for time lags, services not covered, and vouchers not accepted. As long as you can project the real cost of taking government funds, and persuade your leaders to commit to raising the extra money to cover these costs, government funding is a very large source of money for you to consider.

The second challenge is that most government grants and contracts are restricted money, earmarked for a specific project or service. I have worked with community development corporations (CDCs) that received $5 million to build affordable housing, but every dollar was restricted for the housing construction. When they wanted a laptop computer, they needed to hold a raffle. Especially for organizations working in low- and middle-income communities, it takes constant work to educate the leaders about the limits of restricted funding and the need to keep raising nonrestricted funds from nongovernmental sources.

The third disadvantage is that some donors will say they do not need to give to you because they are already paying state and federal taxes. Conservatives will whine that the taxes are too high, so they do not want to give, and the liberals will gripe that the government should be doing a better job on social services (or the arts or education or whatever), so they do not want to let it off the hook by donating to you. In either case, it is your job to enlighten the prospect as to what the government does and does not pay, and why the prospect's vital unrestricted donation is still needed. For example, Medicaid pays for some costs of hospice patient care, but there are no government funds for supporting bereavement care for the family.

If your organization wants to pursue funding from your local, state, or federal sources, ask for advice from other nonprofits in the same jurisdiction. Find out what you need to do in order to apply and what the time lag on payments is, and estimate how much money you will need to raise from other sources.

Add the elected officials for your community to your database, and be sure they receive your newsletters, E-mail alerts, and party invitations. Try to get the politicians or their staff into your office or out to an event at least once per term, and visit them when you are in the capitol. Use every opportunity to educate your elected officials about your issues, your constituents, and your mission.

You Say You Want a Devolution

In most other developed nations, the citizens choose to pay higher taxes and then spend much more government money on health care, public education, and the arts. In America, citizens have chosen to pay lower income taxes and support the social services through other taxes and philanthropy. But the public-sector funding is still very important (the majority of funds in some fields) and must be guided in the future with more input from charities. As funding decisions continue to move from the federal to state and local jurisdictions, nonprofits in America must be more involved in the debates over the use of public funds. We in Chicago, under Mayor Richard J. Daley, learned that elections were about jobs. Now under his son, Mayor Richard M. Daley, we have learned that elections are about contracts. Whether or not your organization chooses to take government funds, if you want public dollars going to the issues you care about, your organization will need to be part of the debates on the allocation of public funds.

Fees for Services—Government Contracts

All the way back in Chapter 3, we discussed the value of fees for service. More and more government agencies, both in the United States and other countries, are moving away from giving grants and more toward fees for service awarded under contracts. The advantages for the governments is they can get competitive bidding to get the best service and the best price; they can get out from expensive union contracts, and they can make jobs for the politicians' relatives supervising the contract procedure. The disadvantages are there is often just as much paperwork whether it is a grant or a contract, there may be more restrictions, there may be less protection such as affirmative action safeguards, and you may have to deal with the mayor's campaign chairman's son Bubba. However, since this is clearly the trend in most countries, and it may be the only source of funds for the most-expensive work nonprofits do, such as quality health care, fundraisers will need to learn the ropes on getting fees for service.

Get the official guidelines from each agency, then ask some other agency they fund about how it really works and how to deal with the people involved. Always remain rigorously nonpartisan so you will not get cut off when the party in power changes.

Conclusion

Successful fundraisers can use foundation grants as the seed money for new projects and then replace that money with renewable income from dues, donations, fees, and sales. You know that your organization cannot depend on foundation grants to pay your everyday core budget. Operating expenses have to come from the people who need and want what you do.

On the other hand, many United Ways, religious congregations, and civic clubs are willing to support their favorite nonprofit groups year after year. Once your organization has been approved, these grants should be a dependable source of funding. Keep local grant makers involved as members and guests at your events and informed through your mailings and personal contacts. Working together, you will all be able to achieve more for your community.

Endnotes

Chapter 1–Fundraising in the Information Age: The Road Ahead for Fundraisers

1. Virginia A. Hodgkinson and Murray S. Weitzman, *Giving and Volunteering in the United States*. Washington, D.C.: Independent Sector, 1996, 34.
2. Ibid., 45.

Chapter 2–The Fundraising Team

1. Virginia A. Hodgkinson and Murray S. Weitzman, *Giving and Volunteering in the United States*. Washington, D.C.: Independent Sector, 1996, 243.
2. Letty Cottin Pogrebin, "Contributing to the Cause." *New York Times Magazine*, April 22, 1990, 22–23.
3. Sandford D. Horwitt, *Saul Alinsky*. New York: Alfred A. Knopf, 1989, 401–402.
4. Hodgkinson and Weitzman, op. cit., 54.
5. Emmett D. Carson, "Valuing Black Benevolence." *Foundation News*, May/June 1990, 39.
6. Janet Moore, "Retailers Eye Generation Y." *Star Tribune*, April 26, 1998, D1.

Chapter 3–Selling Products and Services: Raising Money from Customers and Clients

1. *Fall/Winter 1998 Greeting Cards and Gifts* catalog. New York: U.S. Committee for UNICEF, 1998.
2. David H. Pill, *The English Reformation 1529–58*. London: University of London Press, 1973, 22.

Chapter 4–Special Events

1. Peter Jacobi, *The Messiah Book*. New York: St. Martin's, 1982, 37, 89.

Chapter 5—Getting Started: How to Ask for Money

1. "United Ways Raise $2.98 Billion, Up $200 Million in a Year." *Chronicle of Philanthropy*, May 1, 1990, 6.

Chapter 6—Building the Base by Yourself: With Direct Mail, E-Mail, Phones, and Door-to-Door

1. "SOCM Adds 236 New Families to Membership Rolls in 1989." SOCM *Sentinel* (Jacksboro, Tenn.: Save Our Cumberland Mountains), spring 1990, 13.
2. "Organizers Talk About What They Do and How They Do It—Mary Gonzales, Associate Director, United Neighborhood Organization." *Forum* (Chicago: Donors Forum), spring 1986, 5.
3. "Seasonality Study Released." *Fund Raising Management*, June 1989, 12.Most profitable months for mailers were (1) November, (2) August, and (3) February.

Chapter 7—Mass-Marketing Your Message: How the Professionals Use the Internet, Direct Mail, Telemarketing, and Door Canvassing

1. Jill Smolowe, "Read This." *Time*, November 26, 1990, 65.
2. Mal Warwick, "Reaching Donors the Second Time Around Is Key to Successful Program." *Nonprofit Times*, May 1990, 33.

Chapter 8—How to Find the Big Givers

1. Kwame Anthony Appiah, Introduction to *Things Fall Down* by Chinua Achebe (1958) for Knopf Everyman's Library Edition, 1992.
2. "The Challenge for America's Rich." *Economist*, May 1998.
3. Albo, Amy, "The Benefactor 100: The Most Generous Among Us." *North Magazine*, April 1999.
4. Thomas J. Stanley and William D. Danko, *The Millionaire Next Door; The Surprising Secrets of America's Wealthy*. Atlanta: Longstreet Press, 1996, 8–11.
5. "U.S. Trust Survey of Affluent Americans XV." *U.S. Trust*, December 1998.

Chapter 9—Major Gifts: The Big Gift—Now

1. Elaine Steiner, "Continuing Gifts: Lila Acheson Wallace's Floral Legacy." *Elle Decor*, April 1990, 34–36.
2. Tom Herman, "Tax Report." *Wall Street Journal*, July 29, 1999.
3. Beverly Sills and Lawrence Linderman, *Beverly: An Autobiography*. New York: Bantam, 1987, 328. In 1980, at the age of fifty-one, Beverly Sills retired from being a superstar soprano and began her second career as the chief executive officer/fundraiser of the New York City Opera. She used her drive, humor, chutzpah,

and connections to take the company from the brink of bankruptcy to raising $20 million a year. Includes great examples of soliciting wealthy donors.

4. *Chicago Tribune*, November 22, 1998, 18.

5. Anne Matthews, "The Thoughts That Count." *Forbes*, February 10, 1989, 126–128.

6. Calvin Tomkins, "For the Nation." *New Yorker*, September 3, 1990, 48–90. Profile of J. Carter Brown, director of the National Gallery of Art, Washington, D.C.

7. Jordan Bonfante, "Lady Power in the Sunbelt." *Time*, March 19, 1990, 21–24.

8. Bob Geldof and Paul Vallely, *Is That It?* New York: Ballantine Books, 1988, 332. The Irish rocker who raised $117 million to fight famine in Africa through a global broadcast of concerts in London and New Jersey tells with great insight, anger, and humor how he did it. Plus great stories of '80s rock stars, England's Prince Charles, and another world-class fundraiser: Mother Teresa.

Chapter 10—Planned Gifts: The Big Gift—Later

1. *Historical Products* catalog. Cambridge, Mass.: Historical Products, spring 1990, 4.

2. "Miscellany." *Historic Preservation*, May/June 1990, 11.

3. "Disney Housekeeper Leaves $4.5 Million." *Fund Raising Management*, January 1995, 47.

4. Beth Austin, "Gloria Steinem." *Chicago Tribune*, January 11, 1987, 6: 3.

5. Elizabeth Brown Pryor, *Clara Barton, Professional Angel*. Philadelphia: University of Pennsylvania Press, 1987, 184.

Chapter 11—Corporate Grants

1. *Taft Corporate Giving Directory*, 19th edition. Farmington Hills, Mich.: Taft Group, 1997.

2. Dun & Bradstreet, interview with author, July 25, 1990.

3. "Many Big Companies Increase Donations to Match Employees' Charitable Gifts." *Chronicle of Philanthropy*, July 16, 1998, 20.

4. "Corporate Contributions in 1997." New York: Conference Board, 1999, 6.

5. Sales letter for "John Naisbett's Trend Letter," July 1990.

6. "Cause-Related Marketing Summary." New York: Worldwide Marketing Development & Communications, American Express TRS Co., Dec. 13, 1990, 1–11.

7. Herbert Schmertz, *Goodbye to the Low Profile*. Boston: Little, Brown & Company, 1986, 222. Mobil Oil Company's vice president for public affairs devotes a chapter to "Affinity of Purpose Marketing: The Case of 'Masterpiece Theatre.'" Schmertz is crystal clear on what his company gets from paying for projects, from

imported television for the upper classes to double-Dutch jumprope competitions for inner-city girls. His book gives you a chance to see the deal from the corporation's point of view.

7. "Rankings of Most and Least Generous Corporate Givers." *Nonprofit Times*, January 1991. Based on percent of net earning before taxes.

Chapter 12—Corporate Marketing Partnerships

1. Interview with Kurt Aschermann, December 4, 1998.
2. National Center for Accessible Media, interview with Jennifer Gormley, April 20, 1999.
3. "Guiding Principles for Strategic Alliances." *Boys & Girls Clubs of America*, Atlanta: Boys & Girls Clubs of America, 1999.
4. "Pro Tours." *Chicago Tribune*, July 25, 1990, 4: 8.

Chapter 13—Foundation Grants

1. "Foundation Center Announces Estimates for 1998 Foundation Giving." New York: Foundation Center, April 7, 1999. Press release.
2. Canadian Directory to Foundations and Grants. Toronto: Canadian Centre for Philanthropy, 1998. Amy Sirianni, program director, E-mail.
3. "Foundation Center Announces Estimates for 1998 Foundation Giving." New York: Foundation Center, April 7, 1999. Press release.
4. Foundation Giving: Yearbook of Facts and Figures on Private, Corporate, and Community Foundations. New York: Foundation Center, 1999.
5. "Tax-Exempt Status for Your Organization." *Publication 557*: Washington, D.C.: Internal Revenue Service, 1998, 39.
6. Jennifer Moore, "Gift Makes Gates Fund No. 1 in U.S." *Chronicle of Philanthropy*, August 26, 1999, p. 7–10.
7. *Foundation Giving: Yearbook of Facts and Figures on Private, Corporate, and Community Foundations*. New York: Foundation Center, 1999.
8. Ibid.
9. Marina Dundjerski, "New Chapter at a Storied Foundation." *Chronicle of Philanthropy*, Washington, D.C., March 11, 1999, 7.

Chapter 14—Other Grant Makers:
Religious Denominations, United Ways and Alternative Funds, Civic Organizations, and Government Grants and Contracts

1. *Foundation Directory.* New York: Foundation Center, 1999.

2. *Pre-Application for 1990 Funding Cycle, Campaign for Human Development.* Washington, D.C.: United States Catholic Conference, 1990, 2.

3. Marilyn Dickey, "United Way Donations Increase 4.7%, to Record Level." Washington, D.C.: *Chronicle of Philanthropy*, August 27, 1998, 25.

4. "Basic Facts About United Way" and "Basic Facts Card." Alexandria, Va.: United Way of America, 1998.

Resource Guide

If knowledge is power, the people's access to information is fundamental to democracy.

—Visitor's Center videotape
Library of Congress

IN THE LAST TWENTY YEARS, THE AFFORDABLE personal computer, easy-to-use software, and ever-expanding Internet have greased the slide into the Information Age for fundraisers worldwide. The Internet can enable fundraisers to find everything from the blue-book value for a car donated for your auction to the current addresses of your alumni. It clearly has more potential for fundraisers than any invention since the printing press.

However, the Internet can also be a mind-numbing time-waster. Many of your best volunteers and prospects are now, and will choose to remain, unplugged. So successful fundraisers will always mix their Internet research with the other excellent resources available today.

This book is intended to give professional fundraisers and experienced volunteers an overview of the tools, techniques, and ethics of effective fundraising. When you are ready to learn more, here are the best resources to guide your search. For more advice, begin by asking the best fundraisers and leaders in your community for their list of favorite titles and bookmarks. You can also ask your librarian or Internet research person to recommend new on-line databases, CD-ROMs, and websites, as well as good old-fashioned books. All prices shown are for single copies as of 1999, including shipping and handling. Contact publishers for bulk rates and foreign prices. Prices are subject to change without notice. Note: bargains are marked with a "¢." These are the best buys for beginners and valuable for professionals to buy for their grassroots volunteers.

This section is arranged in three main parts: Resources for Fundraisers (with topics ranging from "board of directors" to "technology"); Professional Associations; and Foundation Center Cooperating Collections.

Resources for Fundraisers

Board of Directors

¢—Klein, Kimberly, and Stephanie Roth. *The Board of Directors. Grassroots Fundraising Journal* reprint, Berkeley: Chardon Press, (888) 458-8588 or www.chardonpress.com. 1995. $10.Tested advice to motivate your board of directors to ask for money; especially good for new and smaller organizations. Includes Kim's classic, "Fifty-Six Ways that Board Members Can Raise $500."

O'Connell, Brian. *The Board Members Book: Making a Difference in Voluntary Organizations*. New York: The Foundation Center, (800) 424-9836 or www.fdncenter.org. 1985. $24.95. The best book to give your board. Especially good on accountability, board-staff relations, and keeping good board members, written by the man who was the CEO of the National Mental Health Association and Independent Sector.

Resource Catalog. Washington, D.C.: National Center for Nonprofit Boards, (800) 883-6262 or www.ncnb.org. Free catalog of best-selling books and booklets to improve the effectiveness of your board.

Corporations

Corporate Grant Makers

Corporate Foundation Profiles. New York: The Foundation Center, (800)424-9836 or www.fdncenter.org. 1998. $155. In-depth information on the 195 largest corporate foundations that give at least $1.25 million per year, featuring background on foundation officers and board members.

Corporate Giving Watch. Detroit: The Taft Group, (800) 877-TAFT or www.taftgroup.com. Twelve issues per year for $149. Offers new corporate givers, recent grants, and industry news.

Matching Gift Details: 1998–99. Washington, D.C.: CASE Books, (800) 554-8536 or fax (301) 206-9789. 1999. $130 ($90 for members of CASE). Information on gifts and eligibility requirements for more than 6,400 companies, divisions, and subsidiaries that match individual gifts to nonprofits.

Matching Gift Leaflets. Washington, D.C.: CASE Books, (800) 554-8536 or fax (301) 604-2068. 1998–99. From $25 to $170 per thousand depending on list quantity. One-page leaflets listing corporations that match employee, director, retiree, and spouse gifts, sold in quantities from 100 to 50,000+. Four versions are: Higher Education (1,018 companies), Elementary/Secondary Schools (594 companies), Nonprofit Cultural Organizations (479 companies), and Nonprofit Charitable Organizations (395 companies).

National Directory of Corporate Giving. New York: The Foundation Center, (800) 424-9836 or www.fdncenter.org. 1997. $225. Authoritative information with six indexes on 1,905 corporate foundations and 990 direct-giving programs. Data from this is also searchable on the CD-ROM *FC Search*.

Corporate Fundraising

¢—Breiteneicher, Joe, and Bob Hohler. *The Quest for Funds: Insider's Guide to Corporate and Foundation Funding.* Washington, D.C.: National Trust for Historic Preservation, (800) 944-6847 or www.nthpbooks.org. 1989. $6. The most readable and realistic guide to raising money from corporations, written by a man who has been both foundation staff member and CEO of a major corporation.

Plinio, Alex J., and Joanne B. Scanlan. *Resource Raising: The Role of Non-Cash Assistance in Corporate Philanthropy.* Washington, D.C.: Independent Sector, (888) 860-8118 or www.indepsec.org. 1990.

$12.50. Most comprehensive guide to getting (or giving) corporate facilities, people, services, products, supplies, and equipment. Includes a list of national and international brokers.

Corporate Market Sponsors

IEG Sponsorship Tools. Chicago: IEG, Inc., (800) 834-4850 or www. sponsorship.com. IEG offers a biweekly newsletter, *IEG Sponsorship Report*, featuring scoops on corporate and nonprofit sponsorships, a how-to manual, *The IEG Complete Guide to Sponsorship*, software to help you prepare your proposals, and a great Event Marketing Conference every March. All are expensive but worth it, especially for fundraisers new to sponsorship.

Ries, Al, and Laura Ries. *The 22 Immutable Laws of Branding: How to Build a Product or Service into a World-Class Brand*. New York: HarperBusiness. 1996. $23. Most readable book on brands, explains why Body Shop, Coca-Cola, and Heineken brands work worldwide. Learn the vocabulary and concepts to market your organization's brand's qualities to corporate prospects.

Steckel, Richard, Robin Simons, Jeffrey Simons, and Norman Tanen. *Making Money While Making a Difference. How to Profit with a Nonprofit Partner*. Homewood, IL: High Tide Press. 1999. $14.95. This book is written for corporate decision makers. Four veterans of marketing great deals give dozens of examples of cause-related marketing, sponsorships, licensing, and strategic philanthropy, plus clear advice on picking the best nonprofit partners.

Weeden, Curt. *Corporate Social Investing. The Breakthrough Strategy for Giving and Getting Corporate Contributions*. Berrett-Koehler Publishers. 1998. $29.95. Curt Weeden gave away $146 million a year when he was a vice president at Johnson & Johnson, and advises some of the biggest corporate philanthropy leaders. This is the best book to read if you want to understand how enlightened corporations design their giving strategies to achieve their financial, personal, and community-relations goals. Features forwards by Paul Newman and Peter Lynch.

On-line

- Big Yellow—www.bigyellow.com
  Directory to 16 million U.S. business listings.

- CASE—www.case.org.
  Publishes list of corporations that match employee, director, re-tiree, and/or spouse donations.

- Conference Board—www.cf.org.
  Publishes annual survey of corporate giving trends in the United States.

- Conference Board of Canada—www.conferencebd.ca

- Conference Board Europe—fax: (322) 675-0395

- Corporate Giving Watch—www.taftgroup.com
  Research and articles on corporate givers.

- Securities and Exchange Commission—www.sec.gov/edgarhp.htm
  Searchable annual reports of most publicly-held companies in the United States.

Earned Income (Fees, Sales, and Businesses)

The Nonprofit Entrepreneur: Creating Ventures to Earn Income. New York: The Foundation Center, (800) 424-9836 or www.fdncenter.org. 1988. $23.45. How-to advice with case studies by seven experts on launching for-profit ventures.

Internal Revenue Service (IRS) at (800) TAX-FORM or www.irs.gov. Free publications:

IRS Pub. 552: *Record-keeping Requirements and a List of Tax Publications*

IRS Pub. 583: *Record-keeping for a Small Business*

IRS Pub. 598: *Tax on Unrelated Business Income of Exempt Organizations*

On-line

- The National Center for Social Entrepreneurs—
www.socialentrepreneurs.org

- The Roberts Enterprise Development Fund—www.redf.org

- Share Our Strength—www.communitywealth.org

  All three offer great advice and publications for nonprofits going
  into business.

- ¢—Small Business Administration—www.sba.gov
Useful nuts-and-bolts advice on starting a business, including
how to get a loan

Ethics

¢—Danforth, Sandra, Alan Embree, et al. *Honorable Matters: A Guide to Ethics and Law in Fund Raising.* Chicago Chapter of the National Society of Fund Raising Executives. Westmont, IL: NSFRE, (708) 655-0134. 1991. $3 prepaid. Best introduction to ethical issues relating to paid, professional fundraisers, major gifts, planned gifts, corporate and foundation grants, and special events. Good appendix of resources.

Fees

Elling, Ronald. *Making Dollars and Sense Out of Fees for Service.* Illinois Alliance for Aging, 327 S. LaSalle St., Chicago, IL 60604, (312) 922-5890. 1995. Book only, $35; book and software, $55. 1995. Best introduction to setting and collecting fees.

Foundations

Foundation News and Commentary. Washington, D.C., Council on Foundations, (800) 347-6969 or www.cof.org. $35.50 for six issues a year. Articles, essays, and gossip on foundations written for foundation trustees and staff.

CD-ROM

FC Search. New York: The Foundation Center, (800) 424-9836 or www.fdncenter.org. 1999. $1,195 for one user. Updated twice annually. This is a great tool. Fully searchable CD-ROM covers more than 47,000 U.S. Foundation Centers, describes nearly 200,000 grants greater than $10,000, and lists about 200,000 trustees and staff. Includes data from ten Foundation Center directories, including *The Foundation Directory* and *The Foundation Grants Index*. Saves time and simplifies searching. The text-search feature enables you to search by key words such as "sudden infant death syndrome" or "Frank Lloyd Wright" that are not listed in print products' indexes. The same data in print versions will cost $1,017, so if you do a lot of foundation research, the CD-ROM is the better investment. For beginners, use it at the cooperating collections.

Directories

The Foundation Directory. New York: The Foundation Center, (800) 424-9836 or www.fdncenter.org. 1999. $185. The best source of information on more than ten thousand of the largest foundations that each give more than $200,000 per year, organized through six indexes, thirty-three types of support, and 187 subject fields.

The Foundation Directory: Part 2. New York: The Foundation Center, (800) 424-9836 or www.fdncenter.org. 1999. $185. Covers more than 5,700 mid-sized foundations (including 2,100 new to the 1999 edition) with annual grant programs from $50,000 to $200,000.

The Foundation Directory Supplement. New York: The Foundation Center, (800) 424-9836 or www.fdncenter.org. 1999. $125. Midyear update.

All three Foundation Directory volumes: $455.

The Foundation Grants Index. New York: The Foundation Center, (800) 424-9836 or www.fdncenter.org. 1999. $165. Descriptions of more than 86,000 grants awarded by the 1,000 largest independent, corporate, and community foundations, indexed by twenty-eight subject areas. Find out who funds in your field.

The Foundation 1000. New York: The Foundation Center, (800) 424-9836 or www.fdncenter.org. 1998–99. $295. In-depth reviews of the 1,000 wealthiest foundations.

Guide to U.S. Foundations. Volume 1: *The Foundations.* Volume 2: *Foundation Trustee, Officer, and Donor Index and Foundation Locator.* New York: The Foundation Center, (800) 424-9836 or www.fdncenter.org. 1999. $215. Nicknamed "Gus" and "Tod," these are the only published references on all 46,000+ foundations and the people who run them. The best source to find smaller, local foundations and discover the names of the decision makers.

The National Directory of Grantmaking Public Charities. New York: The Foundation Center, (800) 424-9836 or www.fdncenter.org. 1998. $200. Directory to community foundations and nonprofit organizations that are not incorporated as a foundation but still make grants, such as the Alabama Law Foundation, Blue Cross/Blue Shield of Michigan, Detroit Lions Foundation, National Hemophilia Foundation, and New Israel Fund.

Research

The Foundation Center's Guide to Grantseeking on the Web. New York: The Foundation Center, (800) 424-9836 or www.fdncenter.org. 1998. $24.45. Best guide to researching foundations and other grantmakers on the World Wide Web.

The Foundation Center's User-Friendly Guide. New York: The Foundation Center, (800) 424-9836 or www.fdncenter.org. 1996. $14.95. Perfect for beginners (and a great review tool for veterans), this is the tool to get started in foundation research.

Proposal Writing

¢—Kiritz, Norton J. *Program Planning & Proposal Writing: Introductory Version.* Los Angeles: The Grantsmanship Center, (213) 482-9860 or www.tgci.com . $6. The classic guide to proposal writing, in an easy-to-read and easy-to-use booklet; amounts are dated, but the advice is timeless.

Robinson, Andy. *Grass Roots Grants: An Activist's Guide to Proposal Writing.* Berkeley: Chardon Press, (888) 458-8588 or www.chardonpress.com. 1996. $29. Best book on everything from planning your work to managing the grant, including four examples of successful proposals. Written by a veteran, this is the most useful and realistic guide to building long-term respectful relationships with foundations.

On-line

- The Foundation Center—www.fdncenter.org
  Features links to free cooperating collections in every state, D.C., and Puerto Rico; publications and services; a proposal writing short course; and a guide to nonprofit sector literature. The Foundation Finder links to every grant-making organization that has a Web presence. Features weekly news on the *Philanthropy News Digest* and much more. Best site for both new fundraisers and veterans.

- The Council on Foundations—www.cof.org
  Council publications and services as well as links to grant makers.

- *Chronicle of Philanthropy*—www.philanthropy.com
  The Deadlines link lists upcoming deadlines and current requests for proposals; the New Grants link lists recent foundation and corporate grants.

- Ask your local cooperating collection or association of nonprofits if there is an on-line resource on local grant makers. For example, the Donors Forum in Chicago maintains the Philanthropic Database (PhD) to list all grants from its member foundations, down to as low as $50. Link to PhD from www.nponet.net.

- The Canadian Centre for Philanthropy—www.ccp.ca
  Publications and on-line database on more than 1,000 active Canadian foundations in English or in French.

- The European Foundation Center—www.efc.be
  Information on the publications, workshops, and annual conference for European foundations and corporate funders.

French language

Wyman, Ken. *Face à Face. L'art d'obtenir des dons plus importants de personnes très généreuses.* (Major gifts.) Ken Wyman and Associates, (416) 362-2926 or E-mail: Ken Wyman@compuserv.com. 1993.

Wyman, Ken. *Guide De La Collecte de Fonds Au Moyen D'Activités Spéciales.* (Special events.) Ken Wyman and Associates, (416) 362-2926 or E-mail: Ken Wyman@compuserv.com. 1989.

Fundraising

Flanagan, Joan. *The Grass Roots Fundraising Book: How to Raise Money in Your Community.* Lincolnwood, IL: NTC/Contemporary Books, (800) 323-4900 or www.ntc-cb.com. Updated 1995. $16.95. The most popular fundraising book in the United States, this best-seller shares foolproof advice on raising renewable, dependable, internally controlled money. Tested tips will work for any nonprofit organization in any community.

Flanagan, Joan. *Successful Fundraising, Second Edition: A Complete Handbook for Vounteers.* Lincolnwood, IL: NTC/Contemporary Books, (800) 323-4900 or www.ntc-cb.com. 1999. $18.95. The best book for professional fundraisers, executive directors, and serious volunteer fundraisers. You get an overview of all the elements of a successful fundraising strategy, from annual campaigns to major donors. Features very useful Resource Guide with current publications and websites.

Seltzer, Michael, editor. *Fundraising Matters: True Stories of How Raising Funds Fulfills Dreams.* Jossey-Bass Publishers, (800) 956-7739 or www.jbp.com. Eight stories of exciting fundraising start-ups for new ideas and organizations. Includes Joan Flanagan's article on how Horizon Hospice grew from the founders' idea to a $2.7 million a year agency.

Periodicals

Chronicle of Philanthropy, Stacy Palmer, editor. (800) 728-2819 or www.philanthropy.com. $67.50 for one year (twenty-six issues). Tabloid-style paper offers the latest on fundraising issues, case studies of successful fundraising campaigns and events, provocative columnists, and list of recent foundation grants and upcoming deadlines.

¢—*Grantsmanship Center Magazine*, Marc Green, editor. (213) 482-9860 or www.tgci.com. Free quarterly tabloid is one-half catalog of the Grantsmanship Center's workshops and reprints, and one-half useful how-to articles.

¢—*Grassroots Fundraising Journal*, Kim Klein, editor. Berkeley: Chardon Press, (888) 458-8588 or www.chardonpress.com. $32 for one year (six issues). Best nuts-and-bolts advice for fundraisers working with membership organizations. Every issue has good ideas you can apply immediately.

Video

"Ask Somebody for Money Today!" starring Joan Flanagan. Three one-hour tapes: "Getting Started," "Asking for Money," and "Fund Raising Forever," plus a forty-three-page workbook. Winston-Salem, NC: Partners in Caregiving, Wake Forest School of Medicine. 1994. $90. Compiled from a series of four workshops, useful to inform and inspire your volunteers.

McKinnon, Harvey. "How to Build a Highly Profitable Monthly Donor Program." (800) 815-8565 or www.harveymckinnon.com. $69. Good advice to set up a monthly pledge program to build dependable income.

Government Funding

On-line

- Catalog of Federal Domestic Assistance—www.gsa.gov/fdac Catalog of grants available from the U.S. government.

- Federal Register On-Line—www.access.gpo.gov

- FedWorld—www.fedworld.gov Administered by the Department of Commerce, provides access to more than one hundred government agencies' databases.

- States—www.state.il.us (This is the site for Illinois—substitute any state's acronym for "il" in the URL.)

Internet

Allen, Nick, and Mal Warwick, editors. *Fundraising on the Internet: Recruiting and Renewing Donors On-line.* Strathmoor Press, (800) 217-7377 or E-mail infor@strathmoor.com. 1996. $31.50. First book on raising money on the Internet, illustrates how direct-mail expertise can be transferred to raising money on-line.

Bergan, Helen. *Where the Information Is: A Guide to Electronic Research for Nonprofit Organizations.* Alexandria, VA: BioGuide Press, (703) 820-9045. 1996. $32. Most readable introduction to using the Internet, on-line services, E-mail, listserves, and CD-ROMs for nonprofits.

Corson-Finnerty, Adam, and Laura Blanchard. *Fundraising and Friend-Raising on the Web.* American Library Association, (800) 545-2433 or www.ala.com. 1998. $59. This well-written book shares the expertise of two librarians who use the Web to raise money and build support for their libraries. Excellent for beginners or any agency that has to make the case for private funds or unrestricted funds to match their public support dollars. Includes Web-enabled CD-ROM to link you to the sites they discuss, plus the real sites managed by the authors.

Johnston, Michael. *The Fund Raiser's Guide to the Internet.* The NSFRE/Wiley Fund Development Series. (703) 684-0410 or www.nsfre.com. 1999. $34.95. Johnston's years of experience shine through this excellent guide. Most thorough tested advice to set up your organization's website and manage it to get donations, sell memberships, and organize advocacy. Includes a disk with more than one hundred sample sites.

¢—*Nonprofits & Technology*, Todd Cohen, editor. (919) 899-3743 or www.pj.org. Free monthly tabloid, full of great advice on the best new bookmarks and using technology to raise money.

On-line

- *Philanthropy Journal* Online—www.pj.org
  The Philanthropy News Network puts up daily news on philanthropy, technology, and job listings. Get information on their

"Nonprofits and Technology" national conference series at http://conference.pj.org.

Legal

Coletta, Lauren M., et al. *How to Organize and Take Action: Building Strong Communities*. Chicago: Citizens Information Service of Illinois, (312) 939-4636 or www.cisil.org. $25.50. Notebook full of clear, tested advice on how to start and incorporate a new nonprofit organization, build committees, recruit members, raise money, hold positive meetings, research legislation, and lobby effectively.

Colvin, Gregory L. *Fiscal Sponsorship: Six Ways to Do It Right*. San Francisco: Study Center Press. 1993. $25 prepaid. Until your organization receives tax-exempt status, you may want a fiscal sponsor (known on the street as "a funnel") to handle your grants and large gifts. Colvin's book is the best for both charities and fiscal sponsors to use.

Hopkins, Bruce R. *The Law of Tax-Exempt Organizations*, 7th edition. Somerset, NJ: John Wiley & Sons, Inc., (800) 753-0655 or www. wiley.com/nonprofit. 1998. $163. Thorough coverage of state and federal law, IRS court rulings, and Hopkins's commentaries.

Ask your state's attorney general, charitable trust and solicitation division, for current regulations on fundraising, especially any form of gambling, and your secretary of state for corporation regulations.

To incorporate as a tax-exempt nonprofit corporation:
IRS Pub. 557: *Tax-Exempt Status for Your Organization*
IRS Pub. 1023: *Application for Recognition of Exemption*
IRS Form 8718: *User Fee for Exempt Organization Determination Letter Request*
IRS Form SS-4: *Application for Employer Identification Number*
Free from the IRS at (800) TAX-FORM or www.irs.gov.

On-line

- Internal Revenue Service—www.irs.gov

- U.S. House of Representatives Internet Law Library— http://law.house.gov/test/obit.htm

Lobbying

To lobby as a charity and protect your organization's tax-exempt status: IRS Form 5768: *Election/Revocation of Election by an Eligible Section 501(c)(3): Organization to Make Expenditures to Influence Legislation.* Free from the IRS at (800) TAX-FORM or www.irs.gov.

¢—*Lobbying and Political Activity for Non-profits: What You Can (and Can't) Do Under Federal Law.* Washington, D.C.: Children's Defense Fund, (202) 628-8787 or www.cdf.com. 1983. $4.95.

Smucker, Bob. *The Nonprofit Lobbying Guide,* 2nd edition. Washington, D.C.: Independent Sector, (888) or www.independentsector. com. 1999. $25.45. Best guide on how to lobby to win and conform to the federal regulations.

Also check with your national organization or network for their publications on lobbying.

On-line

- Independent Sector—www.indepsec.org
  For information on legislation impacting nonprofits.

- State Governments—www.state.il.us
  (This is the site for Illinois—substitute any state's acronym for "il" in the URL.)

- Thomas—www.thomas.loc.gov
  Recent bills and legislation, information about the legislative process.

- U.S. House of Representatives—www.house.gov

- U.S. Senate—www.senate.gov

- White House—www.whitehouse.gov

Mail and Phones

Lautman, Kay Partney, and Henry Goldstein. *Dear Friend: Mastering the Art of Direct Mail Fund Raising.* The Taft Group, (800) 877-8238 or www.taftgroup.com. 1991. $65. The best advice on direct mail for novices or veteran mailers who want to improve their campaigns.

Warwick, Mal. *Raising Money by Mail: Strategies for Growth and Financial Stability.* Berkeley: Strathmore Press, (800) 217-7377 or www.malwarwick.com. 1994. How to capture new names and turn them into loyal donors, packed with real examples from successful campaigns.

On-line

- Alliance of Nonprofit Mailers—www.nonprofitmailers.org

- AT&T 1-800 Information—www.tollfree.att.net

- Four 11: The Internet White Pages—www.four11.com

- Database America—www.lookupUSA.com
  For when you have a person's phone number and cannot remember who the person is.

Major Gifts

Gary, Tracy, and Melissa Kohner. *Inspired Philanthropy: Creating a Giving Plan.* Chardon Press, (800) 458-8588 or www. chardonpress.com. 1998. $24. This is a great tool written by and for major donors. It is packed with thought-provoking work sheets to use yourself and share with your major donors to help you give money strategically. The appendix includes six sample letters *from* a donor to the director of development, twenty-one questons donors should ask on a site visit, and an excellent resource guide on effective giving.

Grace, Kay Sprinkel. *Beyond Fundraising.* Somerset, NJ: John Wiley & Sons, Inc., (800) 225-5945 or www.wiley.com. 1997. $41. If you've ever gagged when one of your volunteers opined, "But I hate begging," this is the book for you. Great advice on changing your leaders' attitudes from the "tin cup" syndrome toward the pride and power of fundraising.

¢—Klein, Kimberly. Getting Major Gifts. Grassroots Fundraising Journal reprint. Berkeley: Chardon Press, (888) 458-8588 or www.chardonpress.com. 1991. $10. Reprint of the best articles on major gifts; especially good for social-change groups or any fundraiser doing its first campaign for big gifts.

Wyman, Ken. *Face to Face: How to Get Bigger Donations from Very Generous People.* Toronto, ON: Ken Wyman & Associates, Inc., (416) 362-2926 or E-mail: KenWyman@compuserve.com. 1993. $40. How to find the right prospects and overcome the fear of asking.

Money Management

Stevens, Susan Kenny, and Lisa M. Anderson. *All the Way to the Bank: Smart Money Management for Tomorrow's Nonprofits.* St. Paul, MN: The Stevens Group, (651)641-0398 or E-mail: thestevensgroup @larsonallen.com. 1997. $16.95 prepaid. The most sensible and sophisticated guide to money management to help you do more with your funds.

Nonprofit Sector

Chronicle of Philanthropy, (800) 728-2819 or www.philanthopy.com. $67.50 per year (twenty-four issues). Good articles, case studies, recent grants, upcoming calendar of events, job listings, and provocative editorial pages.

On-line

- *Chronicle of Philanthropy*—www.philanthropy.com
  Weekly news on philanthropy and foundations

- Guidestar—www.guidestar.org
  List of data from IRS 990s. Useful to find nonprofits.

Performing Arts–Subscriptions

Newman, Danny. *Subscribe Now! Building Arts Audiences Through Dynamic Subscription Promotion.* New York: Theatre Communications Group, Inc., 1977. (212) 679-5230 or www.tcg.org. $18.95. Unabashed razzmatazz and scores of ideas to sell subscriptions or pledges by the man who revolutionized nonprofit box offices in the United States and Canada.

Planned Giving

A Guide to Starting a Planned Giving Program for Nonprofit Executives and Volunteer Trustees. Indianapolis: National Committee on Planned Giving, (317) 269-6274 or www.ncpg.org. 1998. $40. How to phase-in a new planned-giving program or mesh your planned giving with your other development work; includes a glossary of planned-giving terms, and more.

Leave a Legacy Kit. Indianapolis: National Committee on Planned Giving, (317) 269-6274 or www.ncpg.org. 1998. $35. Clear advice to help all kinds of people work with the development officers at their favorite charity as well as with their own estate-planning professionals. Includes a video and workbook.

Planned Giving Today. Roger Sheynolds, editor, (800) 525-5748 or www.pgtoday.com. Twelve issues for one year, $169. Useful articles by gift planners, calendar of training events, and ads for planned giving services and products.

Schoenhals, David G. *Planned Giving for the One Person Development Office: Taking the First Steps.* Rosemont, IL: Berkley: Chardon Presss, (888) 458-8588 or www.chandonpress.com. 1998. Book, $48; electronic version, $94. Good tool to get started in planned giving, including many easy-to-customize forms.

Sharpe, Robert F., Sr. *Planned Giving Simplified: The Gift, the Giver, and the Gift Planner.* Somerset, NJ: The NSFRE/Wiley Fund Development Series, (800) 753-0655 or www.wiley.com/nonprofit. 1998. $29.70. Great advice from one of the pioneers in planned giving.

Pledges

McKinnon, Harvey. *Hidden Gold.* Bonus Books (800) 815-8565 or www.harveymckinnon.com. $39.95. 1999. Clear advice with many samples to set up a monthly pledge program using mail, phone, or events. Features excellent explanation of implementing electronic funds transfer (EFT) and credit card collection.

Religious Congregations and Grant Makers

> *Ask your own denomination's national and judicatory (the dio-*
> *cese, district, synod, etc.) about its publications, conferences, and*
> *other resources for fundraisers.*

1997–1998 Religious Funding Resource Guide. Mary Eileen Paul and
  Andrea Flores, editors. Washington, D.C.: Resource Women, (202)
  832-8071. 1997–98 plus 1999 update. $82. Best information on
  thirty-five religious funding sources, including application guidelines,
  deadlines, and how-to advice. Next new full edition due in 2000 will
  cost $88.

Dean, Peggy Powell, and Susanna A. Jones. *The Complete Guide to Cap-*
  ital Campaigns for Historic Churches and Synagogues. Partners for
  Sacred Places, (215) 546-1288 or fax (215) 546-1180. 1991. $40.
  Looseleaf notebook packed with samples from successful campaigns,
  especially good on the planning that needs to precede the campaign.

Research Statistics

Giving USA 1999. New York: AAFRC Trust for Philanthropy, (212) 354-
  5799 or www.aafrc.org. $45. Published since 1955, these are the best
  estimates of American giving and an insightful analysis of trends.

Hodgkinson, Virginia A., Murray S. Weitzman, et al. *Giving and Vol-*
  unteering in the United States: Findings from a National Survey.
  Washington, D.C.: Independent Sector, (888) 860-8118 or www.
  indepsec.org. 1996. $35. Survey conducted by the Gallup Organiza-
  tion for the Independent Sector presents very useful data on moti-
  vations of donors and volunteers. New editions in odd-numbered
  years.

Responsive Philanthropy. Washington, D.C.: National Committee for
  Responsive Philanthropy, (202) 387-9177 or www.ncrp.org. Quarterly newsletter. $25. The most candid analysis of giving by founda-
  tions, United Ways, alternative funds, and corporate giving plans.

On-line

- The Nonprofit FAQ (frequently asked questions and answers), the Nonprofit Locator (index of data from more than one million nonprofits' tax returns), and the Form 990 Project (working to get charities' tax returns on the Web) merged in 1999— www.nonprofits.org

- The National Center for Charitable Statistics—nccs.urban.org

- United States Census Bureau—www.census.gov

Social Change Organizations

Bobo, Kim A., Jackie Kendall, and Steve Max. *Organizing for Social Change: A Manual for Activists in the 1990s*, 2nd edition. Santa Ana, CA: Seven Locks Press, (800) 354-5348. 1996. $23.95. The most comprehensive and useful manual on building a permanent, powerful organization. Not just for community organizers; fundraisers also can develop stronger leaders and design better strategies with this book. Features excellent chapters fundraising, using the Internet, and on financial and legal issues.

Grantmakers Directory: National Network of Grantmakers. Berkeley: Chardon Press, (888) 458-8588 or www.chardonpress.com. 2000. $35. Directory of more than 150 grant-making foundations and religious institutions that are committed to social, economic, and political justice.

Klein, Kim. *Fundraising for Social Change*, 3rd edition. Berkeley: Chardon Press, (888) 458-8588 or www.chardonpress.com. 1995. $29. Fundraising advice tailored to the special challenges of social-change organizations, this book is especially good on direct-mail, telephone, and major-donor campaigns.

Spanish Language (en Español)

Klein, Kim, et al. *Como Recaudar Fondos en su Communidad* (How to Raise Money in Your Community). Berkeley: Chardon Press, (888) 458-8588 or www.chardonpress.com. 1995. $14. Fourteen reprints from the *Grassroots Fundraising Journal*, useful for any small organization, with or without paid staff. Available only in Spanish.

On-line

- Resources for Social Change—www.chardonpress.com
  The best resource for political analysis, inspiring stories, and how-to books on fundraising, media relations, and community organizing; also includes links to publishers and organizations plus articles and tips from Kim Klein's *Grassroots Fundraising Journal*.

Special Events

Ask your national organization or network about its publications, consultants, and training for special events organizers. Many offer excellent resources such as the Heifer Project International's booklet, "Fun Fund-Raising Activities."

¢—Anderson, Ann. *From Visitors to Volunteers: Organizing A Historic Homes Tour*. Washington, D.C.: National Trust for Historic Preservation, (800) 944-6847 or www.nthpbooks.org. 1989. $6. Great example of organizing a big event with lots of volunteers, includes sample timeline and management outline.

Chase's Calendar of Events. Lincolnwood, IL: NTC/Contemporary Publishing Group, (800) 323-4900 or www.ntc-cb.com. $64.95. This day-by-day directory includes many ideas; you can find a special theme for any day of the year. Purchase price includes free Windows CD-ROM or on-line access password.

Flanagan, Joan. *The Grass Roots Fundraising Book*. Lincolnwood, IL: NTC/Contemporary Publishing Group, (800) 323-4900 or www.ntc-cb.com. Updated 1995. The best advice on organizing small, medium, and large special events, including foolproof tips on choosing the right event, selling the tickets, and getting the best publicity.

IRS Publication 1391: *Deductibility of Payments Made to Charities Conducting Fundraising Events*. Free from the IRS at (800) TAX-FORM or www.irs.gov.

Taxes

Internal Revenue Service (IRS) at (800) TAX-FORM or www.irs.gov. Free.

To calculate how much is tax-deductible:

IRS Pub. 526: *Charitable Contributions*

IRS Pub. 561: *Determining the Value of Donated Property* (how to estimate fair market value)

IRS Form 8282: *Donee Information Return* (for the charity if you sell any in-kind gift within two years of its receipt)

IRS Form 8283: *Non-Cash Charitable Contributions* (for the donor)

To calculate how much is tax-deductible at special events:

IRS Pub. 1391: *Deductibility of Payments Made to Charities Conducting Fundraising Events*

Professional Associations

Check with your national denomination, organization, or network. Many offer special training, conferences, and publications tailored for their fundraisers, such as the Philanthropic Service for Institutions (PSI) of the Seventh-Day Adventist Church which publishes the excellent newsletter the *Philanthropic Dollar.*

All of the following professional associations offer a written code of ethics, excellent publications, training, local and international conferences, research on giving trends and salaries, and job listings. Contact the national office or website to locate your local chapter. Not only will you have fun and learn a lot, but also once you are on the mailing list you will receive advertisements for many new publications and services.

Association for Healthcare Philanthropy (AHP), (703) 532-6243 www.goahp.org. Publishes annual report on contributing to health care.

Association of Direct Response Fundraising Counsel (ADRFC), (202) 293-9640 or E-mail: adfrc@aol.com. Direct-mail businesses, vendors, and consultants; no nonprofit members. Publishes a free brochure to introduce direct mail and offers a list of direct-mail firms that follow the ADRFC's code of ethics.

Association of Professional Researchers for Advancement (APRA), (630) 655-0177 or www.Weber.u.washington.edu/~d/lamb/apra. APRA members work to oppose government censorship in the United States and Canada, maintain confidentiality of private information, and improve standard reference sources. Dues of $125 includes subscription to APRA *Connections*.

Council for Advancement and Support of Education (CASE), (202) 328-5900 or www.case.org. Voting membership is by school rather than individual; dues are based on number of students. If you work for an American or Canadian independent school, college, or university, your institution's membership in CASE gives you support specialized for the work you do. CASE's newsletter, CASE *Currents*, is available to nonmembers for $95 per year.

CASE also runs the CASE Matching Gifts Clearinghouse, (202) 478-5656 or E-mail matchgifts@case.org. It sells leaflets listing hundreds of corporations that match gifts from employees, directors, retirees, and spouses.

National Committee on Planned Giving (NCPG), (317) 269-6274 or www.ncpg.org. Planned-giving professionals in 110 U.S. cities have formed local councils for support fundraisers who specialize in planned giving and other professionals such as lawyers, accountants, and financial planners.

National Society of Fund-Raising Executives (NSFRE), (800) 666-FUND or www.nsfre.org. Dues: $150 a year for national and $25–$75 for local chapters. Open to all professional fundraisers, NSFRE offers local networking, continuing education programs, an international conference, job notices, and a quarterly journal, *Advancing Philanthropy*.

The Foundation Center Cooperating Collections Network

The Foundation Center operates free libraries with trained experts to help you start your research on grant makers. They will not do the work for you, but they will offer an orientation on how to find the best foundation prospects. There are national collections in Atlanta, Cleveland, New York, San Francisco, and Washington, D.C., and more than 190 cooperating collections throughout every state in the United States and Puerto Rico. Call (800) 424-9836 or link from www.fdncenter.org to find your nearest collections.

The cooperating collections have the Foundation Center directories and how-to books, other fundraising books and periodicals, and copies of any state's foundations' 990-PF tax returns. Most also give you access to their excellent CD-ROM called *FC Search*.

Take advantage of other opportunities offered by your local collection. Some offer excellent, reasonably priced training featuring local foundation staff and trustees, such as the seventy-five workshops presented every year by the Nonprofit Resource Center of Texas in San Antonio. Several collections publish a statewide directory of foundations, and some maintain on-line resources. The Chicago Donors Forum's philanthropic database can research foundations and grants in Illinois at www.npo.net.

Use the Foundation Center's publications by appointment for free at:

Canadian Centre for Philanthropy
Le Centre canadien de philanthropie
425 University Avenue, 7th Floor
Toronto, Ontario M5C 1T6
Canada
(416) 597-2293
www.ccp.ca

Biblioteca Benjamin Franklin
American Embassy, USICA
Londres 16
Mexico City 6, D.F. 06600
Mexico
(525) 591-0244

Index

About the Author

JOAN FLANAGAN IS THE AUTHOR of two bestselling "how-to" books from Contemporary Books. Her classic *The Grass Roots Fundraising Book* is the most popular fundraising book in North America. This book, *Successful Fundraising*, tells you how to go beyond the grass roots to raise big money from individuals, corporations, and foundations.

Fundraiser

Joan worked in the 1970s as the fundraiser for CAP, a direct-action community organization, where she helped grow the budget from $25,000 to $250,000, all of it raised from low- and middle-income people in Cook County, Illinois. She was the executive director in the 1990s for Natural Ties, a national organization linking young adults with and without disabilities, where she helped double the budget and triple the assets in two years. These and other "hands-on" fundraising positions help keep her humble and helpful as a fundraising consultant. As an adviser for diverse groups from the Alzheimer's Association and the American Red Cross to the National Main Street Center and United Way International, Joan has had the privilege of working with scores of fascinating fundraisers. In addition, she has worked for two grant-making foundations—the Youth Project in Washington, D.C., and the W. Clement and Jessie V. Stone Foundation in Chicago—that have made more than $300 million in grants.

Trainer

Joan has trained more than forty thousand professional fundraisers and community leaders in the United States, Canada, and Europe. Joan can lead a fundraising workshop for your staff and volunteers or facilitate a retreat for your board of directors. She can also consult on-site to help you design the best fundraising strategy for your organization. E-mail fundsjoan@aol.com for more information.

Volunteer

Joan practices what she preaches. She was one of the first board members of Horizon Hospice and helped grow its annual budget from $310 to $3 million per year. She has volunteered on dozens of special-event committees, membership drives, stewardship campaigns, capital campaigns, and endowment fund committees for a variety of charities.

Fan

Joan lives in Chicago and is a die-hard Cubs fan. She says it is good training for a fundraiser, because rooting for a baseball team that has not won the World Series since 1908 forces you to plan ahead for next year.